Lewis C. Baker

The Fire of God's Anger

Lewis C. Baker

The Fire of God's Anger

ISBN/EAN: 9783337254612

Printed in Europe, USA, Canada, Australia, Japan

Cover: Foto ©Lupo / pixelio.de

More available books at **www.hansebooks.com**

THE FIRE OF GOD'S ANGER:

OR,

LIGHT FROM THE OLD TESTAMENT UPON THE NEW TESTAMENT TEACHING CONCERNING FUTURE PUNISHMENT.

By L. C. BAKER,

Author of "Mystery of Creation and of Man;" Editor of *Words of Reconciliation.*

"*For a fire is kindled in mine anger, and shall burn unto the lowest hell.*"—DEUT. XXXII. 22.

PUBLISHED AT OFFICE OF "WORDS OF RECONCILIATION,"
NO. 2022 DELANCEY PLACE, PHILADELPHIA, PA.
1887.

PREFACE.

This book is a series of Bible studies, from a new point of view, of the burning question of future punishment. Its author has served for many years in the ministry of the Presbyterian Church. No other church stands more in need of a free discussion of the vital questions raised in this volume. He has herein asserted, both for himself and for his brethren, the right to inquire into matters about which he knows many of the ministers and members of that church are profoundly exercised, but concerning which many of them believe they are bound to keep silent. He cannot, for a moment, accept that low idea of the church which makes it a merely voluntary association, formed in the interests of a certain system of doctrine. It is a living body, formed for growth in knowledge and purity. And to such increase each member is bound to contribute as God may give him light and opportunity. This carries with it the right, and just at this time of excited interest on this subject imposes the duty, to reverently investigate the matters treated of in this volume. The author can render no higher service to his own church than to assert within her, and for her, this principle of liberty.

These pages are prepared also in the interest of that large class of Christians in all churches who believe the Bible to be the Word of God, and yet whose loyalty to it is put to a painful test by their inability to reconcile its teachings about future punishment with what they have learned from its pages, and from their own enlightened convictions, of the character of God. A church, which builds hospitals for the sick, and retreats for the aged and the poor and the insane, which seeks to carry Christ's consolation to men of every class, maimed and wounded in this battle of life, which carries His gospel to the sons of want on heathen shores, and which grows into the life of Christ by so doing, cannot long remain content with a view of His redeeming work which makes death the limit of it, and which estops her from any further priestly ministry toward the ignorant and the outcast beyond the grave. In the present bewilderment of the church upon this subject, this book shows that a perfectly satisfactory solution is to be found in the Scriptures themselves by those who search for it. Two fatal misconceptions have thus far prevented her from perceiving it.

1. She has interpreted the Scripture teaching concerning final judgment as relating chiefly to a remote assize to be held after a general resurrection of the dead Whereas Jesus was careful to teach His disciples that He would enter upon His office as Judge of the world before that generation passed away.

2. She has therefore misconceived the place and meaning of resurrection in the divine economy, as the gracious provision of another life to those who must suffer the wages of sin under that judgment. That which was meant to be a boon, the purchase of the ransom given for all, has been perverted into an untold curse to all who have died unsaved in this life,—the prelude to an aggra-

vated retribution and endless despair. This monstrous mistake concerning the purpose of God in raising the dead has vitiated the eschatology of the church for fifteen centuries. It has drawn a mask over His face, and blinded men to the knowledge of the only true God and of Jesus Christ, whom He has sent.

This mistake has largely arisen from the attempt to fix a meaning upon the words of Christ concerning the punishment of the wicked without a previous study of the Old Testament conceptions out of which this teaching grew, and upon which it was based.

This book carries its readers back to this beginning, and invites them to proceed from it to the study of this whole subject of man's destiny, of God's great plan of grace, and of the church's priestly calling under it. It finds in the principle that resurrection is redemptive the key to the mysteries of this subject. With this in hand, we are enabled to give proper place to the Scripture-teaching about the punishment of sin, in that it makes the death-state, or sheol, to be essentially penal, deepened and prolonged according to the intensity of evil character; and in that it makes resurrection a process of sorting and judgment as well as of deliverance. It thus presents a doctrine of retribution in harmony with the laws of life, as well as with the Word of God, and so erects a barrier against that crude universalism which has come in as a reaction against the old creed-doctrine of hell, and which tends to weaken the bonds of human society by concealing from men their accountability to God. And yet, on the other hand, it makes room for the larger hope, which has made for itself a lasting place in the convictions of enlightened Christians. But it locates this hope in the only place where Scripture gives it warrant. It insists that sinful men must first serve out their death-sentence, and be restored to the life and estate of manhood through resurrection, before they can be amenable to the discipline of the gospel, and capable of winning the prize it sets before them. If there be any probation in Hades, it can only be a probation for resurrection. After that, men who died in ignorance of this great salvation may have their opportunity to win it. The superiority of this scriptural doctrine of the larger hope over that now known as the Andover view, lies in the fact that it preserves undiminished the Scripture warnings of the present peril which overhangs men who die in their sins. It makes no room for intervention in their behalf, until after the righteousness of God is fully vindicated in their punishment, and the sentence of His law executed. Beyond this His grace has provided to again take up their case in the only way possible— through their resurrection from the dead.

It will be seen also that this doctrine of redemption through resurrection, of which a chosen seed are the first recipients, and which proceeds from them in wider circles until all the families of the earth are reached, is in accord with those organic principles which underlie the constitution of the human race, and by which it is seen to be something besides an aggregation of individuals. The laws of race-life and the laws of heredity all receive new meaning from it.

A want of the proper view of human destiny, and of the calling of the church in relation to the mass of mankind, out of which she is an election, has been a most fruitful cause of her debasement and division. A true knowledge of the goal towards which we are all tending, would be a most powerful means of drawing into the unity of the faith her scattered bands. These pages are now sent forth with the conviction that they contain that truth which the church especially needs in this day to reconcile the conflicting views of human destiny by which she is distracted and perplexed, and that they will so help her on in that path to unity, which she must tread before the world will believe that the Father sent the Son to be its Saviour, and before she can fulfil her high mission in the future as the chosen vehicle of His Life and blessing to all mankind.

CONTENTS.

PART I.

CHAPTER I.
INTRODUCTORY 1

CHAPTER II.
THE TRUE METHOD OF INQUIRY 5

CHAPTER III.
THE SONG OF MOSES 10

CHAPTER IV.
JUDGMENT IN PSALM AND PROPHECY 24

CHAPTER V.
CORRECTION THROUGH JUDGMENT 30

CHAPTER VI.
THE LORD SHALL JUDGE HIS PEOPLE 35

CHAPTER VII.
REDEMPTION THROUGH RESURRECTION 43

CHAPTER VIII.
REDEMPTION THROUGH RESURRECTION 50

CHAPTER IX.
REDEMPTION THROUGH RESURRECTION 57

CHAPTER X.
CAPTIVITY CAPTIVE 64

CHAPTER XI.
UNQUENCHABLE FIRE 71

CHAPTER XII.
LATER JEWISH OPINION 77

x   *Contents.*

PART II.

CHAPTER I.
THE AXE LAID AT THE ROOT OF THE TREE 87

CHAPTER II.
GEHENNA 94

CHAPTER III.
ETERNAL FIRE, A FACT OF SCIENCE AS WELL AS OF SCRIPTURE   104

CHAPTER IV.
THE JUDGMENT-SCENE OF MATT. XXV. 31–46 115

CHAPTER V.
THE RESURRECTION OF JUDGMENT 138

CHAPTER VI.
THE JUDGE OF QUICK AND DEAD 151

CHAPTER VII.
THE JUDGMENT OF THE GREAT WHITE THRONE . . 158

CHAPTER VIII.
RETRIBUTION IN APOSTOLIC PREACHING 173

CHAPTER IX.
RETRIBUTION IN ST. PAUL'S EPISTLES 183

CHAPTER X.
RETRIBUTION IN THE CATHOLIC EPISTLES 200

CHAPTER XI.
RETRIBUTION IN THE APOCALYPSE 215

CHAPTER XII.
REVIEW 230
APPENDIX A 254
APPENDIX B 259

PART I.

CHAPTER I.

INTRODUCTORY.

Very many persons are reluctant to admit the right to enter upon such investigations as we now propose. In their view whatever is generally accepted by the church as true and as taught in Scripture, and to which she has given formal sanction in her public standards, should be regarded as settled. And he who would reopen such questions is looked upon as a troubler in Israel.

Such persons, however, need to be reminded that, in all that pertains to The Last Things, there is very wide diversity in the beliefs and the teachings of the best and most enlightened Christians. Every church is compelled to allow great liberty here, because of the obscurity of the subject and the confessed inability of even her wisest teachers to grasp it. Moreover, we have no right to assume that any interpretation of these subjects is, of necessity, correct, because it has been long and widely received. The whole history of the professed people of God proves that they have long and repeatedly acquiesced in the gravest errors, and enforced as orthodox the most meagre and mistaken opinions. The generation of Jews in our Lord's time had been carefully instructed in the Old Testament Scriptures. And yet all the orthodox conceptions of the Messiah's office were painfully wrong.

The whole synagogue were blind to the most important features of His redeeming work, and especially failed to see how the Scriptures taught that He must needs suffer and be killed, and the third day rise again. If the Lord has thus allowed whole generations of His people to misconceive important features of His revealed Word, He may, for some wise purpose, do this again. In view of this past history of Israel, and of similar blindnesses which have come upon the church during the centuries of her experience, how can any one affirm that she may not be mistaken about many things pertaining to the future of which she seems most confident?

It is often said that the Bible is a plain book addressed to plain people. And therefore the common understanding of what it teaches concerning any great matter of doctrine must be correct. And yet these "common understandings" of men have been most faulty in the past. They may be so now. They will be necessarily so unless these prevalent judgments are of a higher order than those which are merely literal or logical. They must be spiritual. Truths may be so stated in the Word of God as that the mere literalist, or the man of mere intellectual insight, shall necessarily mistake. Only he that is spiritual judgeth all things. Moreover, the church will be almost sure to err if she assumes that she "knoweth anything yet as she ought to know." (1 Cor. viii. 2.) So long as she notoriously fails to realize that unity for which her Lord prayed, and which was to be the witness to the world of His divine mission, so long all her conceptions of His truth must be partial. A fragmentary church is but a broken vessel, unfit to contain either the divine life or the divine knowledge in its fullness. The Holy Spirit was given to illumine the One body of the One Lord. It is only *with all saints* that we can comprehend the love which passeth knowledge. If even an inspired apostle could say, "For we know in part and prophesy in part," surely these marred and broken sections of the church cannot be too humble in their claims. The church's divided state is *prima facie* proof of her imperfect knowledge of God's word. She is therefore bound to refuse the assumption that she has nothing more to learn, and to hold herself open to receive light from whatever quarter it may come. Indeed, her constant prayer should be for a deeper understanding of the mystery of Christ, in which are hidden all the treasures of wisdom and of knowledge. And instead of frowning upon any of her children who may reverently believe that God has given him a revelation for the common benefit, she should "despise not prophesyings." She must indeed "try the spirits; because many false prophets have gone out into the world." And yet she cannot be too careful lest, by her harsh tests and her servile adherence to preconceived opinions, she stifle within her the voice of that Spirit whose office it is to guide her into all truth and show her things to come. And just as it was true of the first disciples that there were many things He should hereafter show them because they could not bear them then, so it has been always true that God has caused new light to break forth from His Word as men have been prepared to receive it. There are secret things there which have been brought to light in His good time, and there are yet other things " to be testified in due time." (1 Tim. ii. 6.)

Moreover, it would be strange indeed if there were no new light to be expected from the book of God's works upon dark places in His Word. Both are from the same hand. The wonderful progress made in these last days in the study of nature, however much it may have been marred by the natural blindness and conceit of men, has certainly given us a larger knowledge of the great plans of its Author. And this knowledge cannot but be useful in aiding us to a broader and better understanding of His Word, in which these plans are more fully outlined.

The writer has a firm conviction that there are two great facts of Scripture which must be made the centres of far wider circles of truth than we have yet grouped around them. These are the facts of judgment for sin, and of Redemption through resurrection. He is also persuaded that the times are ripe for, and the church is earnestly crying out for, some such restatement of these great mysteries as shall harmonize them with all that she has learned of the condition of man and of the character of God.

And he enters this field of inquiry not to criticize or to dogmatize, but as an humble seeker after truth, hoping, if he fail to find it, that he may at least point out a path along which it may be sought, and which leads out of our present twilight toward the sun-rising.

CHAPTER II.

THE TRUE METHOD OF INQUIRY.

The church doctrine* of future punishment is wholly drawn from the New Testament. A glance at any of its Confessions or Manuals of Theology will show that all the proof texts, whose support is of any value, are taken from this part of Scripture. The Old Testament economy, through the whole period of its history, a period longer than the Christian dispensation, was carried on without any clear revelation to men of their liability to an everlasting punishment in hell after death. The first five books, in which the principles of this divine economy are fully set forth and its laws and ordinances fixed, are silent as to this point. They contain much concerning God's purposes toward mankind. They reveal Him most plainly as the Righteous One, before the consuming fire of whose anger the wicked are destroyed. But there is no threat of their never-ending torment in hell after death. We find then that, when God was revealing to men such truth about Himself and His relation to mankind as was to be the basis of their moral discipline, and of their worship and obedience for centuries, He gave them no clear warning of such tremendous doom. Nor did the Psalms and Prophets supply this defect. Not a single passage in these later Scriptures would be suspected of teaching this doctrine, did not the reflected light of certain passages in the New Testament seem to invest them with this meaning.

---

* By "church doctrine" is meant the doctrine set forth in the accepted standards, as, e. g. the Westminster Confession, chaps. xxxii. and xxxiii.

The three principal proof-texts quoted from the Old Testament in its support are:

1. Daniel xii: 2, which seems to assert the resurrection of some who sleep in the dust of the earth to shame and everlasting contempt. Tregelles (on Daniel pp. 162-167) makes it probable that it is the unawakened sleepers, not resurrected, who are left to shame and contempt as captives in the realms of death. The same view is ably maintained by Dr. N. West in a recent number of the Presbyterian Review, in an exhaustive criticism upon the passage.

2. Isaiah (xxxiii: 14) asks the question, "Who among us shall dwell with everlasting burnings?" in which the answer is pre-supposed that *none* shall be able to dwell with such devouring fire, unless it be the righteous, of whom the next verses speak.

3. Isaiah lxvi: 24, gives a vision of the dead carcasses of transgressors, whose corruption cannot be arrested, nor can the fire that consumes them be quenched. Similar Old Testament uses of the term "unquenchable fire" occur in Jeremiah xvii: 27; xxi: 12.

We refer to these three passages, however, not for the purpose of advocating any special interpretation of them, but in order to show how doubtful and slender a support is given in even these strongest Old Testament passages to a doctrine of such tremendous weight as the endless torment in hell of all who die in their sins. They confirm what we have said that this is not a plain doctrine of the Old Testament. And yet from all we know of the character of God we should suppose that, if true, He would not have left His chosen people, nor mankind at large for so many generations, in ignorance of it.

And this brings us to remark upon the defective method by which this doctrine has been drawn from the Bible. It has been taken from one portion of it. Men have believed it to be clearly taught in the New Testament. And so they have forced the Old Testament to yield it some support. We cannot, of course, affirm that God might not have concealed this doctrine from the men of past ages, bringing it out at a later age through Him who spake as never man spake. We must affirm, however, that this is highly improbable. It is strangely unlike our God. All other great truths of such immense importance to mankind, the sacrificial death of Christ, His resurrection and the consequent resurrection of all men, the restitution of all things, were spoken of, at least darkly, by the mouth of all His holy prophets since the world began. We understand them, as revealed in the New Testament, because they were all typically and germinally revealed in the Old. Nor is the Old Testament silent upon the great features of human destiny. God's wrath against sin, and the final outcome of His dealings with men and with nations on account of it, stand out luminous upon its pages. The doctrine of future judgment, the awards of life and death, reaching by implication far beyond the bounds of time, the tests of character to which all men should be brought under the Messiah's reign, and the final subjection to it of all men and of all things in heaven and on earth,—the Old Testament pages glow with these themes of living interest.

And hence we are right in insisting that the church has pursued a wrong method in making up her doctrine concerning the final destiny of men.

She has first fixed her faith from the New Testament and then inquired what support she could find for it in the Old. This process should have been reversed. She should have first inquired what God had been teaching for four thousand years concerning the great problems of man's duty and destiny. And then she might have come with a truer intelligence to the interpretation of the later revelation. We are in no proper mood to understand these "hard sayings" of Jesus unless we first "know the Scriptures." They were spoken to men who had been taught from these Scriptures all their lives and who were yet strangely blind to their meaning. They pre-suppose this previous revelation. They were never meant to be understood apart from it. They were surely not meant to annul or supersede it. We are unprepared, therefore, to advance to their interpretation before we have made ourselves familiar with that body of truth upon which they are grafted.

There must be falseness somewhere in a method which leads men to imagine that the words which fell from the lips of Jesus are less gracious than those which God spake unto the fathers by the prophets. We have been compelled to assume that the more fully God has revealed Himself the less is He seen to be Love.

We have formed a portrait of Him on the canvass of our narrow exegesis and with the hard drawn lines of our pitiless logic, until even good men have revolted from the image as if our God were a fiend.

This treatise is an attempt to study this deep subject along the lines of what we have indicated as the only true method. We shall first seek to ascertain what the Old

Scriptures, to which Jesus and His apostles constantly appealed as the source of all their teaching, have to say upon the dark problems of human destiny. And then we shall advance to the interpretation of New Testament teaching by the light thus derived.

We know of no recent attempts to solve this great question in which this method is pursued. Canon Farrar's "Eternal Hope" gives us much that is bright and comforting on one side of this question. His discussion is able and learned and throws much light upon the meaning of special texts. But it is unsatisfactory, in failing to lay down a broad Scriptural basis upon which to rest this hope. The same may be said of his more recent book, "Mercy and Judgment." Dr. Pusey, on the other side, in his able inquiry, "What is of faith as to everlasting punishment?" has linked together a surprising catena of proof-passages from Apocryphal and Rabbinical writers and from the Christian fathers, but he has not told us *what the Old Testament prophets believed*. They are the only "Fathers" who can speak to us with authority upon this matter. Jesus placed His divine seal upon their teaching. We are therefore right in demanding that, before we decide upon the meaning of His teaching concerning human destiny, we examine what is revealed about it in the law and prophets which He came not to set aside, but to fulfill.

CHAPTER III.

THE SONG OF MOSES.
(DEUT. xxxii.)

If any passage of Scripture deserves to be regarded as a key to the whole, it is this passage. It was spoken at a most important period in Israel's history. Their wanderings and long chastisement in the desert were now over and they stood upon the borders of the promised land. Moses had reviewed for them this history and enforced its solemn lessons. He had recited again the law, with its blessings and curses, and entreated them by these weighty sanctions to obey it. And yet he foresaw that they would disobey and that this long catalogue of evils would be visited upon them.

About to be removed from them by death, the Lord commands him to speak this song in their ears and to write it out as a testimony against them.

The passage is a vindication and a prophecy. It surveys the past and gazes far down into the future. It hints at God's deep designs in allowing these failures of His people and in their subsequent chastisements. It foreshadows the calling of the Gentiles. It speaks of a series of revenges upon the enemies who had wrought the ruin of His people and provoked His anger, and ends by summoning the nations to rejoice with His people in the mercy with which this long history of sin and of suffering should close.

Let us now examine minutely what this song teaches concerning the wages of sin; concerning judgment and retribution, and concerning redemption and resurrection, and the final outcome of this deep problem of the world and of man.

1. The importance of the matters which make up the substance of this song is such that Heaven and Earth are invited to hear it.

"Give ear, O ye Heavens, and I will speak; and hear, O Earth, the words of my mouth. My doctrine shall drop as the rain, my speech shall distill as the dew, as the small rain upon the tender herb and as the showers upon the grass." (vs. 1-2.)

Even the song of judgment is for the refreshment and growth of those who hear it.

2. The subject of the song is declared.

"Because I will publish the name of the LORD: ascribe ye greatness unto our God. He is the Rock, His work is perfect: for all His ways are judgment; a God of truth and without iniquity, just and right is He." (vs. 3-4.)

The strain of these verses is the one which is taken up in "the Song of Moses the servant of God, and the Song of the Lamb." (Rev. xv. 3, 4). The subject of this Song is the same as of that, only the redemption phase comes out more brightly in that song of victory. The Song in the Revelation contains but two verses, and these are drawn from the beginning and the ending of this Song of Moses. There can be no doubt, therefore, that the Song of Moses referred to in the Revelation is not the one He sang after the passage of the Red Sea (Ex. xv.), but this Song of Judgment, which was spoken under such impressive circumstances just before his death.

3. It asserts the wickedness and ingratitude of the chosen people and recounts their mercies and apostasies.

"They have corrupted themselves, their spot is not the spot of His children: they are a perverse and crooked generation. Do ye thus requite the LORD, O foolish people and unwise? Is not He thy Father that hath bought thee? hath He not made thee and established thee?

"Remember the days of old, consider the years of many generations: ask thy father and he will shew thee; thy elders, and they will tell thee. When the Most High divided to the nations their inheritance, when He separated the sons of Adam, He set the bounds of the people according to the number of the children of Israel. For the LORD'S portion is His people; Jacob is the lot of His inheritance. He found him in a desert land, in a waste howling wilderness; He led him about; He instructed him, He kept him as the apple of His eye. As an eagle stirreth up her nest, fluttereth over her young, spreadeth abroad her wings, taketh them, beareth them on her wings; so the LORD alone did lead him, and there was no strange god with him. He made him ride on the high places of the earth, that he might eat the increase of the fields; and He made him to suck honey out of the rock, and oil out of the flinty rock; butter of kine and milk of sheep, with fat of lambs, and rams of the breed of Bashan, and goats, with the fat of kidneys of wheat; and thou didst drink the pure blood of the grape.

"But Jeshurun waxed fat and kicked; thou art waxen fat, thou art grown thick, thou art covered with fatness; then he forsook God which made him, and lightly esteemed the Rock of his salvation. They provoked Him to jealousy with strange gods, with abominations provoked they Him to anger. They sacrificed unto devils, not to God; to gods whom they knew not, to new gods that came newly up, whom your fathers feared not. Of the Rock that begat thee thou art unmindful, and hast forgotten God that formed thee." (Vs. 5-18.)

Observe here that, behind the forms and forces of nature worshiped as gods, there were demoniac powers, the real recipients of this homage. "They sacrificed unto devils."

4. It declares the Lord's abhorrence of their sins, their consequent rejection, and the calling out from the Gentiles of a new people.

"And when the Lord saw it, He abhorred them, because of the provoking of his sons and of his daughters. And He said, I will hide my face from them, I will see what their end shall be: for they are a very froward generation, children in whom is no faith. They have moved me to jealousy with that which is not God; they have provoked me to anger with their vanities: and I will move them to jealousy with those which are not a people; I will provoke them to anger with a foolish nation." (Vs. 19-21.)

Their rejection, however, would not be final. So St. Paul affirms in the eleventh chapter of Romans, after his quotation of the last verse of the above passage at the close of the tenth.

5. It affirms that the Lord's anger, which must burn against them on account of their sins, must burn also to the final destruction of this world system under which this depravity in His people had been developed.

"For a fire is kindled in mine anger, and shall burn unto the lowest hell, and shall consume the earth with her increase, and set on fire the foundations of the mountains." Verse 22.

Here occurs the first mention in Scripture of the fire of Hell. It is represented as burning down to the regions of the dead, and to the very foundations of this natural order, as if it were the source of that corruption which had come upon His people.

Here we meet with a principle of the divine judgments whose importance cannot be overestimated; that which views the present cosmos or natural system as sharing in the responsibility for man's evil nature. As subject to vanity and in bondage to corruption, it has put its yoke on its highest creature, and it is therefore bound over to the consuming fire of God's judgments. It may seem to us irrational that accountability should attach in any way to a material system. But if the whole system is pervaded by living forces; if it is the visible representative of "things invisible," which according to Colossians 1 : 14 are living powers, it will not appear so strange that the searching fire of God's anger should find evil intrenched at its very foundations, and that this present order and the powers that rule in it, with the devil, who is declared to be its prince (St. John xii : 31), should be involved in a common judgment.* We shall see hereafter how fully this principle is recognized in Scripture as palliating the moral turpitude of men and as furnishing a plea for divine interference in their behalf.

6. The temporal calamities which should soon overtake His people would be in the line of this consuming fire; manifestations of the same destructive energy against sin which must finally "consume the earth."

The term "fire" stands for the concentrated energy of the dissolving forces of nature. It is the rapid consumer of created forms. But this devouring energy operates in slower ways. It is more or less resisted and for a while baffled. And yet Scripture groups all the forms in which human lives are blighted and destroyed under this one head and refers them to one agency.† "Our God is a consuming fire." And so we read

"I will heap mischiefs upon them; I will spend mine arrows upon them. They shall be burnt with hunger and devoured with burning heat, and with bitter destruction. I will also send the teeth of beasts upon them, with the poison of serpents of the dust.

---

* See upon this subject "Mystery of Creation and of Man," chapters VI and VII.

† See "Mystery of Creation," etc. page 169.

The sword without and terror within shall destroy both the young man and the virgin, the suckling, with the man of gray hairs." vs. 23-25.

7. These judgments would make an utter end of His people, were it not that the enemy's triumph over them would thereby be complete, and his impudent boast against the God of Israel be justified.

"I said I would scatter them into corners. I would make the remembrance of them to cease from among men; were it not that I feared the enemy, lest their adversaries should behave themselves strangely, and lest they should say, Our hand is high and the Lord hath not done all this." (Vs. 25-27.)

These words have primary reference to the taunts of their human adversaries. But they look beyond these. This song deals with secret things yet sealed up among God's treasures. The doctrine of diabolic agency, lying back of human instruments, and as concerned in this warfare against God's people, and of Satan as their chief enemy, had not yet been plainly revealed. But this song is of wide scope. It views as from a height this age-long and world-wide conflict. We have seen that it looks forward to a judgment upon this "present evil world," the fashion of which must pass away. And now it brings to view an "enemy" and certain adversaries who have well nigh brought God's people to ruin, and who would have made an utter end of them, but whom Jehovah, for the love He bears them and for the honor of His name, shall baffle and defeat.

8. If His people were but wise enough to understand this and to act in the faith and hope of this coming deliverance, they would now be able to put all these enemies to flight.

"For they are a nation void of counsel, neither is there any understanding in them.

"Oh, that they were wise, that they understood this, that they would consider their latter end!" (Would that their faith could apprehend the deliverance that must finally be theirs!) "How should one chase a thousand, and two put ten thousand to flight, except their Rock had sold them, and the Lord had shut them up." (Vs. 28-30.)

The closing words of verse 30 give, in parenthesis, the reason why they prevailed so little against their enemies. He, who was their Refuge, had given them up to judicial blindness and bondage on account of their sins.

And yet the Rock of their enemies was not as their Rock, as they themselves must confess. (Verse 31.)

9. Trust in false gods is but a delusive and poisonous exhilaration, a draught of deadly venom. And yet of such wine would Israel drink.

"For their vine is of the vine of Sodom, and of the fields of Gomorrah, their grapes are grapes of gall, their clusters are bitter: Their wine is the poison of dragons, and the cruel venom of asps." (Vs. 32-33.)

10. The mystery of God's people as thus enthralled is next referred to. And the "times" during which this "mystery of iniquity" should work, with the final issues of it are declared to be in His own power.

"Is not this laid up in store with me, and sealed up among my treasures?" (Verse 34.)

11. Jehovah now asserts himself as a God of vengeance and recompense. He had already declared the woes that He would send upon His people. But now His thought turns to the enemies, who had been the instruments of His punishment. They had seduced and

enslaved His people. And for this and for all their sins His wrath must come upon them.

> "To me belongeth vengeance and recompense; their foot shall slide in due time: for the day of their calamity is at hand, and the things that shall come upon them make haste." (Verse 35.)

12. He will judge His people, and turn toward them, after they have been brought low, and have become convinced that their false gods can bring them no help.

> "For the Lord shall judge His people, and repent himself for His servants, when He seeth that their power is gone, and there is none shut up or left. And He shall say, Where are their gods, their rock in whom they trusted, which did eat the fat of their sacrifices, and drank the wine of their drink offerings? let them rise up and help you, and be your protection." (Vs. 36-38.)

His judgment of His people, however severe, would be for their salvation.

He would bring them into such humiliation that they will accept of the punishment of their iniquity, (see Lev. xxvi. 41-43,) and confess the impotence of the false gods in which they had trusted.

When men are brought low with no power to help themselves, and with every refuge failing them, then at such a time the grace of God comes to the rescue.

13. And so the Lord proclaims himself as their only Saviour, in that He alone is Lord of Life and of Death. His judgments must fall upon His people unto death. They must be handed over to the great Destroyer. And one generation after another must go down as captives into his gloomy realms. In this, the triumph of their enemy over them seemed complete and irreversible. But nothing is too hard for a God who can heal as well as

wound, who can make alive as well as kill, and out of whose hands none can fall.

"See now that I, even I, am he, and there is no strange god with me: I kill and I make alive; I wound and I heal; neither is there any that can deliver out of my hand." (Vs. 39.)

Here we have an early intimation of that grand truth which runs through the Bible and underlies its whole redemptive system. Our redeeming God can make alive from death. He is the God of resurrection. So that not even death, which holds of right his people captive, can annul or defeat his gracious designs toward them. He can redeem them from the power of even the last enemy.

14. Hence, this song passes on to declare his sworn purpose to defeat and destroy all their enemies. He now makes His people's cause His own. And so we have, in grand outline, a series of revenges upon all their enemies, human and diabolic; a triumph which looks forward to their deliverance from death and from their chief enemy, which can be no other than "him that hath the power of death, that is, the devil."

"For I lift up my hand to heaven and say, I live forever." Vs. 40.

He swears by Himself, the Living One. This name, itself, is the defeat of death.

"If I whet my glittering sword and mine hand take hold of judgment; I will render vengeance to mine enemies, and will reward them that hate me." Vs. 41.

Israel's enemies are now Jehovah's enemies.

"I will make mine arrows drunk with blood, and my sword shall devour flesh, and that with the blood of the slain and of the captives, from the beginning of revenges upon the enemy." (Vs. 42).

These words evidently cover a wide sweep of judgments. They predict the slaughter of their human enemies, the overthrow of them that had held them in captivity, and of the "*head or chief of the princes of the enemy.*"

The English version translates the last clause of this verse, "from the beginning of revenges upon the enemy." The Septuagint give the sense as above. And this is the meaning assigned to the word *peraoth* by Gesenius. See also Robert Young's version and his Concordance under the word "revenges." The reference is to the chief enemy, before spoken of in vs. 27. The song looks forward, therefore, to a culminating triumph over the great Adversary of God and man, the Prince of this world and head over all its evil powers. All Scripture teaches that he must be held to a final responsibility for the evil and misery which have come upon the people of God and upon the human race. And hence this song, among its sealed-up treasures (vs. 34), declares God's purpose to finally bind and destroy this great enemy. We should not have known that this purpose is here concealed, had not all subsequent Scripture taught us that the work of redemption must reach on to this consummation. But now we go back to this key-passage of the Old Testament and find it there.

15. And so the song closes by calling upon the nations to join with Israel in their joy over this coming deliverance.

"Rejoice, O ye nations, with His people : for He will avenge the blood of His servants, and will render vengeance to His adversaries, and will be merciful unto His land and to His people."*

That a triumph over other than mere human enemies of Israel is referred to is manifest from the fact that the nations are summoned to rejoice with them. They are also sharers in its joy and blessing. And hence this passage is quoted by St. Paul (Romans xv: 10,) as proving that, in the mission of Jesus Christ to the world to confirm the promises made to the fathers, the Gentiles also should glorify God for his mercy. All God's adversaries shall finally be trampled out under the conquering feet of His Son, who, in His resurrection, led captivity captive. He has defeated and shall finally destroy death and him that hath the power of death, that is, the devil. (Heb. ii: 14.) He shall destroy all the works of the devil, and all God's enemies shall perish.

Such is the close of this song of judgment. It breaks out at the end into a song of redemption. And hence it furnishes the deeper tones in that splendid song of triumph which the victors sing, standing on the sea of glass, (Rev. xv: 3, 4.) "The Song of Moses, the servant of God, and of the Lamb," saying; *Great and marvellous are thy*

---

* It is interesting to observe how the Septuagint translators have amplified the doxology in the closing verse of this song, showing their sense of the importance of this passage, as looking beyond all temporary deliverances to a final redemption from all the power of the enemy. They call upon the Heavens and all the angels of God and all the sons of God to join with Israel and the nations in joy and praise. "Rejoice, ye heavens, with Him, and worship before Him, all ye angels of God. Rejoice, ye nations, with His people, and let all the sons of God strengthen themselves in Him; because He revengeth the blood of His sons. And He shall judge and requite justice to his enemies and recompense them that hate Him. And the Lord will thoroughly cleanse His land and people."

works, Lord God Almighty; just and true are thy ways, thou King of nations. Who shall not fear Thee, O Lord, and glorify thy name? for Thou only art holy: for all nations shall come and worship before Thee; for thy judgments are made manifest.

The two focal points then around which the far reaching lines of this prophetic song curve are these, *Judgment* and *Redemption*. These are the two great principles of the divine dealing which appear in the history of Israel and of mankind. The two are not antagonistic but supplementary. "All His ways are judgment," (vs. 4,) but they issue in redemption. And "*His ways He made known unto Moses;*" how He chides His people for their sins, but keeps not His anger forever. (Psalm 103: 7-9.)

As to these principles, we have seen

I. The wide scope of His judgments.

a. His people must receive at his hand double for all their sins. (vs. 21-26.)

b. The nations who oppress them must, in their turn, suffer under the heavy hand of His judgments. (vs. 35.)

c. The invisible spiritual enemies, of whom men are often the puppets, and who use them to carry on their warfare against God's people, must fall under His wrath. The fire of His anger shall burn against even the present system of Nature in which these foes are intrenched, the Earth and the foundations thereof. (Verse 22.)

d. He shall bruise the head and finally destroy the great adversary of God and man, and death, the last enemy. (Vs. 42-43.)

II. But these judgments are in order to redemption. They issue in the redemption of His people, of mankind and of the Earth. The oppressors' yoke is broken by them. And death's captives are liberated through a triumph over death. The God who lives forever, who kills, can also make alive, (verse 39.) Not even death can remove any of His creatures out of His hand. This indeed is the vital, the essential fact in His redeeming work. Death is the worst and apparently the most invincible of all our enemies. All other agencies of divine wrath, war, famine, wasting sickness, are but handmaids to this supreme foe. No redemption can avail for man which does not redeem from death. No deliverance from captivity amounts to anything which does not reach the captives in the realms of death. Hence it is the deepest truth of redemption that our Redeemer is the God of resurrection. This truth is but dimly traced through the Old Testament, as compared with its bold outlines in the New. But it is there. And here, in this grand key-passage to all subsequent psalm and prophecy and history, we find it.

Proof that the Jews had some understanding of the great truth of redemption as dependent upon resurrection, and of this truth as taught in this passage, (verse 39) is found in the paraphrase of it given in the Jerusalem Targum:

"See now that I in my Word am He, and there is no other God beside me. I kill the living in this world and make alive the dead in the world that cometh; I am He who smiteth and I am He who healeth, and there is none who can deliver from my hand."

So also in the Jewish liturgies, (Horne's Introduction Vol. 2. p. 107,) we find the prayer:

"Thou, O Lord, of thy abundant mercy makest the dead to live. Thou raiseth up those who fall; thou healest the

sick, thou loosest them who are bound, and makest good thy word of truth to those who sleep in the dust. Who is to be compared to thee, O thou Lord of might! And who is like unto thee, O our King, who killest and makest alive, and makest salvation to spring as the grass in the field! Thou art faithful to make the dead to rise again to life. Blessed art thou, O Lord, who raisest the dead again to life!"

CHAPTER III.

JUDGMENT IN PSALM AND PROPHECY.

Most important principles of God's dealings, of the relations of Israel and of mankind to His government, and of the destiny of man and of the created system to which he belongs, have now been brought to view. The Song of Moses has declared to us God's righteousness and the far-reaching judgments required for its vindication. The human race at large must pass under the power of death. The chosen people must suffer all kinds of temporal disaster and go down into the common grave. The nations who oppress them must be given over to destruction. The unseen powers of evil, who seduce men to worship them as "gods," but who are only "devils," the instigators of this reign of discord and misery, must be tracked to their fastnesses in this system of creation and punished. The earth must be baptized with fire. The prince of all these enemies must be cast out. And death, the last enemy, must be destroyed.

If these judgments, however, were to issue in the final and total extinction of Israel and of mankind, God would be defeated and the enemy would triumph. Hence the Song casts a horoscope to see "what their end shall be." Man's extremity proves to be God's opportunity. "I was brought low and he helped me." Not even death can defeat the least of God's gracious purposes toward His people or annul His design in the creation of man and the world. The secret of relief and of victory is all contained in the fact that He is the Living One, the Lord of both death and life. After the fullest vindication of His righteousness, after punishment has done its worst, and death and hell seem to be complete masters of the field, then the way is only the more clear for the God of grace and resurrection to work.

In His wonder-working counsels Redemption through death and resurrection is provided, and all God's enemies are overthrown. Even Death itself is vanquished and destroyed. And so all mankind, who have been shut up in this bondage to sin and death, share in the benefits of this deliverance and are summoned to rejoice because of it.

It remains for us now to see how these principles give tone to all subsequent Psalm and Prophecy.

That Israel, the nations who oppressed them, and all the Gentiles must suffer for their sins such wrath from God as should fully vindicate His righteousness is the plainest fact of Scripture. No Bible reader will require us to prove this by quotations. It is found on every page. The prophets all denounce Israel and foretell his coming desolation. But their prophetic glance takes in also the nations with which Israel had been in any way associated. It includes, indeed, within its horizon, all mankind. After the burden of Israel is declared we have, as in Isaiah, the burden of Babylon, of Moab, of Damascus, of Egypt, of Ethiopia, of Arabia, of Tyre, and finally of the whole earth, (ch. xxiv.) which is made empty and desolate, because it is "defiled under its inhabitants, and the transgression thereof is heavy upon it." These judgments would reach them through all the channels by which the curses of God find out evil doers, and which

Moses had vividly set forth in his farewell address (Deut. xxviii). Sickness, mildew and drought, famine, war, desolation of home and fields, slaughter, cruel exactions and tortures by triumphant enemies, captivity in distant lands, these were the scourges to be inflicted upon them beneath the rod of God's anger.

But these woes are only the handmaids of a worse evil. They are the avenues of death. And hence the final culminating evil they must suffer under would be a long captivity in the realms of death. Their individual, their national hopes would be buried here. " Thou has visited and destroyed them and made all their memory to perish." (Is. xxvi. 14.)

Here it is to be observed that death, bondage in Sheol, is viewed in the Old Testament as a final vindication of Jehovah's righteousness, the supreme expression of His anger against sin. This was the original sentence. "In the day thou eatest thereof thou shalt surely die." "The wages of sin is death."

The idea attached to this term "death" in the Old Testament was the one which properly belongs to it. It was "cessation of being." Some passages seem to view this end of being as absolute. For instance, Job says (xiv. 10-12) "Man dieth and wasteth away; yea, man giveth up the ghost, and where is he? As the waters fail from the sea, and the flood decayeth and drieth up: so man lieth down, and riseth not: till the heavens be no more, they shall not awake, nor be raised out of their sleep." In Jeremiah (li. 39.) death is viewed as a "perpetual sleep. And yet the hope of a future reawakening is often expressed. Even Job, in connection with the above passage, affirms his belief (vs. 15) that in the end, "Thou shalt call and I will answer thee: thou wilt have a desire to the work of thy hands."

But, before resurrection, the dead, in the Hebrew conception, were not men who had passed into another form of being. They were *dead*; not absolutely extinct; otherwise they could not be resurrected. But their being was only "the miserable consciousness of not being." Doubtless in their later Scriptures, and as the result of their religious development, they advanced to a more definite conviction of the conscious happiness of the righteous in Hades, and of the conscious misery of the wicked. But still the shades (Rephaim*) were viewed as prisoners in Sheol, without the proper prerogatives of being. The Hebrews never conceived of man as properly existent apart from the body. The body was an essential constituent in that form of being called "man." It was not, therefore, judgment *after* death that men were taught to fear, but judgment *in* death. Man, in Sheol, was but a powerless shade, an exile, a captive in the darkness and silence of that gloomy realm. There, they *rest together as prisoners*, (Job iii. 18). They go down *to the bars of the pit* [Sheol] (xvii. 16). *Prisoners of the earth*, Lam. iii. 34. They are *hid in prison houses*, Is. xlii. 22, given up for a spoil by Jehovah for their sins (vs. 24).

In Isaiah (xxii. 14) it is affirmed that no temporal disasters would suffice to purge the Jews of their iniquity. *Surely this iniquity shall not be purged from you till ye die, saith the Lord of hosts.*

---

*See Gesenius upon this word, and also its use in Isaiah xiv. 9; xxvi. 14, 19. Psalm lxxxviii. 10, *et. al.*

The complaints of Israel (Psalm cxli. 7 ; Ezek. xxxvii. 11), under the ravages of death show that they viewed the great enemy as the destroyer of all their individual and national hopes. "Our bones are scattered at the grave's mouth." "Our bones are dried, our hope is lost: we are cut off for our parts." While, as regards the heathen, their kings and captains, in all their pomp and pride, with their multitudinous hosts, are viewed as brought down to hell and shut up there as in a prison house. Isaiah xiv. depicts the descent of the proud monarch of Babylon from his pinnacle of earthly glory down to Sheol, whose inhabitants are stirred up to meet and to mock this great one of the earth, now become as weak and nerveless as one of themselves. In Ezekiel xxxii. we have a similar picture of the casting down of "the multitude of Egypt," "into the nether parts of the earth, with them that go down into the pit." "Asshur (Assyria) is there, and all her company: his graves are about him: all of them slain, fallen by the sword: whose graves are set in the sides of the pit, and her company is round about her grave, all of them slain, fallen by the sword, which caused terror in the land of the living." The same dirge is repeated concerning Elam, Meshech, Tubal, Edom, the princes of the north and all the Zidonians. All these uncircumcised nations were "gone down to hell" where they would be companions of Pharaoh and his multitude, denizens with them of that land of gloom and forgetfulness, fast locked in the embrace of death.

We thus find that one uniform conception of the divine judgments against sin is current through the Old Testament. Sinners, whether viewed as individuals or in masses as nations, were to be visited with all kinds of temporal evils in their persons, their families, their property, their civil liberties, until finally death should carry them away as captives into his dark realm. The final result of the divine dealing with sinners is stated in such passages as these: " The wicked shall be turned into hell, *(Sheol) and all the nations that forget God," (Psalm ix. 17.) " For lo, thine enemies, O Lord, for lo, thine enemies shall perish." (xcii. 9). We shall see, however, as we advance, that not even this dark realm of judgment is beyond the reach of His redeeming power.

CHAPTER V.

CORRECTION THROUGH JUDGMENT.

That the visitations of God's anger, under which men suffer, are *disciplinary* as well as penal is a prime feature in Old Testament teaching. The 26th chapter of Leviticus contains a catalogue of terrible evils that should come upon the people for their sins. They were to be driven out of their own land into captivity, where they should perish among the heathen, and be eaten up by the land of their enemies. (Verse 38.) But if, in the place of their banishment, they should turn again to the Lord in humility and should *"accept of the punishment of their iniquity,"* (vs. 41-43,) Jehovah promises to remember His covenant and to forgive and restore them.

The subsequent history of Israel fully illustrates this gracious dealing. "Many times did He deliver them; but they provoked Him with their counsel, and were brought low for their iniquity. Nevertheless He regarded their affliction when He heard their cry: And he remembered for them His covenant, and repented according to the multitude of His mercies." (Ps. cvi: 43-45.) The prophet Micah (vii: 7-10,) expresses in language beautiful and touching, the faith and penitence of the people when thus humbled under the mighty hand of God. "Therefore I will look unto the Lord; I will wait for the God of my salvation: my God will hear me. Rejoice not against me, O mine enemy: when I fall, I shall arise; when I sit in darkness, the Lord shall be a light unto me. I will bear the indignation of the Lord, because I have sinned against him, until He plead my cause, and execute judgment for me: He will bring me forth to the light, and I shall behold His righteousness." In this passage two principles are distinctly asserted. 1. Those who sin against the Lord must be borne down under the burden of His indignation. 2. If, in their low estate, they "accept the punishment of their iniquity," the Lord will rise up for their relief and plead their cause, and execute judgment upon their enemies. Isaiah (xl: 1-2), at the beginning of the second division of his prophecy, which is so full of the hopes and triumphs of the future, breaks out with this message of grace to Israel.— "Comfort ye, comfort ye my people, saith your God. Speak ye comfortably to Jerusalem, and cry unto her, that her warfare is accomplished, her iniquity is pardoned:* for she hath received of the Lord's hand double for all her sins."

Here again a return of the Lord's favor is declared after His people had suffered a double, that is, a most ample punishment for their sins. Humbled and penitent, the Lord now turns toward them in grace. And the subsequent chapters are bright with the splendors of their glorious future.

It is unnecessary to multiply proofs from the Old Testament of this important feature in the dealings of God with men. All our readers recognize it and will admit without hesitation its application to the history of ·

---

* Robert Young translates this phrase "*accepted hath been her punishment.*" As the Hebrew words are the same as occur in Lev. xxvi: 41-43. it seems just to make their translation in Isaiah conform to this previous usage.

individuals and of nations in this sphere of time. God's judgments are, without doubt, disciplinary and restorative this side the grave. In this world, at least, "He will not always chide, neither will He keep His anger forever."

But here the inquiry must be raised whether this principle of divine dealing does not reach beyond this sphere of temporal suffering. To this we reply that there is nothing in the Old Testament, and it will be borne in mind that our investigation is now confined to these older Scriptures, which requires us to limit it to this life. God cannot change. If there be no restorative effect in His judgments beyond this life, it cannot be from any change in Him or in the principles of His government. It must result from the obduracy of the creature, whose character for evil becomes fixed at death. There is a class of texts in the Old Testament which seem to imply that this is the case. We read, for instance (Prov. xxix. 1), "He that being often reproved hardeneth his neck, shall suddenly be destroyed and that without remedy." But then, it may be asked, do such passages announce the only and the *ultimate* principle of God's dealing with sinners. They certainly announce this important principle, that "the soul that sinneth, it shall die." But it is also an equal principle, set forth, as we have seen, in the Song of Moses and verified in all subsequent Scripture, that God's judgments are corrective as well as penal. In the case of His people they are even redemptive. Now death is the final form of His judgments. Into the hands of this enemy they should finally be delivered. (Lev. xxvi. 25.) Of this captivity all others were but a type. But from it there was to be a deliverance. And this implies that there could not be in them such fixedness of evil character as to preclude their turning to the Lord from out the emptiness and gloom of this bondage. And, therefore, the frequent promises of God to hear the cry of His imprisoned people, to loose their bonds, to plead their cause against the enemy, (Micah vii. 8, 9,) and to bring the prisoners out of the pit wherein is no water (Zech. ix. 11)* must reach over to and include their bondage in death. The words of Moses, (Deut. xxx. 4,) seem to imply precisely this: "If any of thine be driven out unto the *outmost parts of heaven*, from thence will the Lord thy God gather thee, and from thence will He fetch thee." We shall see hereafter that God's promises of redemption are well nigh meaningless and his plan of redemption fruitless, unless they include this very purpose to ransom His people from death, after He has sent them, for their sins, far away into this land of captivity, and after they have there reaped the bitter fruits of their iniquity, and have been brought to accept its punishment. We shall be obliged to admit that, in the case of sinning Israel at least, the promise reaches even to the captives in the realms of death, "For I will not contend forever, neither will I be always wroth: for the spirit should fail before me and the souls which I have made." (Ish. lvii. 16.)

If this be so, it establishes the important principle that, in the view of the Old Testament, God's covenant people did not pass beyond the bounds of His disciplin-

---

* See Jeremy Taylor's use of this passage, as quoted by Dean Plumptree. *Spirits in Prison*, page 97.

ary dealing into an unalterable state of rewards and punishments, when they passed the bounds of death. The realm of death was, to them, the land of their worst captivity, where they came under the severest discipline of Him who is the Judge of His people, and where there could be no escape from the fire of His anger. To suppose there could be no change in them, under this punishment, except an ever increasing hardening in wickedness, is to run counter to the whole spirit of its teaching concerning God's ways toward them, and to deny to Him and to His moral government the attributes which it is the very purpose of these Holy Scriptures to reveal.

CHAPTER VI.

THE LORD SHALL JUDGE HIS PEOPLE.

These words announce a most important principle of the divine dealings. As quoted in Heb. x. 30, they appear to be wholly vindicatory. But as they first occur in the Song of Moses, Deut. xxxii. 36, they are both vindicatory and redemptive. It is a prevalent and a striking misapplication of Scripture to wrest such solemn warnings as occur in the Book of Hebrews from their use as addressed to unfaithful Christians and apply them chiefly to unbelievers. It is the Lord's own people whom He shall judge, and they are warned that "It is a fearful thing to fall into the hands of the living God."

But it would be a still more fearful thing to fall out of His hands. There is grace concealed in even such minatory passages. *Our* God is indeed a consuming fire. (Heb. xii. 29.) And yet the fire burns up our sins, which are our greatest enemies. And all His and our enemies are burnt up by it round about. (Ps. xcvii. 3.) There is always this double aspect in God's judgments. They vindicate His righteousness and punish evil-doers. But they tend also to deliver His people from the evils that make punishment necessary. Hence, it is a cause for deep thankfulness, as well as salutary dread, that " the Lord shall judge His people." And hence, as these words first occur in Moses' song, these two things are closely connected, Judgment and Deliverance.

"*For the Lord shall judge His people, and repent Him-*

self for His servants, when He seeth that their power is gone, and there is none shut up, or left.

His judgments are a great deep. (Ps. xxxvi. 6.) And this Song shows how much more there is in them than penal visitation. They chastise His people indeed, but they reach beyond them over to their enemies, visible and invisible, and pursue their strange work until they smite even the last enemy, which is death.

And thus we see how they may be viewed as a "pleading of their cause." (Micah vii. 9.) We also see why this grateful aspect of the divine judgments is made so prominent in Scripture. In the Psalms, Zion, the nations, and the whole earth, animate and inanimate, are often summoned to "rejoice because of His judgments."

These all-embracing judgments are based upon the principle that the righteousness of Jehovah, which requires that His people suffer for their sins, must vindicate itself also against their enemies who have tempted them to sin. The fire of His anger must burn against the created system in which their spiritual enemies find lodgment, and through whose laws and forces they pursue their work of sin and death. It is only in the light of considerations like these that we can perceive the deepest meaning of such words as these from Moses' Song :

> I said, I would scatter them into corners, I would make the remembrance of them to cease from among men: Were it not that I feared the wrath of the enemy, lest their adversaries should behave themselves strangely, and lest they should say, (margin,) Our high hand, and not the LORD, hath done all this." (vs. 26-27.)

> If I whet my glittering sword, and mine hand take hold on judgment; I will render vengeance to mine enemies, and will reward them that hate me. (vs. 41.)

The Lord Shall Judge His People.

Rejoice, O ye nations, with His people: for He will avenge the blood of His servants, and will render vengeance to His adversaries, and will make expiation for His land, for His people. (v. 43.)

Other Old Testament Scriptures bring to view this deep purpose to plead the cause of His people. Passing by the many passages which denounce judgments upon their human enemies, we refer to such as are directed more or less plainly against the invisible enemies to whom we have referred. The "gods" of the nations who are idols, but whose worship is the worship of demons (Lev. xvii. 7; Ps. cvi. 37), "He shall utterly abolish." (Isaiah ii. 18.) It will be permitted us to observe here that the subject of "demons" and the personal existence of spiritual powers, good and evil, as connected with, and perhaps identical with, the forces of nature which idolaters deify, will be discussed further on in these studies. It will suffice to say at this point that all the Old Testament writers, and the people whom they addressed, believed in the existence of such demoniac powers. And these the judgments of God should reach. The gods of Egypt He would punish. (Jer. xlvi. 25.) Her idols should be destroyed. (Ezek. xxx. 13.) "The gods that have not made the heavens and the earth, even they shall perish from the earth, and from under these heavens." (Jer. x. 11.) Zephaniah ii. 11, declares God's purpose to "famish all the gods of the earth," in order that men everywhere, "even all the isles of the heathen," may worship Him. Isaiah (ch. xxiv.) gives an appalling picture of the tide of judgments which should overwhelm the whole earth, ending thus, "And it shall come to pass in that day, that the Lord shall punish the *host of the high ones that are on high,* and the kings of the earth upon the earth. And they shall be gathered together, as prisoners are gathered in a pit, and shall be shut up in prison, and after many days shall they be visited." The phrase "the host of the high ones that are on high" is a Scriptural expression for powers that rule in the heavens. The antithesis in this passage requires this meaning. It may designate either the angelic powers, (Ps. cxlviii. 2,) or the stars, as the abode of those powers. (Isa. xl. 26) These powers are often viewed as the beneficent agents of God's government in Nature and the almoners of His bounty. (Ps. ciii. 20, 21.) But, as objects of worship, they draw away men's faith and affections from the living God.

Hence, Israel was warned against this. " Lest thou lift up thine eyes unto heaven, and when thou seest the sun and the moon and the stars, even all the host of heaven, shouldest be driven to worship them, and serve them, which the Lord thy God hath divided unto all nations under the whole heaven." (Deut. iv. 19.) In a similar passage (xvii. 3,) these objects are called "other gods." It does not enter into our purpose at this point, to delve into the mystery of this subject, but nothing is more plain than that Scripture views this present natural system as pervaded by living powers, which the ancients worshipped as divinities. It is plain also that while the agency of these powers is in the main beneficent, it has also its hostile side toward man. Not only was he corrupted by this worship and service of the creature. But its powers are the source to him of both physical and moral evil. The sun is the mediate source of life and light to men. But the sun also smites by day and the moon by night.

In the vast reservoir of Nature there would seem to be two kingdoms of forces, those which build up men in the strength and beauty and purity of embodied life, and those which inflame and debase and enfeeble and finally destroy this life. Whether there be indeed two hostile kingdoms, or whether these evils be due to the still untamed operation of forces otherwise beneficent, we cannot determine. But the point upon which we now insist is that such passages as Isa. xxiv. 21, bring before us the mystery, which the New Testament more distinctly affirms, that the judgments of God, in pleading the cause of His people, must finally reach and dethrone all powers in Nature which are hostile to man; which have come in, in any way, as objects of worship, and as a vail between him and God, or which have perpetuated this reign of physical and moral evil under which he has been dragged down into the mire of sin and death. "*Then the moon shall be confounded, and the sun ashamed, when the Lord of hosts* shall reign in Mount Zion and in Jerusalem and before His ancients gloriously." (v. 23.) Too long has the true meaning of such passages been evaporated into the misty realm of figures. They affirm that deep truth of redemption, of which we found hints in the Song of Moses, that this present cosmos, with the powers that rule in it, must be held to a responsibility for the evils that have come upon the human race. The judgments of God must reach and subdue and clarify this whole realm of "the world-rulers of this darkness." (Eph. vi. 12, R. V.)

It is only from this point of view that we can grasp the deep meaning of the Old Testament promises that Jehovah shall confound and defeat all our enemies. The Song of Moses refers to a chief enemy, head of these adversaries, whom the judgments of God must finally overtake and destroy. Many later passages refer to this triumph over "the prince of this world." (cosmos.)

> In that day the Lord with his sore and great and strong sword shall punish leviathan, the piercing serpent, and He shall slay the dragon that is in the sea. Thus saith the Lord, even the captives of the mighty shall be taken away and the prey of the terrible shall be delivered; for I will contend with him that contendeth with thee, and I will save thy children. (Ish. xxvii. 1; xlix. 5.)

> The eternal God is thy refuge, and underneath are the everlasting arms; and He shall thrust out the enemy from before thee and shall say, Destroy. (Deut. xxiii. 27.)

The Psalms also abound in reference to "an enemy and an avenger," (xliv. 16,) strength to subdue whom should come through the channel of this feeble human race. (viii. 2.) This enemy reproaches God's people and blasphemes His name. (lxxiv. 10.) They go mourning under His oppression. (xlii. 9.) They shall be redeemed out of his hand. (cvii. 2.) We are aware that commentators are accustomed to minify the meaning of such passages, referring them to merely human enemies. Such interpretations accord with present low views of inspiration and fall in with the arrogant pretensions of the worldly mind, which demands that all that is supernatural in the Bible shall be reduced within the sphere of its ability to comprehend. The same "wisdom" would deny that there are any references to resurrection and a future life in the Old Testament, whereas the doctrine of redemption through resurrection is the key to the whole of it. Our generation seems almost as blind to this luminous feature of these old Scriptures as were the men of our Lord's day, which knew not the Scriptures nor the power of God, and who failed to see how Moses and all the prophets taught that the Christ must suffer and die and be raised again from the dead. We expect to show, as we advance, that a vail is before the eyes of those Bible readers who fail to see that it assumes that this world, or cosmos, as now constituted, is the seat of mighty invisible foes, the roots of whose power strike deep down into the foundations of this present order, that the moral and physical evil of the world are but two sides of its one disorder, that it is therefore only a training ground for the human race, which must reach its perfection the other side of it, that God's hidden purpose is to overthrow all these enemies, and to deliver the whole creation from this bondage to corruption, to renew it and transform it into a new heavens and earth wherein dwelleth righteousness. (Ish. lxv. 17.) This purpose requires specially the casting down of the great enemy from his seats of power. The Song of Moses and all God's holy prophets anticipate this triumph. And so the Holy Spirit in Zacharias, (Luke i. 70-71,) sums up their teachings, " that we should be saved from our enemies, and from the hand of all that hate us." Even the judgment fires, of which the New Testament distinctly speaks, are foreshadowed in Moses' Song. (v. 22.)

Such is the wide scope of that judgment which the Lord must execute for the deliverance of His people. In in all their affliction, He is afflicted. (Ish. lxiii. 9.) And this affliction, as we have seen, comes from the pressure of more than human enemies. Invisible powers, the very system of nature, are also responsible. And, in judging His people, He must also judge them, "A fire goeth before Him to burn up His enemies round about. His lightnings enlightened the world. The earth saw and trembled. The hills melt like wax at the presence of the Lord, at the presence of the Lord of the whole earth. The heavens declare His righteousness and all the people see His glory." (Ps. xcvii.) Highly poetic and figurative language! we exclaim. True indeed, but it is not fiction. The vail of figures conceals the deepest facts. The fire of God's anger shall not cease its burning until it consumes all that is evil even in the foundations of the earth and down to the lowest hell. And all this strange work of judgment is in behalf of His people, who wait for His salvation.

"*Therefore saith Jehovah, the Lord of hosts, the Mighty One of Israel, Ah, I will ease me of mine adversaries and avenge me of mine enemies. . . . Zion shall be redeemed with judgment and her captives* (Young) *with righteousness.*" (Ish. i. 24, 27.)

"*Yea, in the way of thy judgments, O Lord, have we waited for thee; the desire of our soul is to thy name and to the remembrance of thee.*" (xxvi. 8.)

"*For the Lord is a God of judgment; blessed are all they that wait for Him.*" (xxx. 18.)

CHAPTER VII.

REDEMPTION THROUGH RESURRECTION.

The Lord's triumph over His enemies would be fruitless did it not require and issue in a triumph over death. Hence He must judge also this last enemy. He must rescue His captive people who have been carried away as prisoners into his realm. The Bible was written to reveal this grace of God in providing redemption for man, the first fruits of which he now receives, but whose full results are achieved on the other side of death. Hence, if our view of the Old Testament promises is not carried forward to this point, we shall fall short of their meaning. Failure to give this principle its full value is a main cause of those mistifying and minifying glosses, which, under the specious plea of "spiritual sense," have so obscured the true meaning of God's Word, that multitudes have been led to doubt whether it is indeed His Word. A sad proof of the blinding effect of this process is the fact that "the hope of the resurrection of the dead" which God gave to the fathers (Acts xxvi: 6,) and of which all His holy prophets testify to those who have ears to hear, is taken out of a multitude of passages, in which it is embedded as the hidden kernel, and robbed of which, they lose their chief value.

Old Testament passages which speak directly of judgment to be executed upon this last enemy are the following: "He will swallow up death in victory; and the Lord God will wipe away tears from off all faces; and the rebuke of His people shall He take away from off all the earth: for the Lord hath spoken it." (Ish. xxv: 8.) The whole background of the portion of Isaiah's prophecy on which this splendid promise is projected is one of judgment.

Hosea's prophecy is also burdened with premonitions of wrath to come, especially upon Ephraim, the schismatic kingdom of Israel. The issue of these judgments would be death to a great portion of the people. But in the wonder working of God the pains of death become the pangs of parturition.* The prophet foresees "the breaking forth of children," and exclaims in Jehovah's name, " I will ransom them from the power of the grave (sheol); I will redeem them from death: O death, I will be thy plagues; O grave, I will be thy destruction; repentance shall be hid from mine eyes." † (Hosea xiii; 14.) This promise explains that given in verse 9. " O Israel, thou hast destroyed thyself; but in me is thy help." The ultimate issue of Israel's self destruction was death. The grave covered all his hopes. But Jehovah who kills also makes alive. The honor of his name, His

---

* This figure occurs also in Ish. xxvi; 17, 18, before a promise of resurrection.

† The readiness of interpreters to eliminate resurrection teaching from the plainest Old Testament passages is illustrated by a late writer in the Andover Review, (Nov. 1884.) After adopting an unusual and infelicitous rendering of the above passage, in face of the fact that the Lxx. and St. Paul, in his free quotation of it, (1st Cor. xv: 55) endorse the obvious view of it, he maintains that it teaches the very opposite. His argument that such an outburst of promise is out of place in the midst of a context which speaks only of judgment amounts to nothing. The prophets abound in such instances. One is found indeed in this very chapter, and in the closest proximity to the passage in question. (vs. 9, 10.)

gracious convenant, required that not even death itself should remove His people beyond His power to help. And so He rises to the dignity of this exultant promise to ransom His people even from the power of Sheol. It is a just principle that a great and luminous promise like this sheds light upon the interpretation of all others of its class. There is a large class of these passages which speak of redemption from death, individual and national And many, which promise deliverance to the captives, and the opening of prison doors to them that are bound, reveal their deepest meaning only as we view them as looking forward to a ransom from captivity to death. The name of Egypt (Mitzraim in Hebrew) signifies the "place of straitness." It thus furnishes a suitable type for the empire of Death. And redemption from its bondage stands out upon the pages of Scripture as a primal type of Jehovah's redemption of His people from Sheol.*

We have before seen (Ch. iv.) that the dead in Sheol are viewed as prisoners, (Job iii.: 18,) shut up by bars in the pit, (xvii: 16.) The righteous, however, did not expect to remain there, "But God will redeem my soul from the power of Sheol; for He shall receive me."(Ps. 49: 15.) In Psalm lxxxviii: 10-12, we hear the sighing of these prisoners. "Wilt thou show wonders to the dead? Shall the dead (rephaim) arise and praise thee? Shall thy loving kindness be declared in the grave? or thy

---

* It is interesting to trace through the Old Testament its use of the term "captivity." It will be seen that it often describes a worse than human bondage; and that the promise to Israel and to other nations to " cause their captivity to return and to have mercy upon them," (Jer. xxxii : 7, 11, 26 : xlix : 6, 39,) implies more than redemption from human slavery. It looks forward to their ransom from the power of Sheol.

faithfulness in destruction? Shall thy wonders be known in the dark? and thy righteousness in the land of forgetfulness?" Psalm lxxix: 10, 11, is a prayer that God would avenge Himself upon the heathen who had filled His land with slaughter and requite the blood of His servants. " Let the sighing of the prisoners come before thee; according to the greatness of thy power preserve thou the children of death," (margin.) So wide-spread was the work of death in this case that no vindication of Jehovah's name and people would suffice that did not provide for triumph, not only over their human enemies, but over death. He must hear the sighing of its prisoners and loose their bonds. That this is the ultimate deliverance sought is apparent from Ps. cii. The prophet declares that Jehovah will hear the prayer of the destitute and appear in glory to build up Zion. "This is written for a generation to come; and the people which shall be created shall praise the Lord." (vs. 18.) This coming generation, a people to be created for the Lord's praise, seems to be the resurrected *children of death* (vs. 20, margin) spoken of afterwards. " For He hath looked down from the height of his sanctuary; from heaven did the Lord behold the earth; *to hear the groaning* of *the prisoner: to loose the children of death;*" to declare the name of the Lord in Zion, and His praise in Jerusalem." We are well aware that interpreters may readily reduce the meaning of such passages down to the low level of "things present" and deny that they refer at all to that transcendent order of things of which the resurrection of Christ was the pledge. But we are quite sure that any one who accepts that great fact as the focal point toward which all the lines of God's working in the past converge, and from which they sweep away into the ages to come, will not accept any interpretation of such expressions in the Psalms and Prophets which does not view them as looking forward 1, to the Messiah's victory over death; 2, to the rescue of His people from its bondage, and 3, to an ultimate recovery of the generations of mankind who have gone down as prisoners into its realm.

Bondage in Egypt, captivity in Babylon and among all nations, stands out, no doubt, on the foreground of such passages. There is also a hidden reference to the spiritual darkness and bondage into which the people had fallen by reason of their sins, and a promise of quickening from this spiritual death. But the deliverance promised would be no message of mercy to the men to whom it was spoken, it would not meet the case, it would not execute the judgment written against all God's enemies, nor vindicate the honor of His name, did not these prophecies look forward to the ransom from Sheol of these very generations of men whom the wrath of their enemies and the justice of God had consigned to its gloomy prison.

The 68th Psalm is a glowing anticipation of this deliverance by one who ascends on high, *leading captivity captive*, and obtaining " gifts for men, yea for the rebellious also, that the Lord God might dwell among them." (vs. 18.) " He that is our God is the God of salvation, and unto God the Lord *belong the issues of death.*"* (The out-

---

* Conant translates " God is to us a God for deliverances and to Jehovah the Lord belong *ways of escape from death.*"

goings of death.—*Young.*) This Lord over death shall " wound the head of his enemies," and bring again His people from Bashan, and from the depths of the sea, (vs. 21, 22.) Bashan was a region on the further side ot Jordan, type of death. That this deliverance is more than that of an elect remnant, or even of the nation of Israel, is manifest from the scope of the whole Psalm, which celebrates a salvation for which all the kingdoms of the earth are invited to sing praises unto God, (vs. 32.)

These promises of deliverance are both personal and national. Psalm cxlii is a resurrection Psalm, to be understood first of the Messiah, but also of those in whose behalf He went down to death. The writer expresses his confidence that while no man "sought after his soul," (vs. 4, margin,) the Lord would be His portion in the land of the living *and bring out his soul from prison,*(vs. 7.) In Psalm cxliii, we hear the same complaint, " For the enemy hath persecuted my soul, he hath bruised my life to the earth; hath caused me to dwell in dark places as the dead of old." (vs. 3.—*Young's Translation.*) We have the cry for deliverance, " Hear me speedily, O Lord: my spirit faileth: hide not thy face from me, for I am become like unto them that go down into the pit."(vs. 7, margin.) " Cause me to hear thy loving kindness in the morning (the time of awakening) for in thee do I trust." And then we have the confident expectation; " For thy name's sake, O Lord, thou wilt quicken me; in thy righteousness thou wilt bring my soul out of distress. In thy loving kindness thou wilt cut off mine enemies, and will destroy all the adversaries of my soul: for I am thy servant." (vs. 11, 12, see *Young's* and *Conant's* versions.) Psalm cxvi. records a similar experience, " Compassed me have the cords of death and the straits of Sheol have found me : Distress and sorrow I find, and in the name of the Lord I call : I pray thee, O Lord, deliver my soul . . . . for thou hast delivered my soul from death, mine eyes from tears, my feet from over-throwing. I walk* habitually before the Lord in the land of the living," (vs. 3–9, *Young.*) Whatever application these words may have to release from spiritual death, verse 15 makes it clear that the ultimate deliverance in view is from death in Sheol. For this must be the "death of His saints" which remains " precious in the eyes of the Lord," and rescue from this the reason for the thanksgiving, " Thou hast loosed my bonds," (vs. 16.)

Without denying then that such passages, which abound in the Psalms, may be properly applied to spiritual quickening, for these two forms of death are one in essence, we are sure that their ultimate and highest meaning is seen only as they speak to us of resurrection.

---
* By a common Hebrew idiom the future is viewed as present.

CHAPTER VIII.

REDEMPTION THROUGH RESURRECTION.

Passing on to the Prophets, we find many similar promises of release from a captivity, the roots of which lie in the realms of death. The promises, however, become less personal. The nation's bondage is more in view. But as we have already seen from Isaiah xxv, and Hosea xiii, only a ransom from Sheol can fully meet the case. Such a deliverance is proclaimed in Isaiah xxvi: 14-19, a passage which speaks plainly of resurrection from death, as even rationalistic interpreters admit. The prophet had just declared that the judgments, by which Jehovah would restore His people and bless all nations, would be carried on to this climax,—" He will swallow up death in victory." (xxv: 8.) A careful reading of the whole of the magnificent prophecy, (Chs. xxv.-xxvii.), shows that there is before the writer's mind the burden of woes under which, not only Israel, but all the earth's inhabitants suffer. And the deliverance foreseen is as wide as the misery. And yet it comes "in the way of judgments." (xxvi: 8.) Only in this way will "the inhabitants of the world learn righteousness." (v. 9.) If favor be shown to the wicked, he will not learn righteousness. (v. 10.) Therefore Jehovah's hand must be lifted up against him in judgment. The fire of His enemies must devour them. (v. 11.) They must go down to death. Their condition is thus described. "Dead, they shall not live; Rephaim (shades) they shall not rise: therefore hast thou visited and destroyed them, and made all their memory to perish." (v. 14.) This removal of all the ends of the Earth * had enlarged the nation of Israel, that is, it had given it wide scope for the accomplishment of its mission. (v. 15.) At the same time it had compelled these banished ones to cry in their trouble unto the Lord for relief. (v. 16.) The mission of Israel to the world was Messianic. That nation was raised up to bring to mankind the salvation for which it cries. Like a woman with child the nation had been pregnant with this great boon. Its sorrows had been its parturition pangs. (v. 17) And yet it had not wrought deliverance in the earth, neither for itself nor for the nations. "The inhabitants of the world had not fallen," that is they had not been subdued to Israel's God. (v. 18.) And then comes the announcement of redemption for Israel, whose mission had ended in failure, and for mankind, through resurrection. "Thy dead shall live, my dead body they shall arise." The Lord here asserts His property in them, foreshadowing His identification with them in Christ, who went down to death with and for them. The ransom from death of His people, the first fruits, should be as dew upon the dust of the earth in which all the dead lie buried. "Awake and sing, ye that dwell in dust: for thy dew is as the dew of herbs (Heb. "lights," *i. e.* vivifying dew). And the land of the Rephaim thou wilt cause to fall." †

---

* That is, of its inhabitants into Sheol. The italics in the English version obscure the sense.

† The English version reads " And the earth shall cast out the dead." The form of the Hebrew verb and the collocation of the words are such that either rendering is admissible.

(v. 19.) The verb is the same as at the close of v. 18. Hence, Young gives it a similar rendering. The idea is that, while the inhabitants of the world had not fallen before Israel and Israel's Lord, yet, as captives in Sheol, they should be forced to confess His name. The resurrection grace and power which should some day reach Israel, would finally subdue and rescue them. This deliverance, however, could only be in the way of judgment: and hence Jehovah invites His people to shelter themselves from the coming storm of His indignation, which should beat upon the earth's inhabitants, the issue of which would be that the earth should disclose her blood and no more cover her slain. (vs. 20, 21.) How deep this work of judgment would be the next verse brings to view—" In that day the Lord with His sore and great and strong sword shall punish Leviathan, the piercing serpent: even Leviathan that crooked serpent; and He shall slay the dragon that is in the sea." (xxvii: 1.) We have already seen that this passage foretells judgment upon "him that hath the power of death, that is the devil." The whole scope of the prophecy accords with what we have in view in this essay, which is to show that, from Moses onward, all his holy prophets foretell a triumph over His enemies and over death and hell which shall bring salvation to Israel and to all mankind. In the passage we have been reviewing we detect a principle, more fully unfolded in the New Testament and of which we shall have much to say hereafter, that this salvation reaches *first* His people, who are made the mediums of wider blessing. We shall also see that it has respect to previous character, and that it is a harvest in which every man must reap as he has sown. But at this point we fasten attention simply upon the great principle that, guilty as all men are on account of sin and worthy of death, there is a class of spiritual enemies behind them, involved in the guilt, who must share in its punishment, and for whom there is preparing a final overthrow that shall bring to all men at least this blessing, rescue from the power of death. The dead stock of Israel "shall blossom and bud and fill the face of the world with fruit." (v. 6.)

We urge then our readers to bring to bear upon the interpretation of the numerous passages of this class these considerations.

1. Israel and all nations, by the righteous judgments of God, have been consigned to Sheol. They suffer under this worst of all captivities, bondage to death.

2. God has wrought for them a redemption which proceeds in the way of judgment upon themselves, their enemies, seen and unseen, and over the empire of death which holds them captive. The meaning of the word "captivity" is at once broadened in this view. "The perishing in the land of Assyria and the outcasts in the land of Egypt" (v. 13) are at once seen to be typical of the victims of a real and lasting captivity in the land of death, for whom "the great trumpet shall be blown." The people "robbed and spoiled," "snared in holes," "hid in prison houses," "a prey whom none delivereth," "a spoil, of whom none saith, restore," (Is. xlii: 22) are the people who are bound in the prison-house of death. And to such comes the promise (xliii: 1), "But now, thus saith the Lord that created thee, O Jacob,

and he that formed thee, O Israel, fear not: for I have redeemed thee, I have called thee by thy name; thou art mine." Neither the waters nor the floods nor the flames should destroy them. (v. 2.) "I even I, am the Lord; and beside me there is no Saviour." We again repeat that we have no desire to strip these passages of their spiritual meaning, nor deny to them any reference to Israel's spiritual bondage and subsequent conversion. Spiritual death, as the New Testament constantly affirms, is one in essence with bodily death. The last is a deeper and more fatal bondage than the first, but the captivity and degradation are the same in kind. We maintain, however, that we shall fall far short of their meaning if we *limit* these passages to the lesser evil, and see in them no promise of redemption from the greater. Indeed, we shall mistake in our whole interpretation of the Old Testament, if the light that guides us is not that of "the hope of the resurrection of the dead." It is only on the other side of death that the splendid promises that glow along these pages of Isaiah can find fulfilment. For the men to whom they were made are long since dead. They never realized the promised salvation. They "died without the sight." Israel missed the blessing himself, and failed to become the instrument of it to all mankind. But Israel, (and this name includes the Messiah, the First Born of that princely seed which has power with God and prevails), on the other side of death and in the power of resurrection, shall realize and accomplish this deliverance. Plain do these promises become if we allow them their full and proper scope.

Another such occurs in Is. xlix: 5-10. Jehovah commissions His "servant" to raise up the tribes of Jacob and to bring back the preserved of Israel, and to be His salvation unto the end of the earth, to be a covenant of the people, to raise up the earth, to cause to inherit the desolate heritages; " To say to the prisoners go forth, to them that are in darkness, be uncovered. They shall feed in the ways, and their pastures shall be in all high places. They shall not hunger nor thirst; neither shall the heat nor sun smite them: for He that hath mercy on them shall lead them, even by the springs of water shall He guide them." The quotation of the latter verse in the Revelation (viii: 16,) makes it clear that the promised deliverance reaches beyond the grave, and harmonizes with all that we have said concerning the meaning of the "captivity" so often alluded to. The unbound "prisoners" are the released from Sheol. They are again referred to in the 25th verse. The question of the possibility of such a deliverance is raised in the 24th verse. "Shall the prey be taken from the mighty, or the lawful captive delivered?" The next verse replies, "But thus saith Jehovah. Even the captives of the mighty shall be taken away, and the prey of the terrible shall be delivered: for I will contend with him that contendeth with thee, and I will save thy children."

Again we say, if we limit such words to release from Babylon, or even from spiritual bondage, we shall fall far short of their meaning. "When God says so much He cannot mean so little." No release which does not provide for and include the exiles in Sheol, where the vast majority of the nation were gathered, and which does not wound the head of their chief enemy and avenger, could meet the case or fulfil the terms of the promise. In the next chapter we hear Jehovah again declaring that though the heavens and earth must fade away and "they that dwell therein must *die in like manner*," * yet " His salvation shall be forever (unto all generations. v. 8. R. V.) and His righteousness shall not be abolished." (li: 6.) He stretched forth the heavens and laid the foundations of the earth. The huge grinding wheels of nature, under which all the earth's inhabitants are ground out in death, are subject to His will who is Lord of Creation and of Life. And therefore He asks exultingly, why His people should fear continually every day the fury of the oppressor, as if he were able to destroy. "And where is the fury of the oppressor? The captive exile hasteneth to be loosed, that he die not in the pit, nor that his bread should fail." (vs. 13, 14.) That is, he dreads death, as if this enemy would put him beyond the help of even the Maker of heaven and earth. And so Jehovah appeals to His former wonder-working in behalf of his people, smiting Rahab, (Egypt, type of Sheol,) wounding the dragon, and drying up the sea. (v. 10.) And so they need not fear that even death can put them beyond the redeeming power of the Lord, their God, "the Lord of hosts is His name" (v. 15.)

---

* Or *like gnats* (margin R. V.).

CHAPTER IX.

REDEMPTION THROUGH RESURRECTION.
(Continued.)

In the prophecy of Jeremiah we find ample illustrations of the same principles of divine dealing which we have traced out in that of Isaiah, and which were so significantly announced in the Song of Moses. "The spirit of judgment and the spirit of burning" by which the Lord should purge away the sin of His people (Ish. iv: 4.) had begun to burn fiercely against them in Jeremiah's time. A pious remnant humbled itself under the mighty hand of God during these judgments. We hear their prayer, "O Lord, correct me, only in judgment: not in thine anger, lest thou bring me to nothing." (Jer. x: 24.) The mass of the people, however, were unrepentant, and were either destroyed by the sword and by pestilence, or carried into captivity. The prophet's eyes ran down with tears, because the Lord's flock was carried away captive. (xiii: 17.) He intercedes with Him for His stricken people. The Lord reveals to Him that the people must not only go into captivity, but that in their own land and the land of their enemies, they should die of grievous deaths and be consumed. (xvi: 4-13.) Before He could interfere for their deliverance He must "recompense their iniquity and their sin double." (vs. 18.) And yet He promises that in days to come He would prove Himself the Living One who could rescue even from such bondage and death. "Behold I will send for many fishers, saith Jehovah, and they shall fish them; and after will I send for many hunters, and they shall hunt them from every mountain and from every hill, and out of the holes of the rocks." (vs. 16.) A mere promise of national restoration, we say. But no national restoration in the past, nor any possible restoration of some future generation of Jews, can ever fulfill these prophecies, either in letter or spirit. The generations to whom these promises were made were carried away into a worse captivity than that of Babylon. They went down to death. Only a conqueror of death could meet their case and bring them release. From this point of view alone can we get the full meaning of such passages as these. "Therefore fear thou not, O my servant Jacob, saith Jehovah ; neither be dismayed, O Israel : for lo, I will save thee from afar, and thy seed from the land of their captivity; and Jacob shall return and shall be in rest, and be quiet, and none shall make him afraid." (xxx: 10.) And this by a judgment upon their enemies:

"Therefore all they that devour thee shall be devoured ; and all thine adversaries, every one of them, shall go into captivity; and they that spoil thee shall be a spoil, and all that prey upon thee will I give for a prey. For I will restore health unto thee, and I will heal thee of thy wounds, saith the Lord ; because they called thee an outcast, saying, This is Zion, whom no man seeketh after." (vs. 16, 17.) " Hear the word of the Lord, O ye nations, and declare it in the isles afar off, and say, He that scattered Israel will gather him, and keep him, as a shepherd doth his flock. For the Lord hath redeemed Jacob, and *ransomed him from the hand of him that was stronger than he*. . . . And they shall not sorrow any more at all." (xxxi : 10-12.) "Thus saith the Lord ; a voice was heard in Ramah, lamentation and bitter weeping ; Rachel weeping for her children refused to be comforted for her children, because they were not. Thus saith the Lord ; Refrain thy voice from weeping, and thine eyes from tears: for thy work shall be rewarded, saith the Lord ; *And they shall come again from the land of the enemy.* And there is hope in thine end, saith the Lord, that thy children shall come again to their own border." (xxxi: 15, 16.)

It is at least certain, in respect to the limited and local application of this prophecy by St. Matthew (ii: 17, 18.) to the slaughtered infants at Bethlehem, that the land of the enemy from which they should return must be the land of death. It is certain also that the captivity to which the bulk of the nation was at this time delivered was a captivity to death. (See chs. xvi: 4; xxxiii: 5; xxxii: 36.) And therefore the repeated promise to regather them, to "cause their captivity to return," (xxxiii: 44.) to bring to them "health and cure" and "reveal unto them the abundance of peace and truth," to do this for both Judah and Israel, and to restore and "build them as at the first," to cleanse and pardon them, to repair all their desolations, and fill their cities with joy and praise to Him "whose mercy endureth forever" (xxxii: 3-11.) must reach to the captives in the realms of death. Nothing short of this would fulfill such promises, nor perform "the good thing which He hath promised unto the house of Israel and to the house of Judah," (vs. 14.) to "cause their captivity to return and have mercy upon them." (vs. 26.) The most meagre criticism must fail to find such words justified by the paltry return from exile in Babylon. Nothing in the subsequent history of Israel has answered to them. To suppose that Israel stands here as a mere type of the Christian church and that the blessings promised him find their fulfilment in the spiritual blessings which have come to Abraham's "spiritual seed," is to suppose that Jehovah's words do not mean what they say, and that He mocked His ancient people with the promise of blessings which were to be bestowed on some one else.

There is, no doubt, truth to be gained in interpreting such Old Testament words as pledges of spiritual blessing. But this may be had without excluding their plain literal meaning. The mistake of both "literalist" and "spiritualist" in their interpretations of Scripture has been that one assumes that his system of interpretation necessarily excludes the other. Whereas both may be true. The Bible comprehends more of truth than any of us have yet grasped.

We might trace through the prophecy of Ezekiel the same threatenings of judgment and promises of restoration. We notice, however, but one passage which conspicuously illustrates the danger, of which we have just spoken, of missing the real intent of a passage by a process of "spiritualization" which empties the words of their obvious meaning. The 36th chapter, after specifying the sins of the house of Israel and their consequent punishment, affirms that Jehovah, for His own name's sake, will cleanse and restore them. In the 37th chapter, He gives to the prophet a vision of a valley of dry bones, the design of which was to show him, and through him the people, how such promises of restoration could be fulfilled to a people the vast majority of whom were already dead. He sees a skeleton multitude rise up out of death, and made to live by the animating breath of Jehovah. He is told that these bones represent the whole house of Israel, whose complaint was "Our bones are dried, and our hope is lost: we are clean cut off." The prophet is then commanded to assure them that not even death can defeat Jehovah's purpose or annul the least of his promises. He is the Conqueror of death.

"Therefore prophesy and say unto them, Thus saith the Lord God; Behold, O my people, I will open your graves, and cause you to come up out of your graves, and bring you into the land of Israel. And ye shall know that I am the Lord, when I have opened your graves, O my people, and brought you up out of your graves, and shall put my spirit in you and ye shall live, and I shall place you in your own land; then shall ye know that I, Jehovah, have spoken it and performed it, saith the Lord."

And then follows the promise to reunite the severed fragments of the nation into one people in the land, and to gather their captives from among all nations and on every side, to purify them, to make an everlasting covenant of peace with them, to set His sanctuary in the midst of them forevermore. "My dwelling place also shall be with them; yea I will be their God, and they shall be my people." All these closing features enter into St. John's sublime description of the new heaven and earth. (Rev. xxi: 1-4.) This fact of itself proves that the prophecy, as its terms imply, has to do with post-resurrection scenes and connects itself with "the times of the restitution of all things." The re-settlement of some subsequent generation of Israel in Palestine, some twenty-five or more centuries later in the world's history, would not fulfill it to the men to whom it was spoken. A word of promise to me is not fulfilled by a good thing bestowed upon some very remote descendant. Still less would there be any comfort to me in the thought that I stand merely as the type of a class of some other persons who are to receive the blessing. God's words are too true and plain to admit of any such belittleing. They must mean here, therefore, what all true Israelites have always understood them to mean, that, however death may seem to have triumphed over Jehovah's people, to have made void His covenant and annulled His promises, He will avenge their cause upon even this last and greatest enemy, and bring them back in triumph even from the power of Sheol, and perform every good thing He has spoken concerning them.

We have already seen that the Lord, through Hosea, gives a promise, if possible more distinct than this through Ezekiel, to do this very thing. (xiii: 14.) "I will ransom them from the power of Sheol; I will redeem them from death; O death, I will be thy plagues; O Sheol, I will be thy destruction." Nor is the promise by either prophet restricted to a pious remnant. It is given by Ezekiel to "the whole house of *Israel*," to the schismatical section as well as to Judah. Hosea deals throughout with an Israel of the present as well as of the future. It is the Israel who had "fallen by his iniquity," and "destroyed himself," whose backsliding was to be healed (xiv: 4.) who was to be freely loved, and from whom God's anger was turned away. There is no possible escape from the conclusion, if the language of Scripture is to be allowed its proper meaning, that the promises of God to Israel require that, after adjudging them to death on account of their sins, and after their long and bitter bondage in that dark realm, He shall interfere to rescue them from the hands of this enemy and avenger, and so bring them into a new relation to Himself of life and blessing, in which He can make good to them all His sure Word.

Some of our readers will be repelled from this conclusion because it seems to require their acceptance of the whole system of millenarianism; and they have already prejudged this as absurd and impossible. The mistakes made by many advocates of that system have brought it into a disrepute which it does not deserve. We shall have occasion hereafter to notice these. We observe at this point, however, that the restoration of Israel, which we have found to be taught in the Old Testament, is quite different from that looked for by many advocates of that system. They concern themselves largely about Israel's pre-resurrection destiny and the present hiding places of the lost tribes. Our view affirms that, while the living remnant of the nation is under the eye of God and has its place in His plans for the future, the most of Israel are in the prison house of death. It is from thence that God will search them out and bring them. The glorious destiny in reserve for them lies on the other side of death. These are *post*-resurrection promises upon their face. And all our views of Scripture and of things to come will be greatly simplified by regarding them as such.

CHAPTER X.

CAPTIVITY CAPTIVE.

We shall not detain our readers by any minute examination of the minor prophets. Their testimony, while it confirms, would only repeat that already given. We cannot forbear, however, to cite these few passages which we ask them to read in the light of the truth we have already gained.

"Sing, O daughter of Zion; shout, O Israel; be glad and rejoice with all the heart, O daughter of Jerusalem. The Lord hath taken away thy judgments, He hath cast out thine enemy: the King of Israel, Jehovah, is in the midst of thee: thou shalt not see evil any more, . . The Lord thy God in the midst of thee is mighty; He will save, He will rejoice over thee with joy; He will rest in His love, He will joy over thee with singing. Mine afflicted from the appointed place I will gather; from thee they have been bearing for her sake reproach.* Behold I will undo all who afflict thee at that time, and will save the halting one, and the driven out ones I will gather, and set them for a praise and a name in all the land of their shame. At that time will I bring you again, even in the time that I gather you; for I will make you a name and a praise among all people of the earth, when I turn back your captivity before your eyes, saith the Lord (Zeph. iii: 14-20.)

"And He shall speak peace unto the heathen: and His dominion shall be from sea even to sea, and from the rivers even to the ends of the earth. As for thee also, because of the blood of thy covenant I have sent forth *thy prisoners out of the pit wherein is no water.* Turn ye to the strong hold, ye prisoners of hope; even to-day do I declare that I will render double unto thee." (Zech. ix: 11, 12.) †

---
*Young's Version.

†Jeremy Taylor, in his *Life and Death of the Holy Jesus*, C. xvi, in referring to this passage, speaks of the dead "whom the prophet Zechariah calls 'prisoners of hope.'"

"And I will hiss for them, and gather them ; for I have redeemed them : and they shall increase as they have increased, and I will sow them among the people ; and they shall remember me in far countries; and *they shall live with their children* and turn again." (x : 8, 9.)

It is, of course, an easy matter to find an explanation for all this class of passages lower than the one we have given. Most readers are satisfied to regard them as prophetic either of Israel's future return to their own land or of their future conversion. Our extended examination, however, has shown that, whatever of preliminary blessing they convey, the remote and final release from captivity to which they refer is Israel's rescue from bondage in Sheol, to which the vast majority of them have been consigned. All their other captivities were but types of this. And all minor deliverences foreshadow this. We shall not fully penetrate the meaning of Old Testament prophecy until we discover that this great promise underlies the whole, and that behind the veil of these passages, which seem to deal only with the temporal fortunes of the chosen people, there is concealed the secret of God's covenant to perform the mercy promised to their fathers, which the death they must needs suffer for their sins seemed to make forever impossible. We shall only skim the surface of these great promises until we learn that the "outcasts" of Israel so often referred to by the prophets, and for whom the great trumpet is to be blown (Is. xxvii : 13), are in reality, as the word signifies, the *perished* ones.* The true "outcasts in the land of

---

*The corresponding word in the Septuagint is always ἀπολόμενοι. It occurs twice in this verse. See also Young's version. The Hebrew word means literally the " thrust down ones."

Egypt" (type of Sheol) are the lost ones in the realm of death.

It remains for us to observe further that ultimate release from captivity to death is promised also to the Gentile nations which were not within the pale of Israel's covenant. Thus, for example, we find Isaiah coupling Egypt and Assyria with Israel in a promise of blessing. "In that day shall Israel be the third with Egypt and with Assyria, even a blessing in the midst of the land: Whom the Lord of hosts shall bless, saying, Blessed be Egypt my people, and Assyria the work of my hands, and Israel mine inheritance." (xix: 24, 25.)

So also Jeremiah, after denouncing judgments upon the nations who were enemies of Israel, declares, "Yet will I bring again the captivity of Moab in the latter days, saith the Lord. Thus far is the judgment of Moab." (xlviii: 47.) "And afterward I will bring again the captivity of the children of Ammon, saith the Lord." (xlix: 6.) "But it shall come to pass in the latter days, that I will bring again the captivity of Elam, saith the Lord." (vs. 39.) We read (Ezek. xvi), concerning Sodom and Samaria that inasmuch as Israel had become as vile as they, they would be restored from their captivity, with Israel's restoration.

"When I shall bring again their captivity, and the captivity of Sodom and her daughters, and the captivity of Samaria and her daughters, then will I bring again the captivity of thy captives in the midst of them. . . When thy sisters, Sodom and her daughters, shall return to their former estate, and Samaria and her daughters shall return to their former estate, then thou and thy daughters shall return to your former estate. . . Then thou shalt remember thy ways and be ashamed when thou shalt receive thy sisters, thine elder and thy younger; and I will give them unto thee for daughters, but not by thy covenant. And I will establish my covenant with thee; and thou shalt know that I am the Lord : that thou mayest remember and be confounded . . . when I am pacified toward thee for all that thou hast done, saith the Lord."

Whatever might have been true of Samaria, there was no captivity under which Sodom was then held but captivity to death. It had been utterly destroyed, "suffering the vengeance of eternal fire." (Jude 7.) No recovery could therefore reach its people except it reached them in the realms of death. The release referred to must be granted to them as "spirits in prison." Under the administrations of the Messiah, in whom "all shall be made alive," even the men of Sodom should be at last set free.

We thus see why, in the Song of Moses, the Gentiles were invited to "rejoice with His people." That song, as we have seen, looks forward to such far reaching triumphs over death, and such riddance of this created system of the enemies who have put upon it the yoke of "bondage to corruption" (Rom. viii: 19-21), that all mankind, living and dead, must share in the blessings of that redemption. All shall at last be freed from captivity to death.

We are aware that it is the custom of interpreters to find some way of escape from the plain meaning of such passages. The most plausible of these explanations is that which makes these names, Egypt, Assyria, Moab, Sodom, etc. stand as symbols for various classes of mankind, all of whom were to be reached by the gospel.

There is a sense indeed in which we are now surrounded and live in the midst of Sodom and Egypt and Babylon. The New Testament carries over these names and applies them to systems which exist, some of them in towering proportions, to the end of the age. Still further, it may be truly said that all these systems hold men in bondage. Every form of Old Testament captivity has its correspondence now in the various forms in which the god of this world leads men captive at his will. Some are in bondage in "Egypt," which represents the world as dominated by natural laws. These compel men to yield them service above the claim of the living God of Nature, debasing them into a hard, grinding, pitiless slavery to natural appetites and necessities and so treading them into the mire of sin and death. Others are in bondage in "Assyria," the representative of social progress and world-conquest. They are inflamed by a desire for expansion and acquisition, slaves of worldly ambition, worshippers of Mammon. This is also a cruel and often a fatal bondage. Others, and especially multitudes in Christendom, are enslaved in "Babylon," type of that mixed system of world-religion, which seeks to throw the charms and sanctions of religion over the pleasures and pursuits and ambitions of the world, worshipping Mammon under the forms of godliness, and prostituting the church to the ends of its own lust for wealth and dominion. This is a more seductive bondage but no less dangerous. We may admit then a reference to all these forms of spiritual bondage which still dominate mankind in the prophetic promises which proclaim "deliverance to the captives and the opening of the prison doors to them that are bound."

But we shall greatly mistake if we cramp and limit these words of Holy writ to this region. Spiritual emancipation is but a "first-fruits" blessing (Rom. viii. 23), the possession of which leads us to long for "the redemption of the body." Nothing short of this can give man that place of freedom and ownership and lordship in creation, to which he was destined when God made him in His own image. These Old Testament promises, therefore, must reach on to this consummation, or the major part of the blessing to which they give title is never conveyed. They certainly require that all the past generations of mankind, in due time and order, shall be "made alive." This gift of life, indeed, does not exempt from judgment. There is a "resurrection unto judgment." Only men in Christ, whether in this world or the world to come, are set free from judgment. It must pursue, even to a second death, those who persistently reject Him. All God's truth concerning judgment for sin must be firmly held along with all He promises concerning redemption. But the one must not nullify the other. He has promised to Abraham that in his seed *all the families of the earth* shall be blessed. And hence David could sing, " All nations whom thou hast made shall come and worship before thee, O Lord; and shall glorify thy name; for thou art great and doest wondrous things: Thou art God alone." (Ps. cxiv: 9.) Are not the dead generations of mankind a part of "all the families of the earth?" By what right or reason can we exclude them? Are not they a part of the "all nations whom thou hast made?" To shut them out from these promises is to deny that He is the God of the dead as well of the living. It is to ignore the deepest truth in His Word and in His redemption plan.

CHAPTER XI.

UNQUENCHABLE FIRE.

We have seen that there are two radical principles of the divine dealing with mankind unfolded in the Old Testament.

1. The principle of far reaching *judgment*; rendering to every man according to his work, shutting up the wicked as prisoners in sheol, extending itself also to the diabolic and cosmical enemies who have put this yoke of bondage to sin upon man, and so merging into

2. A second principle of far reaching *redemption;* providing forgiveness and salvation for all men, securing to all at least a ransom from the power of death, and freeing the system of creation to which man belongs from the yoke of those enemies which, to both, has been a bondage to corruption.

We come next to see that in all this strange work "our God is a consuming fire."

In our study of the song of Moses we found (vs. 22) that this deep work of judgment is represented as a fire of God's anger, burning down to the lowest hell. We found there also an unmistakable reference to a future renovation of this natural system, which is viewed as under the yoke of sin with man, through the agency of fire. We have now to observe that "fire" is a common Scripture term for these judgments, through the whole range of them, and that the one feature, common to them all, is destruction, which is not extinction. Fire is the most rapid consumer of human lives and of creature forms. But slower destructive agents, such as famine and disease, consume them also. Hence (Deut. iv. 24) in the judgments threatened against Israel, Jehovah is declared to be a "consuming fire." So also in the judgments by which He was to go before Israel to disposess and destroy their enemies, He would be a " consuming fire." "A fire goeth before Him and burneth up all his enemies round about." (Ps. xcvii. 3.) War, famine, pestilence, death, all destructive agencies are included in this term. " Before Him went the pestilence, and a burning flame goeth out at His feet." (Hab. iii. 5.) In Isaiah the special judgments by which Jehovah shall accomplish the deliverance of His people are thus described : " The hand of the Lord shall be known toward His servants, and His indignation toward His enemies. For, behold, the Lord will come with fire, and with His chariots like a whirlwind, to render His anger with fury, and His rebuke with flames of fire. For by fire and by His sword will the Lord plead with all flesh: and the slain of the Lord shall be many." (Ch. lxvi. 14-17.) In verse 24, these " slain of the Lord " are represented as dead " carcasses." And the remediless destruction which has overtaken them is thus described: " For their worm shall not die, neither shall their fire be quenched ; and they shall be an abhorring unto all flesh." It is only by ingrafting upon this passage our pre-conceived opinions that we can make it teach an eternity of torment for these dead transgressors. The picture is that of thickly strewn dead corpses, upon which the worm and the fire feed with a destructive gnawing which nothing can arrest.

A similar scene of judgment is described in the 34th Chapter, in which, although the land of Idumea, or Edom, is mentioned as the special object of Jehovah's anger, His indignation is upon all nations and the prophetic vision reaches forward to the great day of His wrath. " For it is the day of the Lord's vengeance, and the year of recompenses for the controversy of Zion. And the streams thereof shall be turned into pitch, and the dust thereof into brimstone, and the land thereof shall become burning pitch. It shall not be quenched night nor day; the smoke thereof shall go up forever; from generation to generation it shall lie waste; none shall pass through it forever and ever. . . . And He shall stretch upon it the line of confusion and the stones of emptiness." (vs. 8-11.) Here, not only a people, but a whole territory, is represented as consumed under the quenchless fire of God's anger. This passage is specially to be observed as determining the Old Testament import of the similar terms employed in the Apocalypse.

A similar use of the term "fire that cannot be quenched" is frequent in Jeremiah. It is used to describe the judgments threatened against His own land and people. "Therefore thus saith the Lord God: Behold, mine anger and my fury shall be poured out upon this place, upon man, and upon beast, and upon the trees of the field, and upon the fruit of the ground; and it shall burn and shall not be quenched." (vii. 20.) "And I will cause thee to serve thine enemies in the land which thou knowest not; for ye have kindled a fire in mine anger, which shall burn forever." (xviii. 4.) " Lest my fury go out like fire, and burn that none can quench it." (xxi. 12.)

So also Ezekiel. "Thus saith the Lord God; Behold, I will kindle a fire in thee, and it shall devour every green tree in thee, and every dry tree; the flaming flame *shall not be quenched*, and all faces from the south to the north shall be burned therein. And all flesh shall see that I the Lord have kindled it; it shall not be quenched." (xx. 47.) In the 38th Chapter we have a vision similar to the one already noticed in Isaiah lxvi., in which the final decisive judgments by which Jehovah shall deliver His people are described. Judgment is visited upon Gog and his armies, and all the powers of nature are engaged in its execution; earthquake, the sword, pestilence, great hailstones, fire and brimstone. The land becomes one vast sepulchre. This vision also reaches on to the terrors of that final consummation, which shall be a day of birth-anguish in creation as well as for mankind.*

It is not necessary to trace the same forms of expression through the minor prophets. The language of Zephaniah (iii. 8.) condenses their testimony. "For all the earth shall be devoured with the fire of my jealousy." It is summed up in the last book of Old Testament prophecy. "For, behold the day cometh, that shall burn as a furnace, and all the proud, yea, and all that do wickedly, shall be stubble: And the day that cometh shall burn them up, saith the Lord of hosts, that it shall leave them neither root nor branch." (Mal. iv. 1.)

From these extended quotations, which might be easily multiplied, it is manifest that God's consuming anger

---

*See also Ezek. xxi. 31, 32; xxii. 20, 21, 31; xxx.

against men and nations is everywhere represented in the Old Testament as an unquenchable fire, and its work as a work of destruction and death. These denunciations do not carry with them the idea of torment beyond death. They do not exclude it. But retribution beyond the grave is never in view in the Old Testament only so far as captivity in sheol is such a retribution. We have already seen that bondage in that prison-house is a part, or rather it is the culmination of the divine judgment for sin. What horrors may come upon the ungodly in that region of outer darkness, or what mitigations, what relief of light and blessedness from the Lord of light and life may come to the godly, is not there revealed. But one thing is made clear. This destruction in death is not final extinction. The hope of resurrection, of ransom from this captivity, we have found gleaming all along these Old Testament pages. Even the heathen nations, who were Israel's seducers and persecutors, are not shut out from it. In Jeremiah xlviii., for example, we have the judgments against Moab described in the very terms we have been considering. "Fear, and the pit, and the snare, shall be upon thee, O inhabitant of Moab, saith the Lord. . . . A fire shall come forth out of Heshbon, and a flame from the midst of Sihon, and shall devour the corner of Moab and the crown of the children of Shaon. Woe be unto thee, O Moab! The people of Chemosh perisheth; for thy sons are taken in captivity and thy daughters in captivity. *Yet will I bring again the captivity of Moab in the latter days, saith the Lord.*" (vs. 43-47.) So in the next chapter the same thing is said of Ammon and of

Edom, both of whom were to be consumed by His fierce anger.

The importance of thus fixing the use of the term "unquenchable fire" in the Old Testament, and of observing the character, the scope, and the issue of the judgments it portrays, will be apparent as we proceed.

CHAPTER XII.

LATER JEWISH OPINION.

The phrase, "eternal fire," does not occur in the Old Testament, although the idea is contained in passages already quoted which speak of God's anger as a "fire which shall burn forever." This judgment by fire we have seen to be compatible with the idea of purgation and restoration. (Isa. iv. 4.) There crept, however, into Jewish theology, and especially after the exile in Babylon, and the close of the Old Testament canon, the idea that a future torment in eternal fire awaits the desperately wicked. In this class, however, but few Jews were included. This doom was, in the main, reserved for incorrigible heathen.

We do not find the roots of this conception in the Old Testament. God's judgments there terminate in the destruction which brings men and nations down to death, and shuts them up in Shoel. We are assured, however, that this period of death is, for all men, in their own order, brought to an end. And all the Old Testament views of resurrection imply that it is a redemptive act. It must bring to all the subjects of it some order of blessing.

As to the origin of the idea of an eternal torment in hell, its sources are heathen, and not Jewish. "This doctrine was, as an historical fact, brought back from Babylon by the Rabbis. It was a very ancient primary doctrine of the Magi, an appendage of their fire kingdom of Ahriman, and may be found in the old Zends, long prior to Christianity."* Hence we must pass beyond the region of the Old Testament into the Apocryphal books, and into the wide waste of Rabbinical traditions and conceits before we find proof that this doctrine was held among the Jews. The song of Judith, (xvi. 17) closes thus: " Wo to the nations that rise up against my kindred! The Lord Almighty will take vengeance of them in the day of judgment, in putting fire and worms in their flesh; and they shall feel them, and weep forever." In 2 Maccabees, vii. 14, we read of a " resurrection unto life," from which the tyrant Antiochus should be shut out, receiving through the judgment of God "just punishment for his pride." (vs. 36.) These earlier apocryphal books, which the Roman church receives as part of Holy Scripture, furnish, however, no clear outlines of the later doctrine of everlasting punishment, and especially of such a doom as following resurrection. Passages may be quoted from them which seem to teach the annihilation of the wicked; others, the final restoration of all men. " The congregation of the wicked is like tow wrapped together, and the end of them is a flame of fire to destroy them."† (Eccl. xxi. 9.) " After this the Lord looked upon the earth and filled it with His blessings. With all manner of living things hath He covered the face thereof; and they shall return into it again." (xvi. 29-30.) " The mercy of man is toward his neighbor; but the mercy of the Lord is upon all flesh. He reproveth and nurtureth, and teacheth, and bringeth again, as a shepherd his flock." (xviii. 13.)

---

*Life and letters of Chas. Kingsley, pg. 194. See Alger's History of the doctrine of a future life (Chs. vii-ix.)
†See also 2 Esd. xv. 23-26.

"And after seven days, the world, that yet awaketh not, shall be raised up, and that shall die that is corrupt. And the earth shall restore those that are asleep in her, and so shall the dust those that dwell in silence, and the secret places shall deliver those souls that were committed unto them. And the most High shall appear upon the seat of judgment, and misery shall pass away, and the long suffering shall have amend." (2 Esdras vii. 31-33.)* The writer of this book was profoundly exercised over the problem of God's dealings with His people and with mankind. Instruction concerning these mysteries is given him in a series of visions. He is assured that God's covenant mercy toward His people cannot fail, that by His unchanging law of righteousness the good will be rewarded and the wicked punished; that these rewards and punishments are not limited to this life, and that the divine administrations are directed toward this end: "That all the earth may be reached, and may return, being delivered from thy violence, and that she may hope for the judgment and mercy of him that made her." (xi. 46.)

When we pass, however, still beyond this post-exilian period, we find that the later Jewish apocryphal books contain fuller and more definite allusions to the fate of the wicked. The Book of Enoch declares that "they shall be cast into the damnation of fire, and shall perish in anger and in the mighty damnation which lasts to eternity." The fourth book of Esdras, written about the close of the first century, contains these words: (vii. 46.) "A lake of torment shall appear, and over against it a

---

*See also Wisdom of Solomon, xi. 22—xii. 2.

place of rest. And the oven of Gehenna shall be shown, and over against it a paradise of delight; and then shall the Highest say to the risen nations: See and understand Him whom ye denied, or whom ye did not serve, or whose observances ye despised; behold, on this side and that; here is pleasure and rest; and there fire and torments." Any one who cares to examine many similar passages found in this class of Jewish writings, will find them collated at length by Dr. Pusey in his work "What is of faith as to everlasting punishment." (pp. 55-98.) There is no doubt that the doctrine of an eternal punishment for the wicked may be derived from selected passages drawn from the Hebrew books of that period, and also from the Talmud, which contains the teachings of the Rabbins and their traditional interpretations of the law. We are not to suppose, however, that there is any approach to agreement in their teachings.

For, in the first place, there is confusion in the Persian sources from which the doctrine was drawn. It is only from exceptional statements in the Zoroastrian theology that it may be derived. The general drift of that system was toward restoration. The fire was to purge all things. "Through the glowing flood all human kind must pass. To the righteous it will prove a pleasant bath, of the temperature of milk; but on the wicked the flame will inflict terrific pain. Ahriman will run up and down Chinevad in the perplexities of anguish and despair. The earth-wide stream of fire, flowing on, will cleanse every spot and everything. Even the loathsome realm of darkness and torment shall be banished and made a part of the all-inclusive Paradise. Ahriman himself, reclaimed to virtue, replenished with primal light, abjuring the memories of his envious ways, and furling thenceforth the sable standard of his rebellion, shall become a ministering spirit of the Most High, and, together with Ormuzd, chant the praises of Time-without-bounds. All darkness, falsehood, and suffering shall utterly flee away, and the whole universe be filled by the illumination of good spirits blessed with fruitions of eternal delight."* In like manner very many of the passages from the Rabbis do not consist with the idea of unending torment. One passage of the Talmud affirms that after twelve months of expiatory sufferings, "the bodies of the wicked cease to exist, their soul is burned, and a wind scatters their cinders under the feet of the just." This is annihilation. The general drift of Rabbinical teaching was toward the idea that Gehenna was not endless torment, but purgatory, for at least the wicked Jews and the more righteous among the Gentiles. The famous Akiba taught that their sufferings would last but twelve months.† The severest doctrine of the Rabbis was more merciful than the modern dogma which consigns all but an elect company of believers to the unspeakable torments of an eternal hell. For even the better class among the heathen, as well as wicked Jews, would finally escape from these torments. Without attempting to go over the ground so exhaustively explored by such recent authors as Drs. Pusey and Farrar, we think it is plain from the quotations which they abundantly cite‡ that, amid all

---
*Persian doctrine of a future life. Alger. pg. 143.
†See Dr. Pusey's "What is of Faith," etc. pp. 83-89.
‡See "Mercy and Judgment," by F. W. Farrar, D.D. Ch. viii. Also "What is of Faith," etc., by Dr. Pusey, pp. 50-104,

this variety of teaching, the prevalent opinion among the Jews during this period concerning the Gehenna of fire was that it meant:

1. For the majority of their own people a temporary punishment, followed by forgiveness.

2. For worse offenders, long, but still terminable punishment.

3. For the worst offenders of all, especially Gentile offenders, punishment either followed by annihilation, or, issuing in hopeless despair, through failure to attain unto the resurrection of the dead.

And this suggests the point which has been overlooked by most of the writers who have surveyed this field. And that is, that future punishment precedes resurrection. Resurrection was deliverance. Most of the Rabbis either denied the resurrection of the hopelessly wicked, or if admitting it, regarded it as only a brief embodiment to be terminated by a second death. Thus in the comment upon Is. xxii. 14, the Jonathan Targum explains the second death to be " that which happens when a soul that has animated a body a second time separates from it." Alger, in his *History of the Doctrine of a Future Life*, pp 170-171, states that "most of the Rabbins made the resurrection partial." He quotes one as saying: "Whoever denies the resurrection of the dead shall have no part in it, for the very reason that he denies it." Rabbi Abbu says: "A day of rain is greater than the resurrection of the dead; because the rain is for all, while the resurrection is only for the just." " Sodom and Gomorrah shall not rise in the resurrection of the dead." That this was the belief of the Pharisees in our Lord's day

Josephus repeatedly affirms. "The righteous shall have power to live again, but sinners shall be detained in an everlasting prison."* "The Pharisees say that all souls are incorruptible, but that only the souls of good men are removed into other bodies."† We have seen that the general drift of Old Testament allusions to resurrection is that it is a "hope," a deliverance to all the subjects of it. And, although the narrower, because uninspired teaching of this later period shut out a large portion of mankind from this hope, it was still true to this great principle, that resurrection is a boon, inasmuch as it is essentially redemption from that estate of death and captivity in the gloom of Sheol, to which men are consigned for their sins, by the just judgment of God.

In the light of this great principle then, that resurrection is a redemptive act, and that the threatened punishment in the eternal fire for the *sins of this life* lies this side of resurrection and not beyond it, we shall advance to the study of the New Testament teaching. That we shall find there hints of a punishment reserved for a class of sinners beyond resurrection we do not doubt. But that punishment which is concisely described as "the second death," we shall see to be a doom, not for the sins of this life, but of a life restored in resurrection, and again forfeited by incorrigible sin.

---

*Antiq. Book 18, Ch. 1.
†Jewish War. Book, 2. Ch. 8. See also "Spirits in Prison," by Dean Plumptre, pp. 50-51.

PART II.

CHAPTER I.

THE AXE LAID AT THE ROOT OF THE TREE.

Certain great principles of the divine administration have been clearly brought out by our study of the Old Testament. They may be stated thus:

1. Notwithstanding the ruin brought upon the race by sin and its adjudgment to death, God has a gracious purpose of blessing toward it.

2. This purpose, first manifested in the selection of a chosen people, flows on in ever widening channels of blessing, until it shall reach all the families of the earth.

3. It does not arrest, however, the operation of that primal law which adjudges sinful men to death.

4. It must reach mankind, therefore, through such a triumph over death as shall secure the ultimate recovery to life of all men, each in his own order, after they have served out their sentence in death's prison-house.

We shall see, however, as we advance, that this restoration to life does not lift all men into the rank of that eternal life which is the gift of God through Jesus Christ, and which is given only to "as many as receive Him, even to them that believe on His name," nor does it require the final salvation of all.

We proceed now to study the New Testament upon these points, and to show how all our Lord's teaching, and that of His apostles, concerning God's designs toward the world, the punishment of sin, the responsibilities of life, and the tremendous issues of the future are in harmony with, and in fulfillment of, what we have found to be taught in the law and the prophets.

The Old Testament closes with a solemn arraignment of the covenant people for infidelity and the declaration of Jehovah that He would send His messenger, even the messenger of the covenant, to sift and try the nation as in a refiner's fire. "For, behold, the day cometh, it burneth as a furnace; and all the proud, and all that work wickedness, shall be stubble; and the day that cometh shall burn them up, saith the Lord of hosts, that it shall leave them neither root nor branch." (Mal. iv. 1, R. V.) Accordingly we find that John the Baptist, who came in the spirit and power of the predicted Eljiah, announced that this Messenger of Jehovah was now come to do precisely this work of judgment.

"And even now is the axe laid unto the root of the trees; every tree therefore that bringeth not forth good fruit is hewn down and cast into the fire. I indeed baptise you with water unto repentance; but he that cometh after me is mightier than I, whose shoes I am not worthy to bear; He shall baptize you with the Holy Ghost and with fire; whose fan is in His hand, and He will thoroughly cleanse His threshing-floor; and He will gather His wheat into the garner, but the chaff He will burn up with unquenchable fire." (Matt. iii. 10-12.)

This primary announcement of the Forerunner gives the key to the meaning of Messiah's mission. The Old Testament had plainly taught that all the forms of proud and wicked and pretentiously pious manhood must be adjudged to death as unworthy of a place in the kingdom of God. The religious men of our Lord's day, as has been true in every age, were slow to receive this lesson. In John's day they were building their hopes upon the boasts and claims of a mere natural manhood. "We have Abraham for our father." They would not learn the lesson of their Scriptures, a lesson confirmed to them by every open sepulchre, and by the long and universal reign of death over them and their fathers, that this old flesh and blood nature cannot inherit the kingdom of God, and that His promised salvation must therefore come through a hewing down of the old man, with all his pride of ancestry, his hypocrisies and self-righteousness, and a casting of him into the fire for complete destruction. In no other way could room be made for the God of resurrection to come in and work out His salvation for man upon a new basis, and in the power of a new life, to be given to the world from a new fountainhead, even His anointed Son. That the baptism "with the Holy Ghost and with fire" is a work of the same character as the burning up of "the chaff with unquenchable fire," is proved in the fact that it is a part of this one announcement, and also by the subsequent teaching of the New Testament that the new Spirit of life from Christ is a spirit of judgment and of burning against the flesh with its affections and lusts, and that the whole trunk of the old manhood is by it consigned to the fire. For it is only as we bear about in our bodies the dying of the Lord Jesus that His life can be manifested in our mortal bodies. We must die with Him, if we are to rise with Him into the life eternal.

This fundamental feature of the Messiah's work is in perfect harmony with the Old Testament principles above mentioned. No salvation is possible for sinful man except through this way of judgment unto victory. And this first mention in the New Testament of the unquenchable fire determines for us the meaning of all subsequent uses of this phrase, or of its cognates, such as "eternal fire," "the Gehenna of fire." These words set before us vividly the operation of that unchanging, resistless law of God, by which a consumption is determined upon all flesh, not only upon all its evil ways and practices, but upon "the root of the tree," the old manhood itself, the form and vices of which we have all inherited from Adam. It must be cast into the fire. An evil tree cannot bring forth good fruit. Hence, God declares His purpose, at the outset of His Son's mission, to cut the old trunk of humanity down. A new tree had already been planted, even Christ. And out of the grave of the old the new should rise into the life immortal and bring forth much fruit. In Him all nations should be blessed.

The " unquenchable fire," therefore, instead of burying the myriads of mankind in a sea of tormenting flame, and forever beyond the reach of His salvation, is needed in order to clear the way for that salvation. The Christian world has been long and wearily oppressed with a horrible nightmare, induced by its wrong conception of the place and use of this "eternal fire" in the economy of God. That this expression does apply to a terrible work of judgment, and to an irresistible work of death, in which God appears as a consuming fire to the ungodly, is evident. But so also is *our* God, the Christian's God, a consuming fire. There is no escape for any of us from that destroying flame. The axe is laid at the root of the tree of every plant of the human race. The old man must be slain in the Christian, as in every other man. If he sows to the flesh he must reap corruption. This warning is specially addressed to him. (Gal. vi. 7, 8.) He is saved, not by escaping the just judgments of God against him for his sins, but by submitting to them. He confesses judgment against himself, when he believes on the Lord Jesus Christ for salvation. He then and there hands over his old nature to judgment and death, and accepts God's sentence against it as just, and confesses that his only hope is in the salvation wrought *for* him by Christ, who has redeemed his life, and wrought *in* him by the Spirit, whose office it is to create him anew in Christ Jesus. It is in this way that, while the tree of the old man is hewn down and cast into the fire, we become graffed into the new man and so become plants of righteousness, to be transplanted to the Paradise of God.

Now all this accords with the Old Testament teaching that the promised salvation could come to the world, not by a rescue of sinful men and nations from well-deserved death for sin, but only after death, and through a triumph over it. The seed of the woman was to bring rescue to all her seed from their captivity to death. The trees were to be cut down and burned, but a new tree of life was to be planted. The outcast spirits, of all the sons of the first Adam were to be revived through the life of the last Adam, made a quickening Spirit. We have already said that this resurrection of all is not the final salvation of all. For evil types of life and character may appear again in the resurrection, as required by the unchanging law, "To every seed his own body." And God's eternal fire burns on forever against all such. But this does not set aside the great truth, which we have traced through all Old Testament Scripture, and which Jesus Christ came to confirm, that there is a promised deliverance of all mankind from the pit of death into which their sins have cast them, through a resurrection from the dead. What we shall find in the New Testament plainly set before us, is the Person of the promised Deliverer, and the unchanging principles of righteousness by which His salvation proceeds, and the inflexibility of its first principle that, "without holiness no man shall see the Lord," and that every tree which does not bring forth such fruit must be cut down and cast again into the lake of fire.

The one point at which so many Christians have been misled as to the meaning of this judgment by fire, is in their mistaken view of its relation to the resurrection. They have placed it *after* that event, and regarded resurrection as only preparatory to it, and as a mere heaping up of untold anguish upon those who were already damned. They have failed to see that as death is the wages of sin, incurred by the whole race in Adam, so resurrection is the antidote of death, and hence a provision of redeeming grace, the fruit of Christ's triumph over death. The true Scriptural place of the "fire that cannot be quenched," the "eternal fire," the "fire of Gehenna" is *before* resurrection. These expressions all pertain to the realm of death and dissolution. They describe a punishment which even now gnaws in the bodies and souls of men like a consuming fire, and which issues in the destruction of both in hell. But all this lies this side of resurrection and not beyond it. There is indeed "a second death, which is the lake of fire" into which those will finally be cast who despise and abuse the grace that intervened to raise them out of death. But our Lord's fearful words relate to the retribution which follows the sins of this life, not those of the life to come. It was the trees planted in the soil of this world, not those of the world to come, which He came to consign to the unquenchable fire. And as it would be absurd to think of a tree as burning forever in such a fire, or of chaff as endlessly preserved in a fire which is expressly declared to burn it up, so it is a monstrous *non-sequitur* to infer that, because the "fire cannot be quenched," it must be a fire of endless torment to all who are cast into it. These phrases imply the rejection and handing over of the old man to utter destruction, as unworthy of any place in life or inheritance in the kingdom of the Son of Man. Thus it was that He came to lay the axe at the root of the tree. And thus it is that He is daily hewing down these corrupt trees of humanity around us with which the world abounds, and casting them into the unquenchable fire.

CHAPTER II.

GEHENNA.

In conformity with John the Baptist's announcement of the Messiah's mission, we find Jesus beginning his ministry with the searching, sifting doctrine of the Sermon on the Mount.

Nothing that was false or corrupt or pretentious or unjust could find place in the new kingdom which He came to found. To enter into the life of that kingdom all that was evil in the old life must be given to the burning. "If thy right eye causeth thee to stumble, pluck it out, and cast it from thee." "And if thy right hand causeth thee to stumble, cut it off, and cast it from thee: for it is profitable for thee that one of thy members should perish, and not thy whole body be cast into hell" (Gehenna) (Matt. v. 29, 30).

At various other times we find Jesus warning men against this great danger. In sending out His disciples to preach, He urged them not to fear them which kill the body, but are not able to kill the soul: "but rather fear Him which is able to destroy both soul and body in hell" (x. 28). In Matthew xviii. we have the warning repeated that it is far better to sacrifice hand or foot or eye, rather than having two hands or two feet or two eyes "to be cast into the eternal fire." This expression in verse 8 is only another form of stating that which in verse 9 is described as a being "cast into the hell of fire." A comparison of these two verses shows that these two Scripture phrases, "eternal fire" and "Gehenna of fire," are equivalent. They denote one and the same punishment.

We find the same word again in the denunciation of the Pharisees (Matt. xxiii. 15, 33), who would compass sea and land to make one proselyte, and who, under their tutelage, would become two-fold more a child of hell than themselves. In still more bitter words he calls them the offspring of vipers, who could by no means escape the damnation of hell. In Mark ix. the words in Matthew xviii. are repeated, except that here we have the phrases "unquenchable fire," the "fire that is not quenched," used to describe the fire of hell. Another expression, "where their worm dieth not," is added here derived from Isa. lxvi. 24. The words in Isaiah, which furnish the Old Testament basis for the New Testament usage, relate to the utter destruction of the Lord's enemies. "And they shall go forth, and look upon the carcases of the men that have transgressed against me: for their worm shall not die, neither shall their fire be quenched; and they shall be an abhorring unto all flesh." In this passage there can be no reference to an endless torment of these transgressors. It is their dead bodies which are in view, upon which the worms prey unceasingly and the fires feed with a consuming energy which nothing can avert. That this passage does not imply the eternal torment of those cast into the fire, is manifest from the words appended in verses 49 and 50 (R. V.,) "For every one shall be salted with fire. Salt is good: but if the salt have lost its saltness, wherewith will ye season it? Have salt in yourselves and be at peace one with another." This whole discourse of Jesus was designed to enjoin humility and self-sacrifice upon his disciples, who had been disputing one with another as to who should be greatest. By setting a little child in the midst of them, by shewing them that their honor and reward would be found in lowly service, He taught them that whatever in them caused them to offend against this principle of self-sacrifice they should lop off and cast away. In this way, by a loss of a part, they should save the whole. It was far better thus to "enter into life" and "into the kingdom of God." For it is the law of life that it can be preserved only in this way. "Every one shall be salted with fire." Salt is itself enduring, and it preserves other substances from decay. The salt here is this spirit of self-sacrifice. This preserves the life from destruction. It gives over to the burning the evils of the life. If men possess it not, they must themselves be cast into the fire. For every one, saint and sinner, must be salted with this fire which burns up self-seeking and destroys the old man. If men lose this spirit, what shall take its place or do in them its saving work? "If the salt lose its true character, wherewith shall ye season it?" "Have salt in yourselves, and be at peace one with another." That is, admit this principle of self-surrender into the core of your being. This will silence all such disputes and make you at peace one with another. How men can derive a doctrine of the everlasting torment of sinful men in a hell of fire from these words, spoken not to men indiscriminately, but to *disciples* to teach them the law of self-preservation, is marvelous indeed. The most that could possibly be drawn from it would be the *destruction* in the fire of those who will not submit to this sacrifice of self. But even this inference is made to be an uncertain one by the comparison of this fire, to which every one must be subjected, to salt, the effect of which is to preserve.

We have already seen that, before the coming of Christ, there was current among the Jews an idea of such a destroying fire, as awaiting the wicked in Sheol. The name Gehenna, which is the original word for "hell" in all the above passages, was derived from Ge Hinnom, the valley of Hinnom, adjacent to Jerusalem, into which the offal of the city and putrid carcases of beasts, and sometimes of criminals, were cast. Purifying fires were kept constantly burning, to aid in consuming the corrupt mass. It furnished, therefore, a vivid picture of that destructive work of judgment by which God consumes, by the fire of His anger, the vile refuse of wicked men.

As to the difference between *Gehenna* and *Sheol* or *Hades*, we are unable to discern that it is a radical one. We have already found that the Old Testament writers constantly look upon Sheol as a realm of destruction. The righteous indeed had hope in his death that God would preserve his soul from being devoured in this pit. There was a place of refuge and repose, which in later times was called "Abraham's bosom," for the righteous. But the wicked must sink into the abyss, and this was Gehenna, a place not radically differing from Hades, but only a deeper pit in the same gloomy abode. Accordingly we find that Jesus sometimes uses the word Hades as the equivalent of Gehenna, and notably in describing the punishment of the rich man who had despised Lazarus

(Luke xvi.). It was in *Hades* that he lifted up his eyes, being in torment. And there he was "tormented in this flame." It was down to *Hades* that Chorazin and Bethsaida and Capernaum should be cast. This equivalent use of the two terms, *Hades* and *Gehenna*, by our Lord, is proof that both radically represent the same idea of a place of destruction—only in Gehenna the destruction seems more complete and hopeless.

It thus appears that all these terms, Hades, Gehenna, eternal fire, the fire that cannot be quenched, furnace of fire, belong to the same category.

We pass now to the important inquiries: 1. What punishment do these terms describe? 2. When is it inflicted? We have no doubt that the one idea in which they all unite is that of complete destruction. This is the uniform Scriptural penalty of sin. Man was made an embodied image of God. The idea that this image consists only in a spiritual likeness does not fully explain the narrative of man's creation. Nor does it agree with the New Testament definition of the Christ who is the perfected Man, the true "Image of the invisible God," and in whom "dwelleth all the fullness of the Godhead *bodily*." Our ordinary conceptions of man's dignity of nature depreciate embodiment. And so we miss the meaning of the threatened punishment of sin, and also of the "hope toward God" which illumines all Scripture, of resurrection.

Man forfeited his life and his high place of dignity by sin. The wages of his sin was death. This involved not only spiritual blight, but the destruction of his being as a *man*. The earlier Scriptures contain only here and there a gleam of hope that personal being could survive this dissolution and reappear as man. A few, like Abraham, were lifted on to a summit of faith, from which they discerned the promise of resurrection. Later, however, among the Jews, the security and final recovery from death of the godly became more and more assured, while the wicked were viewed as sinking more and more deeply into the abyss of destruction under the consuming hand of God. This was Gehenna. But the radical idea of its punishment was banishment from the light of life, the loss of embodied being, a loss, to those confirmed in wickedness, beyond the hope of retrieval through resurrection.

Gehenna, therefore, is essentially the pit of destruction. The death-idea underlies all Scripture allusions to the punishment due to man for sin. All the words employed contain this idea of perishing; and the agents of this destruction are the forces of nature, which Scripture views as the angels of God. By the ministry of these forces, man has been built up into the highest form of creaturehood, and they are the powers who destroy it. They execute God's judgments through blight and famine and disease and plague and war. For all human lusts and unbridled passions are set on fire by forces that move on the course of nature. And as "fire" is the form in which these forces exhibit their most destructive energy, it stands in Scripture as the type and representative of all destroying agents. They are often grouped together under this one term, "consuming fire" (Deut. ix. 3; xxxii. 22–24. Ezek. xx. 47, etc.). This is the "fire that cannot be quenched" of the Old Testament. And the "eternal fire" of the New Testament is but the same devouring energy of Nature, which, as God's minister, consumes all created forms, and especially man, as now a sinner, condemned by the law of nature as well as of God, to go into its Gehenna of fire. In the earlier days of Christianity this was commonly viewed as material fire. Now it has been thinned down to a mere figure of mental torment. It is not, indeed, a gross material flame, but it is more than a mere fever of the mind. Eternal fire is the one term which comprehends all those devouring forces which destroy man from off this heritage of creation, of which God made him the heir and lord, and quench in him the light of life; and Gehenna is the *maw of these whirling forces down into whose vortex man disappears at death.*

What our Saviour, therefore, warns men against in these fearful words is this loss of their lives and this destruction of their bodies in hell. It was evidently a destruction that went beyond physical death. Men were warned to fear Him who was able not only to kill the body, but to destroy both soul and body in hell. The parable of the rich man and Lazarus makes it evident that the process of destruction in Gehenna lasts longer than the death of the body. The rich man died, and was buried, and in hell he lifted up his eyes, being in torment. It was, therefore, not annihilation. Indeed, the declaration of Jesus (John v. 29), which is the first clear Scriptural announcement of the purpose of God to raise the unjust dead, proves that the continuity of their being is somehow preserved. Our own explanation is that these uniform Scripture terms which describe man as perishing, as destroyed in hell, refer to what we have spoken of as his destruction out of manhood. So constant is the use of these terms that we are obliged to regard them as involving, either the extinction of man's existence, or his destruction *qua homo*, that is of his being *as a man*. The former cannot be true; for, in that case, there would be nothing of the person left to be raised. The newly-created being, at the resurrection, could not retain the consciousness nor the responsibility of the old. There must be, therefore, a survival of the human spirit through this abyss of death. As to how long it may retain the intense personal consciousness shown by the rich man in the parable, we do not know. The passage already referred to (Matt. x. 28) seems to distinguish between the "soul" and "spirit." It speaks of a threatened destruction of the *soul* in hell with the body. What seems death to us is not the whole of it. The death of that physical frame which we call the body may not completely disembody the *spirit*. There may be finer qualities of substance entering into its embodiment than those of which our senses take cognizance. These may pertain to the *soul*, which would, therefore, furnish the spirit with that more subtle embodiment which outlasts the gross body. But the soul also may be destroyed in hell. Hence, it may be more than a mere figure of speech by which Dives in Hades is represented as still having the bodily organs of eyes and tongue. He was not yet a naked, outcast spirit. Whether "the spirit of a man" is also destructible is an inquiry beyond our present purpose, which is to show that the punishment in Gehenna, while it includes material death, lasts beyond it and involves a prolonged suffering of the "soul," which also, as distinct from the spirit, is a constituent part of man's embodied being, the whole of which may be destroyed in hell. And this is the fearful doom against which Jesus warns us men.

But the important inquiry yet remains, When is this punishment inflicted? On the answer to this question the whole of any system of eschatology turns.

We do not hesitate to reply that these words of Jesus refer to an *immediate* punishment, and they can be properly explained in no other way. The Church, for centuries and with amazing uniformity, has interpreted these words as descriptive of a doom to be visited upon the wicked after a remote resurrection and a general judgment. Obscure passages in the Apocalypse, which speak of a future casting into a lake of fire of a class of resurrected men, and which we shall have occasion hereafter to examine, have fixed the meaning of all these earlier and plainer passages. These words of Jesus, and the subsequent references of the apostles to an eternal destruction to be visited upon the ungodly, relate to men in flesh and blood, and not to dead men raised. There is not the slightest warrant for the assumption that, when Jesus urges men to cut off a hand or a foot, if need be, rather than having two hands or two feet, the whole body should be cast into hell, He means, not the present body, but a resurrection body of the far-distant future. His words evidently refer to a now-impending loss of this present embodied life in a present Gehenna. For that Gehenna is a present fact is directly certified by James in his Epistle (iii. 6), where he speaks of the tongue as now "set on fire of hell" (Gehenna). And that the casting of the wicked into hell is not a remote, but an immediate punishment, is made as plain as it can be, by the plainest of all passages which refer to it, the parable of the Rich Man and Lazarus.

And yet, just at this point, as to the *time* when this Gehenna punishment is inflicted, our long-accepted systems of eschatology have stumbled and gone astray, and so the deepest and most vital truth of the Bible—redemption through resurrection—has been long hidden from our eyes.

CHAPTER III.

ETERNAL FIRE, A FACT OF SCIENCE AS WELL AS OF SCRIPTURE.

We have thus far examined the Scriptural use of the term "eternal fire" and its cognates sufficiently to determine,

1. That the one radical idea, common to them all, is that of destruction.

2. The term comprehends and is the exponent of all the agencies by which the consuming energy of Nature wastes and destroys the bodies and souls of men.

Thoughtful men have long been waiting for some statement of the doctrine of future punishment which should be scientific as well as Scriptural. If we are not yet able to arrive at this, we may at least indicate the direction in which it may be found.

Our primary source of knowledge upon this subject is the Holy Scriptures. But its interpreters have too often forgotten that God has revealed Himself to men in other ways than through His Word. As man was made in His image, no conception of God's government of the world can command permanent assent which violates what He has revealed of Himself in man and in the constitution of human society. And, as all things were made by Him, nothing can be true which does not accord with what He has made known of Himself in the system of Creation. The mistake of Theology has been in its too exclusive view of God as the moral governor of the world, and of man as His subject. Whereas man is also the product of a created system of which God is the Author, and the subject of natural as well as of moral law. His place and destiny in this system of nature needs to be studied before we can appreciate the Bible terms which define his destiny as a subject of God's moral government.

We therefore pause here to inquire whether there is anything in Nature corresponding to the Bible doctrine that sinful men must be cast into eternal fire.

The observations of Science convince us that the primary condition of the elemental substances out of which all created forms have been built up, was one in which their atoms were held apart by great heat. The visible universe is for the most part a wilderness of fire. The nearest star to us in space is the Sun, a vast incandescent globe of fire, in whose photosphere vaporous masses of iron and sodium, and other minerals are glowing with intensest heat. On the Earth these same substances have been cooled down, and have combined according to their chemical affinities. In this process of combination the heat-energy has been rendered latent. There has thus been a progress in the creative process from the state of primeval fire, to one of chemical combination and equilibrium, and cosmical order, by which these elements have become subordinated to the ends and uses of Life. Two antagonistic forces seem to have been contending for the mastery on this arena of the universe, the eternal fire and the eternal Life. The fire resolves all things into their primary elements. It is constantly claiming back the things that have been wrung out of its bosom. All processes of decay are but the slower gnawing of the tooth of this eternal fire. Life, however, has been from the first capturing and subsidizing these substances to the ends of its manifestation. Under its transforming power they are organized into a variety of creature forms, advancing from one stage of development to another, until finally man has appeared at the summit of the series, the highest embodiment of created life. It has been from the first, however, a law of creation that all defective forms of creature life cannot abide. They are but transient and must give way to higher forms. There has been a constant struggle in Nature toward a perfect and abiding form, but it has not yet been reached. Type after type, race after race, has been suffered to sink back into the womb of the eternal fire out of which they were brought forth. But along all the series the abiding Life has been conserving the fruits of past triumphs and making new conquests.

Still, however, it remains the law of Nature that all defective forms of life must yield to the law of decay and go back to the elemental abyss out of which they sprang. And to this law man is no exception. He exists as yet only in a sinful and imperfect type of manhood. And therefore he is made subject to vanity, and is under bondage to this law of corruption. He must depart into the eternal fire.

The eternal Life, however, has at length been manifested in the person of the perfect Man. It was" with the Father" from the beginning, and has now been "manifested unto us" (1 John i. 1, 2). The man-nature in Christ has reached its ideal as the perfect and indestructible image of God, the depository and vehicle of His Life, the representative of His authority, the inheritor and administrator of His vast estate. As such, Jesus is now triumphant over death and all the powers of the Universe, crowned Lord over all.

It is then not only in obedience to the requirements of a moral law, but also to the law of nature, that sinful men are consigned to the eternal fire, and that only those who, by faith in Christ are made partakers of His nature, enter into the eternal life. This is no arbitrary sentence of an irate Judge. It is according to the eternal order of Nature.

We have already seen that the term " fire " stands in Scripture as the representative of all the death-dealing forces of Nature. In them all God is seen as " a consuming fire." We have also here to notice that a wide generalization of the passages in Scripture which refer to angelic powers, convinces us that they are either closely identified, if not identical, with what we call the forces of nature.* They are the executive forces of the one Supreme force in Creation. And as it is these forces which draw men down into that abyss of dissolution which, in this economy of Nature, may be viewed as its gulf of eternal fire, it is in their agency that we find the proper explanation of the angels which attend the administration of the Son of Man. They "gather out of His kingdom all things that offend, and them which do iniquity and cast them into a furnace of fire" (Matt. xiii. 41-42). And they are the angels of His might who shall attend Him at His revelation from Heaven in flaming

---

* See upon this subject Chaps. I, IV, and VI, of " Mystery of Creation and of Man."

fire (2 Thess. ii. 8). The language of Scripture also accords with Science in assuming that there are two classes of forces in the realm of nature, the one life-giving, the other death-dealing. There are two classes of effects, and if these are not to be referred to two classes of agencies, the one constructive, the other destructive, there must at least be an essential difference in the mode of operation when the forces of Nature transcend the sphere of beneficent action, and become the ministers of evil and of death. Without, however, seeking to penetrate this mystery, which is beyond our ken, it is sufficient to know that the common language of both Science and Scripture recognizes these two realms of cosmic forces, in one of which the energy of Nature is directed toward the production of order out of chaos, of light out of darkness, of life out of death. And in the other its energy is bent to produce the counter class of effects, remanding to darkness and chaos, dissolving the elements that had combined to the production of forms of life and beauty, breaking down organisms, and carrying down into the vortex of dissolution the creature forms which Life had built up and beautified out of the substances it had rescued from their grasp. Now, as the angels of light are identified in Scripture with these beneficent operations, so on the other hand it has a name for these destructive and death-dealing forces. It calls them "the devil and his angels," "the ruler," "the kingdom of darkness." It has been a great mistake to regard these evil powers as operating against man in the sphere of moral agency alone. They are more truly and deeply his physical enemies. They have the power of disease,

(Luke x. 19; xi. 14-18; xiii. 16; Acts x. 38), and of death (Heb. ii. 14). The devil is a prince over all death-dealing forces in Nature (Job i. 12-19; Psalm lxviii. 49; Ephes. ii. 2, vi. 12). The difference between the scriptural and the scientific conception of these forces is that the former always views them as living spiritual agents. But even here science is gradually approaching the scriptural conception. Herbert Spencer admits that the final postulate of science, the omnipresent, inscrutable, unknowable Force may be living and spiritual. Why may not all minor forces in this created system be also living powers? Indeed we were not long ago assured by an able writer upon the "Fallacy of Materialism," that " the theory that the universe consists entirely of mind stuff," and that "mental and physical phenomena, although apparently diverse, are really identical, is the one toward which all the greatest minds that have studied this question in the right way are tending."

There is one sublime luminous truth, however, revealed in Scripture, which is beyond the province of Science. And that is that the Author and Energizer of this created system is directing all its forces, not only to the preparation of it as an abode for the highest forms of life, but toward its ultimate transformation and deliverance from the yoke of these evil powers that have wrought in it this work of corruption and death (Rom. viii. 19-23; Rev. v. 13, xxi. 1-5). The "eternal fire," which is the concrete expression of all these devouring agencies of Nature, must finally consume them all in its own bosom. For we read that it is "prepared for the devil and his angels" (Matt. xxv. 41; Rev. xx. 10, 14). The death-dealing forces contain within themselves the principle of self-destruction. The whole realm of death and hell, with " the devil and his angels," must be " cast into the lake of fire." And the Scripture term for this fate is " destruction " (1 Cor. xv. 24-26; Heb. ii. 14). " There shall be no more death " (Rev. xxi. 4).

But although Science halts here, where Scripture advances with firm tread and lifts the veil, there is yet complete accord in what both teach as to the pit of dissolution which Nature, or rather the God of Nature, has dug for all the imperfect forms of created life which have heretofore appeared, and which contain within themselves the principle of decay and death. And the natural man, as belonging to the same system, must depart, under the common curse, into the eternal fire. The sentence of the Son of Man (Matt. xxv. 41), " Depart, ye cursed," is as truly a sentence of the law of Nature as it is of the law of God. Only one Man has as yet appeared in whom the Eternal Life was so manifested as to enable Him to rise above and out of this pit of death into the glory of a divine and immortal manhood. Union with Him, by faith, is the only power of life that can save our lives from destruction and redeem us out of the hands of all our enemies. It is true only of those in whom this purifying and conserving life-power dwells, that they " go into life eternal."

It is manifest, therefore, that before we can arrive at any true doctrine of future or present punishment for sin, we must learn to view man in his relations to this natural system in which God has placed him, of which he is a product, and with whose destiny his own is involved. The fire of hell is not merely a future torment of the mind. The Scripture terms are too literal for this. Nor, on the other hand, is it a gulf of flame specially created for the endless torment in body and soul of lost men. It is a present fact of nature, a fact the proofs of which are all around us, and the signs of whose activity are everywhere in nature apparent; yea, even in our own bodies and souls, depraving, blighting and consuming. We walk each day along the edge of this bottomless pit. Each night we go to sleep upon the confines of this outer darkness. The fire that burns in our very life-blood is a shred of this eternal fire. The vices that taint and inflame it, that blight the bodies of men and consume their energies of soul are but the outer lappings of the billows that toss on this lake of fire and beat themselves upon these shores of life whereon we tread for a few brief years. And the yawning gulf of this sea of raging forces and of elemental unrest waits to receive us all. The cry of even Jesus, in presence of it, was, " Save me, oh God; for the waters are come in unto my soul. I sink in deep mire, where there is no standing: I am come into deep waters where the floods overflow me . . . Let me not sink . . . neither let the deep swallow me up, and let not the pit shut her mouth upon me . . . Draw nigh unto my soul and redeem it: deliver me because of mine enemies" (Ps. lxix). With such "strong crying and tears" did even this Divine Man "offer up prayers and supplications unto Him that was able to save Him from death, and was heard in that He feared" (Heb. v. 7).

We must, therefore, open our minds to take in this full and Scriptural significance of death, the appointed wages of sin, if we would understand the Scripture terms which set forth its punishment. The meaning of death, in God's economy of nature and of moral government, has been strangely perverted by a satanic perpetuation in the minds of men of the original lie, "Ye shall not surely die." Men have believed themselves of an immortal nature, apart from God. And hence the real significance of the death-sentence has been missed, and also the real value of the gospel record that God hath given us eternal life in His Son. We need, therefore, to know that all these Scripture terms, "Gehenna," the "hell of fire," "eternal fire," the "fire that cannot be quenched," all pertain to this realm of death and dissolution, and describe to us the pit, which not only the law of God, but the law of Nature, has dug for the sin-blighted bodies and souls of men. It is not to a realm of endless torment, but to an abyss of inexorable dissolution, protracted indeed beyond the death of the body, for the soul, as a finer essence of man's being, is longer in its dying (see pg. 101), to which wicked men are consigned. And even the righteous, as to their flesh and blood nature, which is but carnal, and must see corruption, do not escape this pit. It is only as they are made partakers of the divine nature, and become in life and spirit identified with it, that they "go into life eternal." This is the profoundest teaching of the scene in Matt. xxv. 31-41. Their life in manhood has become incorporate with the life of the Divine Man. And so they go with Him into His kingdom of joy and into the life eternal. But here again, this doom of the wicked, and of this we cannot be reminded too often, is immediate and lies this side of resurrection. The eternal fire is a present fact. It pertains to this present economy of nature. This, indeed, is the real significance of the adjective which describes it. It is the *aionion*, the age-during fire. It pertains specially to *this* order of nature and not to the ages to come. Its power then will be gone, for there shall be no more curse nor death (Rev. xxii. 3). It is therefore a present Son of Man, now exalted to Headship over all the forces of the Universe (Ephes. i. 20-23), seated on the throne of an ever-present judgment, and executing the law of this present system of Nature, whose voice we are to hear in the dread sentence, "Depart ye cursed into eternal fire, prepared for the devil and his angels." This is the consignment, not of a future host of resurrected dead, who are not here in view, but of the living generations of unrighteous men, to that present abyss of dissolution which yawns beneath us all as a gulf of consuming fire. It is from this now-impending peril that His gospel is sent out with its glad tidings of rescue. Its gift of eternal life is the divine antidote to this death. And so great is the power of life now deposited in the new Source of Life to men, that " power has been given unto Him over all flesh," to give not only *eternal* life to a chosen seed who are to be associated with Him in His life-giving work (John xvii. 2), but also to raise up out of the abyss of death to lower orders of life (each in his own time and order), the masses of mankind who have gone down into this pit (John v. 28, 29). Their resurrection, although it be to judgment and corrective discipline, is yet the result of His redeeming work and a manifestation of His triumphant power. And it violates the whole order of God's working in this plan of creation, and the whole spirit and meaning of His Word in its dealings with these great problems of life and death, to view this recovery of the unjust dead as anything but a blessing, even though it bring with it new risks with the new opportunities of life.

Moreover this view of God's gracious purpose to recover men from the abyss of eternal fire into which they are cast by the law of Nature, as well as by the sentence of the Son of Man, is necessary to show how His goodness answers to His severity. The eternal fire is not master in this universe, only a servant. The devil wins no triumphs that are not turned into defeats by Him who was manifested to destroy him and his works. Not even death can hold his trophies. "The last enemy that shall be destroyed is death." And death and hell shall be cast into the lake of fire (Rev. xx. 14). There is, indeed, before sinful men a fearful punishment. It is no light thing to die and to sink down, body and soul, into that abyss where burns the eternal dissolving fire. It is no small privation to be shut out from the light and life and blessedness of those of whom Jesus says, "They shall never taste of death." "I give unto them eternal life" (John viii. 52, x. 28). And wicked men, when raised, must still be adjudged unworthy of this life. And yet their recovery will prove the truth of what the book of Creation and the Book of God both teach, that the Eternal Life is master of the realm of Eternal Fire, that Love is stronger than wrath. To take away every element of hope from the resurrection of all but the small class who now receive Christ, is to limit His grace and power as the Prince of Life, and to deny that His gospel is glad tidings of great joy to all people.

CHAPTER IV.

THE JUDGMENT-SCENE OF MATT. XXV. 31-46.

" But when the Son of Man shall come in His glory, and all the angels with Him, then shall He sit on the throne of His glory : and before Him shall be gathered all the nations : and He shall separate them one from another, as the shepherd separateth the sheep from the goats: and He shall set the sheep on the right hand, but the goats on the left. Then shall the King say unto them on His right hand, Come ye blessed of my Father, inherit the kingdom prepared for you from the foundation of the world : for I was an hungred and ye gave me meat: I was thirsty and ye gave me drink: I was a stranger, and ye took me in; naked, and ye clothed me: I was sick, and ye visited me: I was in prison and ye came unto me. Then shall the righteous answer Him, saying, Lord, when saw we thee an hungred, and fed thee? or athirst, and gave thee drink? And when saw we thee a stranger, and took thee in? or naked and clothed thee? And when saw we thee sick, or in prison, and came unto thee? And the King shall answer and say unto them, Verily I say unto you, Inasmuch as ye did it unto one of these my brethren, even these least, ye did it unto me. Then shall He say also unto them on the left hand, Depart from me, ye cursed, into the eternal fire which is prepared for the devil and his angels: for I was an hungred and ye gave me no meat : I was thirsty, and ye gave me no drink : I was a stranger and ye took me not in; naked, and ye clothed me not; sick, and in prison, and ye visited me not. Then shall they also answer, saying, Lord, when saw we thee an hungred, or athirst, or a stranger, or naked, or sick, or in prison, and did not minister unto thee? Then shall He answer them, saying, Verily I say unto you, Inasmuch as ye did it not unto one of these least, ye did it not unto me. And these shall go away into eternal punishment : but the righteous into eternal life."

This passage, which we have transcribed in full from the New Version, is the crucial passage in eschatology.

It is the one passage in the New Testament which, above all others, has determined and fixed the prevalent doctrine of endless punishment.

By all our previous studies in the Bible, especially of the Old Testament, we have been irresistibly led to this conclusion, namely, that no consistent view of its great plan of redemption, and no adequate fulfilment of its promises, is possible which makes death the limit of all God's gracious dealings toward the masses of mankind who have not known Him, and which takes away from their promised resurrection every element of hope. We have already found that all our Lord's previous teaching about the "unquenchable," the "eternal," fire is perfectly consistent with the thought that He is speaking of a present Hell, into which man's present embodied being must be cast for destruction; and that the interpretation which projects this punishment beyond the resurrection, and puts the stress of it there, is wholly arbitrary and unnatural. It is this *present* body and soul of man which is in danger of being destroyed in hell.

We purpose now to examine this passage in Matt. xxv to ascertain whether its teaching harmonizes with this current thought of all Scripture. Does it shut out all the nations of unregenerate mankind from any hope in and beyond their resurrection from the dead, and shut them up to a final doom in an everlasting hell?

Before we proceed, however, to this main inquiry we remark briefly upon this passage.

1. It forms part of an address by our Lord upon "the last things," spoken, not to the multitude, nor even to

Matt. xxv. 31-46.

all His disciples, but, as we learn from Mark xiii. 3 to Peter and James and John and Andrew, "who asked Him privately, Tell us, when shall these things be? and what shall be the sign of thy coming and of the end of the age?"

2. The immediate occasion of their question was the Master's recent prediction of the destruction of the temple.

3. This impending event is made the occasion of directing their minds to other and wider judgments, of which it was to be the forerunner, and reaching beyond the Jews to all nations.

4. As judgment was to begin with the Jewish nation so the twenty fifth chapter declares to us specially, in the parables of the ten virgins and of the talents, how it must begin at the house of God. The closing parable, the sorting between sheep and goats, shows that it must extend to "all the nations," and what the end shall be of them that obey not the gospel of God.

5. The standard of judgment resolves itself simply into this,—similarity of nature with the Judge. All of those in whom the Christ-nature has been begotten, and who therefore have done His works, are adjudged to eternal life. All who cannot stand this test are banished from His presence to "the eternal fire."

And here we come to the main enquiry before us. Is this an irrevocable doom to endless misery in an everlasting hell? Before we can answer this, another and a preliminary inquiry must be raised, the answer to which will go very far in determining the main issue.

It is of prime importance in interpreting this vision of

judgment to give it its proper location. Does it depict a judgment of mankind pertaining to the period during which the gospel is preached to "all the nations," and specially a consummating judgment upon these living nations, with which that period should close, or does the vision pre-suppose a previous resurrection of all the dead?

No Christian will deny that our Lord Jesus Christ is now exalted to be the Judge of both the living and the dead, nor that the principle of judgment here laid down applies to both classes, and must prevail in all realms and ages. But as to this particular vision we have no hesitation in saying that it has no primary reference to the resurrected masses of mankind, but to a test to which the *living* nations of men were to be subjected. And the doom pronounced is to a destruction which those who obey not the gospel must suffer *in death* and before resurrection, and not after it. For

1. The analogies of the whole discourse require this. It begins by describing the approaching judgment upon the Jews. This was to be visited upon a living generation of men and not upon men brought out of their graves. This wider judgment is of the same series, and, therefore, we infer the subjects of it to be living nations and not resurrected men. The fact is, ungodly men who are dead are always viewed in Scripture as already judged and sent down to Sheol or Hell.

2. The phrase "all the nations" is the ordinary Scripture designation of the Gentile world outside of Judaism.

3. There is not a word about resurrection in the whole discourse. This idea must first be read into the passage before it can be read out of it.

4. This judgment-scene is based upon the vision of the coming of the Son of Man given in Daniel vii. Its costume is derived from it. Daniel's vision relates to a kingdom to be administered over men *on the earth*, and one in which all peoples, nations, and languages should serve and obey Him.

5. A convincing proof that this is a pre-resurrection judgment is given in the emphatic way in which Jesus assured His disciples that that generation should not pass away, till all these things be accomplished. We are aware of the efforts made to evade the force of this declaration,—made chiefly, too, by a class of interpreters who are sticklers for the principle that the plain literal meaning of Scripture language is always to be preferred. But the large majority of both Greek and common-sense readers will still believe that Jesus meant to guard His hearers against an impression that these great events of His Messianic rule and judgment were remote. He constantly warned them that they were at the doors. In Matthew xvi. 27-28, after setting before them the radical test of self-denial to which all true disciples must submit, He tells them, " For the Son of Man shall come in the glory of His Father with His angels; and then He shall reward every man according to his works. Verily, I say unto you, There be some standing here which shall not taste of death, till they see the Son of Man coming in His kingdom." Here again the attempt is made to evade the force of these words by referring them to the vision of His coming kingdom granted to some of the disciples on the Mount of Transfiguration. If these words stood alone they might be susceptible of

this explanation. But the passage is one of a class. Every reference of Jesus to His coming and kingdom carries with it this idea of nearness. He was always most careful to guard His disciples against the thought of delay and to urge upon them expectancy. Nor are we to be deterred from putting this meaning upon His words by the majestic accompaniments of the warning.

In the twenty-fourth chapter, in the discourse we are studying, He speaks of a coming tribulation in which the sun shall be darkened and the moon withdraw her light, and the stars shall fall from heaven and the powers of the heavens be shaken, and all the tribes of the earth shall mourn when they shall see the Son of Man coming in the clouds of heaven with power and great glory. "And He shall send His angels with a great sound of a trumpet, and they shall gather together His elect from the four winds, from one end of heaven to the other... Verily, I say unto you, This generation shall not pass away until all these things be accomplished" (vs. 29-35).

Now, whatever consummating fulfilment of these words the future may disclose, we cannot overlook the fact that, as Luke phrases it (xxi. 28), Jesus declared they should "begin to come to pass" during the life-time of His first disciples. On the day of Pentecost Peter assured the people that they might know that God had made the crucified Jesus both Lord and Christ. And Paul assures us (Ephes. i; Col. i) that, in raising Him from the dead, the Father hath now exalted Him Head over all the powers and forces that rule in this system of Creation, which are the angels of His might. In a most important sense He has entered now upon His office as King and Judge of men, with all the powers of Nature as His angels. We most firmly believe in the future *revelation* of Him in this high office. We know that it is now administered behind the clouds, and with a veiled hand. The clouds are to be rent. The King is to be made manifest. But it is none the less true that the Son of Man has already come into His kingdom, and that He is now judging the world in righteousness, and that He is now sorting between sheep and goats, bestowing upon the one class eternal life, and banishing the other to the eternal fire.

6. This interpretation, which locates this judgment-scene in this present age (αἰών) and before the resurrection, which introduces the age or world to come, is required by all the Scripture teaching concerning death and resurrection. If there is anything fixed in its testimony it is that the wages of sin is death. In some form the idea of the dissolution or destruction of man's embodied being enters into every passage which speaks of future punishment. Our previous studies have shown us that the Old Testament " Sheol " and the New Testamen " Hell " alike represent this pit of destruction. All previous references in the words of Jesus to the eternal fire (see Matt. xviii. 8-9; Mark ix. 43-48) show that it belongs under this same category. And, therefore, this sentence, " Depart, ye cursed, into the eternal fire," is essentially a *death* sentence. Our last study of this term is convincing on this point. And resurrection is essentially recovery from death. It lies at the other pole of the divine dealing. It is the rehabilitation of the lost spirit of man, outcast in death. It is its emancipa-

tion from the bands of Sheol, its reinvestiture with manhood. For embodiment is essential to manhood. Hence, resurrection is always referred to the redeeming work of Christ (Rom. v. 12-20; 1 Cor. xv. 22). All this harmonizes with the view we have taken of this passage. The ungodly class spoken of are *living* men, not once dead and raised again, who have been tried by the test of Christ's gospel and are found wanting. Such are adjudged to death as unworthy of eternal life. The eternal fire which consumes them is but another name for that devouring energy of nature which is continually drawing down into the vortex of death the sin-blighted bodies and souls of men.

7. But a most convincing proof that this is not a post-resurrection judgment is that such an interpretation requires us to suppose that God has made promises which can never be fulfilled. This view assumes that the doom of all mankind is irrevocably fixed by death, that the resurrection of the immense portion of it who have not known Christ is simply for purposes of judgment. But all our studies in the Old Testament have taught us that the gracious purposes of God toward mankind can be fully accomplished in no other way than through a resurrection. If death has forever put it out of His power to bless or to show compassion towards these countless myriads, then there are abundant hints and types and emphatic promises which come to naught. We have so often referred to these that it is not necessary again to repeat them. Suffice to say they are all an expansion of that primary redemption promise made to Abraham, which the Bible so often refers to and repeats,

that in a chosen seed all the families of the earth should be blessed, and of that still deeper secret stored up in the Song of Moses (Deut. xxxii) that, while the fire of God's anger against all evil-doers must burn to the lowest hell, this same fire of judgment must burn against the enemies that have fastened this yoke of bondage to corruption upon the human race, and bring to it a deliverance, in hope of which the nations are called upon to rejoice with His people. Nor are these promises confined to the Old Testament. They are taken up and amplified in the New. The prophecies with which the birth of the infant Jesus was accompanied, the Song of Mary (Luke i. 46-55), of Zacharias (68-79), of Simeon (ii. 29-32), condense these precious promises and joyfully declare that now at length they were to be fulfilled. The mercy promised to the fathers was to be performed. Through the tender mercy of God the long-promised day of redemption was about to break upon them who were sitting in darkness and in the shadow of death. The light had arisen to lighten the Gentiles and the glory of His people Israel. It is worthy of remark that during the earthly ministry of Jesus He does not Himself often repeat or refer to these glowing prophecies. Their full meaning was held in abeyance until after His resurrection. A veil was upon the hearts of even His disciples both as to the fact of this great event and its scope. It was only after its occurrence that their understanding was opened to discern what flood of light was cast upon these ancient promises by their Lord's triumph over death. This explains why the views of human destiny given in the words of Jesus seem so much more severe than those given in the first sermons and letters of the apostles. Men were not ready for the light until the Morning Star had risen above the night of the grave and the gloom of hell. But, in the preaching at Pentecost it begins at once to break forth. Peter declares that the crucified Jesus was now enthroned in the heavens as the pledge and the accomplisher of those times of restitution of all things of which God had spoken by the mouth of all His holy prophets since the world began (Acts iii. 21-26). And Paul's preaching sums itself up in the assertion that Jesus Christ had come to fulfil all the promises made to the fathers, and that the Gentiles might glorify God for His mercy (Rom. xv. 8-9). Now, if our study of these old promises has proved anything, it has proved that they require the deliverance of mankind, Jew and Gentile, from that pit of death into which sin has cast the human race. How otherwise can the promised seed bring blessing to all the kindreds of the earth? Are not the dead á part of this "all"? Are they not a part of the all flesh who shall see the salvation of God? and of the "all people" for whom a feast of fat things is prepared in that mountain upon which the Lord God shall swallow up death in victory? (Is. xxv. 6-8.) We have repeatedly discriminated between this hope of a universal redemption from death and universal salvation. But the point we now make is that since the Old Testament in numerous passages, both in type and prophecy, predicts blessing in store for unregenerate Israel (Hosea xiii. 9-14), and for nations lost in death, such as Egypt and Sodom and Moab and Edom, through a redemption from captivity to death, the final destiny of all mankind can not be everlastingly fixed at death. And, therefore, this scene in Matt. xxv cannot be one in which "all the nations" are raised and gathered before a judgment seat for their eternal award. It must relate to a doom to hell which precedes resurrection, and from which it is a deliverance.

8. Nor does the test of character here given agree with the thought that all the generations of the dead are here assembled. There is little doubt but that the human race has lived a much longer time on this planet than our common chronology provides for. How could all the swarming myriads of pre-historic times, how could the men before the flood, or even the heathen and barbarous tribes of our own day, be tried by the test here proposed,—" Inasmuch as ye did it not unto one of the least of these my brethren ye did it not to me"?

These considerations furnish then ample reason for our rejection of the ordinary view that this passage describes a last general judgment of the whole of mankind, dead and living, at one great assize. It is the vision of a work of judgment which Jesus assured His hearers was to begin before that generation passed away. The Son of Man was shortly to enter upon His glory as the King and Judge of men. His gospel was to be preached to "all the nations." Men were everywhere to be tried and sifted by it. Those to whom it proved a word of life, and in whom the Christ-nature was formed, would enter into eternal life. All others, even though they had refused Christ in ignorance, must depart into the eternal fire. No power of divine life in them could carry them safely through the crisis of death or hold them up from sinking into the abyss. Thus, the sorting between sheep and goats has been going on ever since Jesus was enthroned. Nor does this view exclude the thought of a consummation of this judgment work at the close of this gospel age, nor diminish the force of the Scripture testimony to a future *revelation* of Him in this high office. His Apocalypse will be the *unvailing* of Him in His now hidden character as the world's King and Judge, but by no means His first assumption of these offices.

We have thus found that this whole judgment-scene relates to the trial and the punishment to which men are subjected before their resurrection. And, therefore, the terms " eternal fire " and " eternal punishment " must be interpreted in subordination to this thought.

It has been long and widely assumed that the adjective " eternal " is here the necessary equivalent of " endless." And that, therefore, the doom here pronounced must be interminable. This consideration will be enough in the minds of superficial readers to rule out every suggestion of possible change or limit to the damnation of the lost. And, with the ordinary traditional view that the passage describes the judgment, after a general resurrection, of all who have ever lived, this inference from the use of the word " eternal " is almost irresistible. But the falsity of this view has been demonstrated. Moreover, we have found it wholly inconsistent and irreconcilable with the uniform teaching of Scripture concerning the nature and scope of resurrection, and of the promises involved in it and made dependent on it. If this word " eternal " here holds us to a doctrine of endless misery for all who have died in their sins, and to a denial of all those gleams of hope for the unsaved nations of the past which flash out on so many pages of Old Testament prophecy, rather than deny these we had better even resort for relief to a principle laid down in a recent lecture by Dr. A. A. Hodge, in which he said, "When I read the Bible, I confess I am never absolutely convinced by one text. It is a habit of the mind, perhaps, because the thought will arise, How do you know that this text is sure, How do you know there is no error in the transcript, How do you know there is not some error in the interpretation? I do not believe God ever meant us to believe in a great doctrine upon a single text. But, when the truth is interwoven and associated in the record as a condition of the history; when it is taken up and interwoven in the whole scheme of redemption, and afterwards as the very basis of God's treatment of man under all conditions, . . . you cannot touch such a truth without destroying the whole scheme of redemption, and it is just because it has been interwoven into the whole scheme."

Now, this applies to the case before us. It is not too much to say that the doctrine of an endless hell for all who die unsaved rests almost wholly upon this one text, "These shall go away into everlasting punishment." This is its main pillar and its bulwark. By this we do not mean that there are not a great many other passages relied upon. But it will be found that their interpretation takes its coloring from this passage. The falsehood in interpretation which locates this judgment-scene after the resurrection has thrown its baleful glare over these other passages and covered them with its gloom. We have already seen that all the previous references of Jesus to a hell of fire relate to a present impending destruction of man's present embodied being, both body and "soul" (as distinct from "spirit") in that pit which God's natural and moral laws have dug beneath the very foundations of unrighteous being, but that this destruction of the wicked does not preclude the hope of a resurrection out of this abyss. And so with all the plainer passages, Old Testament and New, which set forth the doom of the sinner. The few more obscure passages of the Apocalypse we purpose to examine hereafter. There is, for instance, but one passage in all of St. Paul's recorded sermons or epistles which may be regarded as parallel to this 46th verse, or which appears to teach the doctrine of endless punishment for the sins of this life. We refer to 2 Thess. i. 9, "Who shall suffer punishment, even eternal destruction from the face of the Lord and from the glory of His might, when He shall come to be glorified in His saints" (R. V.). But, if it had not been for the assumption that the sentence in Matthew was to an everlasting punishment of men raised from death to be judged, no one would have thought that the punishment referred to by Paul was to be inflicted on resurrected men. The whole context presupposes a generation of ungodly men, living on the earth, who are overtaken by the fiery judgment which shall accompany the manifestation of the Lord Jesus from heaven. And as even for such there is provided a future resurrection, however long delayed, the destruction threatened must consist with this promised reconstruction. For resurrection is essentially the reconstruction of man's embodied being destroyed in death and hell.

We say then, in accordance with Dr. Hodge's principle, that even if we were tied up to the belief that this 46th verse teaches the common doctrine of endless punishment, the claims of this single passage, the bulwark of all the rest, must yield to the current teaching of all Scripture that even the resurrection of the unjust is included in the great redemption hope (Acts xxiv. 15). Better that its authority be impugned in the way he suggests than that it be allowed to pervert and cloud the meaning of the great promises which God has spoken through all the ages by the mouth of holy prophets, and which underlie His whole redemption plan.

But happily we are not obliged to resort to any such questionable method of dealing with this text. Its authority stands unimpeached, and we would not dare dispute it. All the relief needed, and all that is required to harmonize it with all Scripture, is the simple recognition of this primary principle that resurrection recovers from the eternal fire.

With regard to the force of this adjective "eternal" in connection with "punishment" two explanations are possible.

1. The Greek adjective *aionion*, like the Hebrew *l,olam* which it translates, is not the precise equivalent of the English word "endless." We freely admit that it may have that meaning. When Paul speaks, for example, of the "eternal God" (Rom. xvi. 26), there

can be no limit to the duration which the term implies. But when in the previous verse he uses the same adjective, and speaks of "eternal times" during which the mystery of the Christ had been kept hidden, it is manifest that these "times" were not endless. The force of the word *aionion* cannot therefore be determined apart from the noun with which it is used, and apart from the context. All Greek scholars know that the word admits of this varied meaning. No one claims that the word αἰών from which it is derived equals our word "eternity." It always defines an age, or dispensation, or economy. Its frequent use in the plural shows that there are many such "ages" or "worlds" marked off from the eternity in which God is unfolding His purposes. The "eternal fire" therefore, as we saw in our previous study, pertains to and characterizes this existing economy of creation, out of which the devil and his angels, the evil powers of the system, are hereafter to be destroyed. The eternal punishment would then be that destruction awaiting imperfect and sinful men which is the law of this present order (cosmos), and which wicked men, who belong to it, must experience until the system to which they belong is delivered from its bondage to corruption into the liberty of the glory of the children of God (Rom. viii. 19-23). With this deliverance their resurrection is somehow bound up. And, therefore, their eternal punishment would not be endless, but an age-during one. Such an interpretation not only does not violate, it fully preserves the proper force of the word *aionion*. And no small proportion of our best scholars insist that this is its only etymological and legitimate meaning.

For instance, Robert Young, whose Analytical Concordance is on the book-shelves of every Bible scholar, in his version of the Scriptures, uniformly translates it "age-during" wherever it occurs.

2. But, if any insist that this limitation of the word as applied to punishment must limit also the life promised, and that if the life be endless, the punishment spoken of in the same verse must be also endless, even this view may be harmonized with that Scripture doctrine of resurrection which makes it a "hope." The word punishment here is κόλασις. By consulting Liddell and Scott, or any good Greek Lexicon, it will be seen that there are two principal Greek terms for "punishment." The one, τιμωρια as defined by Aristotle (Rhet. i. 10, 17) means *retributive penalty*. While κόλασις means *corrective* punishment. Its primary meaning is a "cutting off" or "pruning." We have already seen that the sinner is excluded from the life and happiness of the Son of Man's kingdom and shut up in the gloom of hell until delivered through resurrection. But we have never supposed or taught that this recovery would introduce him to the life and blessedness of the righteous. He can never share in the dignity and glory of "the church of the first born." Some of the wicked will rise but to abuse and forfeit again the renewed gift of life and to perish in the second death. Many may be brought back only to those outer circles of life which are far removed "from the presence of the Lord and from the glory of His power," and which shall perpetuate their banishment (κόλασις). They may be *forever* cut off from the honor and blessedness of heirship in His kingdom.

They may experience there forever the "suffering of loss" and the shame of degradation. And yet for all this their restoration to life and to any place in the ranks of God's creatures, and any tenure in His created system, may be a great blessing. Better the outmost verge of the realms of life and manhood than the outer darkness and nakedness of hell. And thus we see how a doctrine of everlasting punishment may be held which is not one of endless misery, and how this banishment from heirship in the kingdom may be perpetual with multitudes of those who are yet brought back from death by the power of Christ's resurrection, and within the sphere of that victorious reign of life and bounty by which He shall reconcile all things unto God. And so the strictest adherence to the verbiage of this text need not quench in any of our souls the light and peace of that universal resurrection hope which is God's sunrise upon the darkness and misery of the world's long night of sin and woe.

It is important, however, to remember that the truth of the main principle in our interpretation of this passage is not dependent upon our efforts to explain this last verse in harmony with it. If neither of the two modes above suggested be satisfactory, we must still hold that the principle is true. Some mode of adjustment will be found when we come to know more of man, of his place in the present constitution of the natural and moral world; and more of God, and of His great plan of Creation and Redemption, the deepest facts of which are a righteousness that adjudges to death all that does not share in the perfect nature of His Son, in whom all things were created and by whom all things consist (Col. i. 16-18), and a love that floods again with restoring and advancing life even the realms of death.

There are two *a priori* arguments which ought to be mentioned as making the proof complete that the view we have taken of this judgment-passage is correct. They might have found place at the outset but they will be just as forcible at the close. Two things make it antecedently improbable, and even impossible, that the long-received interpretation of this passage can be true. The first is the utter silence of the Old Testament upon this doctrine of endless torment; and the second, its utter incongruity with all that Scripture teaches, and all that enlightened Christian consciousness affirms of the character of God.

1. There are three passages indeed in the *later* Old Testament Scriptures (Is. xxxiii. 14; lxvi. 24; Dan. xii. 2) which have been confidently appealed to as teaching this doctrine. We have before shown that they cannot be made to bear this interpretation. All the best modern critics reject it. But, granting all that can be claimed from these supposed allusions to an endless fiery punishment we still ask, How can it be possible, if, from the dawn of history, all mankind have been exposed to the awful risk of this incalculable doom, made dependent upon the issues of this brief human life, not a word should have been said about it for thousands of years? We heard recently a very conservative minister of the most orthodox church admit that his special study of the subject had convinced him that the human race had lived upon this planet for at least thirty thousand years.

However this may be, it is certain that God has suffered countless generations of mankind to come and go without one word concerning this awful fate which overhung them. The five books of Moses, in which He made a special revelation to His chosen people and gave them laws, with penalties and rewards, are wholly silent here. Can it be possible, if such endless woe was to follow the unforsaken sins of this brief life, He would not have warned His own people of the danger? We are asked to believe that Jesus, in a book written expressly to show that He came to fulfil and confirm all that Moses and the prophets had spoken, teaches a doctrine concerning human destiny of the most tremendous and inconceivable importance to every human being, about which His Spirit speaking through the prophets had been, to say the least, so long reticent. And still more impossible is this to believe when we consider that the revelation of God in Christ was designed to bring out more fully the gracious aspects of His character, and to teach men, as never before, to revere and love Him as our Father in heaven. Is the God of the New Testament so incomparably more severe in His dealings with the children of men than was the Jehovah of the old?

2. And this brings us to observe that it is impossible to reconcile the traditional view of this passage with the idea of God as imprinted by His Spirit upon the sacred page and upon the renewed heart. No elaborate proof of these statements is required. The man who does not *see* and *feel* their truth would not be convinced by proof. But, sure we are that, however the lurid fire of His

wrath gleams out along the surface of these pages, the profound student of them will be convinced that His Name is love. Such an one cannot find it possible to believe that that God whose " tender mercies are over all His works," of whom Jesus said that if we would be perfect as our Father in heaven is perfect, we must learn to love our enemies, to be merciful as He is merciful, to forgive them that trespass against us as He forgives, to be kind to the evil and the unthankful (Luke vi. 27·37), and who gave His Son to be the propitiation for our sins, "not that we loved God, but that He loved us" (1 John iv. 10), can be the God which the ordinary theory of this passage requires us to suppose.

Nor can we believe that this view of Him can ever agree with that image of God which it is the office of His Spirit to form within those who are being created in Christ Jesus unto good works. The whole history of His church, the lives of the best Christians we know, show that those who are most like Him are the most merciful and humane and compassionate. They are the ones who build hospitals and endow charities, and visit prisons, and minister to the poor and the sick, just as this passage describes. They lay down their lives for the good of their fellow men, even the vicious and the debased, as well as for the brethren. Can this Christ then, who is thus formed in them, change His attitude so utterly toward the sinful and the undeserving ? Can He make it forever impossible that His saints shall do anything more for these poor lost ones ? " Will the Lord cast off forever ? and will He be favorable no more ? Is His mercy clean gone forever? doth His promise fail forevermore ? Hath God forgotten to be gracious ? hath He in anger shut up His tender mercies?" (Ps. lxxvii. 8.)

Some interpretation of this passage *must* be sought which shall preserve to us all that we have learned of God, and which shall not run counter to all the instincts which His own Spirit has begotten in our breasts. Even if the one we have suggested be not the one, such an one must be sought somewhere, for God cannot contradict Himself.

But we submit that this great Scripture principle, and this true* "eternal hope" of redemption through resurrection, furnishes just the key to solve the mystery. On the one hand it makes ample provision for the satisfying of every claim of God's righteousness in the sinner's perdition. He must lose his body and soul in hell. His spirit must be cast out from that tenure in God's universe which embodiment in manhood gave it, into the outer darkness. But, as in all God's realms life succeeds to death, re-creation to dissolution, so this field of death must yield its harvest. "Every man in his own order" and "to every seed his own body." Now that death has done its work, the sentence executed, and the law satisfied, the field is cleared for grace to come in. And so "all shall be made alive;" the unjust not to eternal life, but to a restored life in manhood that shall bring them once more

---

*We apply this word to this hope in order to distinguish it from the false "eternal hope" which flatters sinful men with the idea that there is no damnation from which they need immediate salvation, and which promises a prolongation of the opportunities of this life through an "intermediate state" before judgment.

within the circle of those administrations of blessing of which Christ the Life-giver is the Source. Many may be brought only within the outer verge of that circle and fall again out of it into a second death. But when once we have apprehended the fact and the scope of God's gracious provision through death to redeem from death, all truth about punishment for sin and about the future of those countless multitudes of the race who have gone down to death under it, will sooner or later fall into its right place. As their " being turned into hell " makes room for the fullest exhibition of God's righteousness in their condemnation, so their resurrection will make room for the amplest fulfilment of all His designs in their creation, and all the purposes and promises of grace with which His word is fraught. Any explanation of these mysteries of the future which leaves out either side of this dealing must draw a veil over the face of our Father God, and hide His true character from men.

CHAPTER V.

THE RESURRECTION OF JUDGMENT.

"Marvel not at this: for the hour cometh in which all that are in the tombs shall hear His voice, and shall come forth; they that have done good unto the resurrection of life; and they that have done ill unto the resurrection of judgment" (John v. 29, R. V.).

This is another of the passages which is generally regarded as teaching that the judgment of wicked men, and their weight of doom, are fixed for a period after their resurrection.

This long-accepted view has been favored by the authorized version which, in this case, is also a commentary. Instead of "the resurrection of damnation," which phrase at once suggests that the wicked are raised in order to be damned, the New Version more correctly reads, "the resurrection of judgment."

I. That the resurrection does not introduce this class to a formal trial to determine their fitness for eternal life is proved from the fact that they have been "judged already" (John iii. 18, R. V.), and the penalty of sin, which is death, has already been inflicted upon them. This "death" is more than the death of the body. Beyond it there is for the wicked the loss of the "soul," which we have seen to be a constituent of embodied manhood. The soul may be destroyed in hell, although as the more subtle part of the spirit's embodiment, it may long survive and suffer there, as the case of Dives illustrates. This rich man was evidently sentenced and doomed before his resurrection. We cannot therefore suppose that "the resurrection of judgment" is preparatory to a trial, or to the infliction of a doom which the unhappy subject has been already suffering under for perhaps a thousand years. It is worth noting that the phrase "*the* day of judgment" occurs uniformly in the Greek without the article, save in one instance (1 John. iv. 17), where the ordeal through which the Christian is to pass is in view. And nothing is further from the teaching of Scripture than the idea that the punishment of the wicked is reserved against some such special day. "After *death* cometh judgment" (Heb. ix. 27). The confirmation which this idea has received from 2 Peter ii. 9, "The Lord knoweth how to deliver the godly out of temptation, and to reserve the unjust unto the day of judgment to be punished," is dispelled by the truer rendering of the New Version, "The Lord knoweth how . . . *to keep the unrighteous under punishment unto the day of judgment.*" This accords with what we have found to be the uniform Scriptural conception of the punishment of the wicked. The Old Testament always views them as turned into hell, or sheol, at death. There they must abide as captives and prisoners. Our Lord's teaching we have seen to be in perfect harmony with this. Only He brings out into greater prominence the fact that the soul of man, as well as his body, may be destroyed in this pit, and that this process of destruction is a process of suffering. The loss of both body and soul leaves the "spirit" naked and outcast. The "soul" of the righteous man is preserved from destruction. Hence he is never compeletely disembodied. Disembodiment, for man, is essentially punitive. It casts him out of his inheritance. The "evil spirits" of

Scripture are always disembodied beings. All this goes to show that the ungodly, through the whole period before resurrection, are "kept under punishment," as the passage quoted from St. Peter states, and not reserved *for* punishment. And with this view we found the leading passage which sets forth their punishment, Matt. xxv. 31-46, to be consistent. Indeed, we believe this notion, that the sinner's punishment is not immediate, and that the bulk of it is reserved for infliction after his resurrection, to be wholly false and unscriptural. It is this which lies at the bottom of all that is defective and monstrous in our modern eschatology. And, therefore, we are required to look for some other meaning for "the resurrection of judgment" than that which makes it preliminary to a doom which has already been pronounced, and to a sentence already executed. We may be sure that God will not bring His doomed creatures out of hell merely for the purposes of a scenic display before a judgment seat, and in order to hurl them back again into the pit from which they were brought out.

Nor is there any weight in the consideration often advanced that, as man sins in the body, his punishment cannot be completed until his entire personality is restored through a resurrection of the body, and that as the body was the instrument of his sin, so it must be made the avenue of his suffering. Those who so urge forget that this is precisely the form in which punishment reaches the sinner *before* resurrection. Even before physical death, sin corrupts and debases the body. Men sometimes suffer the torments of the damned through the channel of its organs and nerves this side of the grave. And the dissolution of the body,—what is this but the direct judgment of God upon this human fabric through which He gives us title and heritage in this created system? In death it is wrenched asunder and taken to pieces. We have already spoken of the protracted torment which the "soul" may experience in this dissolution, before the "spirit" is wrenched from it and driven into the outer darkness. Why then is it necessary to raise up the body in order that it may experience sin's penalty when, under the weight of that penalty, it has already been debased and crushed and dissevered and destroyed? We ask again, of what other body than this present structure in manhood is Jesus speaking, when He exhorts us to pluck out an eye or lop off a limb, if these cause us to offend, rather than lose the whole body in hell? Which one of His hearers would imagine that He was speaking of the sinner's future resurrection body? The Jews, if we may believe the testimony of Josephus and of their Rabbis, did not look for the resurrection of the wicked at all. "Only the souls of good men are removed into other bodies." * It is only through gross failure to recognize what the threatened punishment for sin is, that such perversion of our Saviour's words is possible as this transfer of the destruction which overhangs the embodied life with which men are now endowed, to a resurrected body of the remote future.

II. What then is "the resurrection of judgment?"

1. It is something which is in sharp contrast to the

---

*Jewish War, Book II. Chap. 8. Alger, pg. 170.

"resurrection of life" which is the portion of the righteous. Their resurrection must be a complete investiture in that glorified manhood in which Jesus was raised. The righteous have now eternal life. We have seen also that death does not deprive them of this gift, nor cast them out naked and desolate. The *soul* of the righteous is delivered from going down to hell. Hence he is not found naked. A building of God awaits him upon the dissolution of his earthy tabernacle (2 Cor. v.). And in it he awaits the time of the complete redemption of his body, when it shall be fashioned like unto His glorious body. For his destiny as a joint heir with Christ to all the Father's vast estate requires that he have a body which shall put him into complete possession of these works of God, and be a worthy vehicle for His eternal life. Such is the resurrection of life. *

The resurrection of judgment must be such as shall at once condemn its subjects as unworthy of this life and inheritance. There is but one order of manhood capable of this dignity,—that which is conformed to the Son of Man, to whom the Father hath committed all judgment. He is the standard of admission. All who fall below that standard cannot be raised in eternal life. They fall into a lower rank. Their resurrection is their condemnation. It is to be borne in mind that what we are considering is the resurrection *of* judgment, and not *unto* judgment. The genitive here is of character. It expresses a characteristic quality by which this resurrection is distinguished from the resurrection of life. And this leads us to speak of the nature of this lower order of being in which the wicked dead come forth. *Appendix A.

Scripture speaks of but two orders of manhood, the earthy and the heavenly. Of these two, Adam and the risen Christ are the heads. Each of these has its own embodiment. The one is spoken of as a "body of humiliation," the other as a "body of glory" (Phil. iii. 21). St. Paul speaks also of "celestial bodies" and "bodies terrestrial" (1 Cor. xv. 40). Now we cannot conceive of the wicked as raised in the celestial order. As for wicked spirits and Satan, they have no bodies. They are never once spoken of in Scripture as having bodies of their own, although eager to take possession of the bodies of men and even of swine. The fact that the wicked are raised at all implies that they are lifted above this order of bodiless demons. They are invested again with human bodies; and as these can not be of the heavenly order, they must be of the earthy. Their bodies must be therefore mortal and corruptible. This is further proved in the fact that they are capable of the second death, as distinguished from the bodies of the risen saints who cannot be hurt of it (Rev. xx. 6). To maintain that the wicked are raised in *immortal* bodies we shall have to invent an order of embodied beings of which Scripture gives no instance and makes no mention. No such monstrosity is there conceived of as an evil being, immortally embodied. We are forced therefore to conclude that their risen bodies will be terrestial, mortal, and corruptible. And this will be the main feature which shall mark their resurrection as one of judgment, in contrast with that of the saints which will be to unfettered life. For this Adamic manhood comes of necessity into bondage to corruption. It is only the

Christ-man who is superior to this whole system, and who is its immortal sovereign. Jesus, in rising from the dead, broke through all its trammels, spoiled its principalities and powers, and passed on to its summit, subjecting all its realms of life and all its forces to His control. And to as many as receive Him, to them also does He give power to become the sons of God. But all other men must come back to life still in bondage to the creature, and liable to its corruption and death. Moreover, their resurrection must be long delayed. We shall greatly err if we suppose that the resurrection of all men is simultaneous. " Every man in his own order."

It is manifest also that these harvest fields of death must be reaped according to the universal law, " To every seed his own body." We cannot indeed regard resurrection itself as ever a penalty for sin. It enters into the very idea of it that it is a blessing. It is the deliverance of the unjust from the death-penalty incurred by the sins of this life. Their reinstatement in manhood must be a result of God's gracious provision that all who died in Adam shall be made alive in Christ. And yet judgment must still come in to determine when their captivity shall end, the time and nature of their deliverance. The more the blight of sin has degraded and withered their lives, the lower down on the scale of manhood they must begin again. This principle gives the fullest scope for compensations and adjustments in this resurrection of judgment. We are taught indeed that this principle of award will be applied also to the saints. In a passage frequently misapplied to the judgment of the wicked (2 Cor. v. 10), and whose exact reading is,

"For we must all be made manifest before the judgment seat of Christ that every one may receive the things through the body, according to what he hath done, whether good or bad," it is implied that the future bodies of saints will gather up and perpetuate the fruits of previous character. For the "we" of this chapter refers to this class alone. But the same principle must apply also to the resurrection of the wicked. For if there is anything universal in the economy of God, and profoundly true to all the laws of life, it is that embodiment carries with it both reward and penalty. It organizes character and determines destiny. The kind of body which a man has measures his possession and use of created things. It ennobles life or debases it. It unfetters the man for large aspirations and achievements and joys. Or it narrows his sphere, cripples and clogs his activities, and clouds his sky with despair and gloom. There must be room in God's future administrations for all orders and degrees of created life, as there is in the present. This law of resurrection, "To every seed his own body," must insure that there shall be not only a resurrection of life, and one of judgment, but in each of these fields every variety of career and destiny, according as it is written, "Whatsoever a man soweth that must he also reap."

2. And this leads to the further observation that the resurrection of the unjust *introduces* them to judgment. Not as we have seen to another judicial trial to determine their doom to hell. They have already suffered an utter bankruptcy of their being *as men* in that pit of destruction. Now they are brought out of it and rein-

vested with the human life. But they are compelled to begin it over again, and perhaps far down the scale. And during it all they are under process of judgment, as men are in this world, subject to the judicial administration and the corrective discipline of God. The primary use of the Greek word here ($κρίσις$), as distinguished from its synonyms, is of judgment as a process rather than an act. It often carries with it the idea of prolonged judicial administration, during which motives are sifted, results of conduct brought out, and character made manifest. It is in this broad sense that the word is used in the 23d verse, which declares that unto the Son, as the Quickener of the dead, hath the Father given all judgment; that all may honor the Son, even as they honor the Father.

Here it is pertinent to remark that nowhere do the views of Christians concerning God's dealings with men need broadening more than in their notions of judgment. Our theology has but little use for this word save in its narrow, legal, and technical sense. But in Scripture this represents but a small part of the divine work of judgment, which is a benevolent as well as a judicial administration, and one for which the nations were to be glad. "All His ways are judgment; a God of truth and without iniquity, just and right is He." And all nations shall come and worship before Him when His judgments are made manifest (Rev. xv. 4). His judgments are often directed to the benefit of those to whom they bring penalty. Nothing was more conspicuous in Israel's history than the judgments constantly visited upon them for their sins. The Lord must judge His people. And yet when they humbled themselves under His mighty hand, He repented Himself for His servants when He saw their power gone (Lev. xxvi. 41-45; Deut. xxxii. 36-43). Then, His judgments which seemed to be turned against them were made to be for them, and against the enemies who had brought them into their sad plight. His judgments are indeed a great deep, for they contemplate the overthrow of all those hostile powers who have brought this curse of sin and death upon man, and upon the created system of which he is the head. And, therefore, we are not to think it strange if to this resurrection of judgment there is a delivering and redeeming aspect. Man's present life is a process of judgment. The natural man is throughout it under judgment, yea, under an abiding wrath of God (John iii. 18, 36). So the unjust, in resurrection, continue under judgment. But as this brings to men now corrective discipline, we may infer that this will be its character and issue in the life to come. Not that all men will by correction learn righteousness and be made heirs of eternal life. In some, sinful character will have hardened into such permanence as to become "eternal sin" (Mark iii. 29, R. V.). And for such as suffer the second death there would seem to be no second resurrection. And yet we shall fall far short of the intent and meaning of this resurrection of judgment, if we suppose that it is only preliminary to the sinner's deeper damnation. It is to all its subjects a recovery and a boon. It gives them another standing and opportunity in life. It brings them within the sphere of those gracious operations of God of which the resurrection of

Christ is the centre. It makes room, as we have seen, for the fulfilment of great and precious promises to the human race, and to nations specifically mentioned as to be blessed through the Christ, and who are dead and gone.* These promises must prove a nullity if there is no such room beyond death for God to make them good. It provides also for the infant and imbecile portion of the race, without the necessity of supposing that all of this class belong now to the redeemed church of God. All that is necessary to make this passage fit in with all we have learned from the study of these ancient promises, and of the grand outlines of God's redeeming plan, is to divest our minds of that narrow view of His judgment which has become traditional, and we shall see that the resurrection of judgment makes room for all these features of blessing. While at the same time its punitive character is preserved. Even the setting of the judgment and the opening of the books in Daniel's vision (vii. 11) was preparatory to something more than a judicial trial. It introduced an administration by which all peoples, nations, and languages were brought under the gracious dominion of the Son of man. And so in all His judgments, which are unsearchable, and His ways which are past finding out, we are to view them as connected with His great redemptive economy. Even the final picture of universal judgment given in Rev. xx. 11-15 is accompanied by that glorious triumph over death and hell

---

*Many obscure allusions to this gracious issue become luminous when once this key to Old Testament promises is found; *e. g.* in Ps. xxii 27-31 where the Messiah's resurrection-triumph is set forth. Among all the kindreds of the nations who shall worship before Him, verse 29 declares, "All they that go down to the dust (that is, the *dead*, see Gesenius *sub voce*) shall bow before Him; even he that cannot keep his soul alive."

which leaves them cast into the lake of fire. And it is followed by the vision of the new heaven and earth which is the goal of all our desires.

It is therefore in accord with all God's wondrous ways that we regard the resurrection of judgment as a prelude to an administration, both gracious and corrective, over those multitudes of mankind who, in this life, were ignorant of God or shut up in unbelief. And such an administration we have seen to be positively required in order to make good to mankind the promises He spake by the mouth of all His holy prophets.

To recapitulate, then, the leading features of this resurrection of judgment, we find:

1. That it is not for the repetition of a sentence already pronounced, and of a penalty already inflicted.

2. It is not unto life, that is, unto life unfettered and eternal.

3. It is to a state of being not yet freed from bondage to death. Its subjects have not yet "passed from death unto life." They are still "under judgment."

4. It is to an inferior, a mortal and corruptible body. No other life can keep a body immortal but eternal life. There is but one kind of immortal embodiment, the glorified manhood of Christ. There is no instance in Scripture of an order of evil beings immortally embodied. And the contemplation of such an order is foreign to the whole plan of Creation and redemption.

5. It must introduce its subjects to that corrective discipline which characterizes every economy of God's judgments, in this age or the age to come.

6. It must issue, in the case of all who prove incorrigible under this discipline, in a second death.

7. The rehabilitation in life of men whom the judgment of God had consigned to death and hell is, however, essentially a blessing, the fruit of that far-reaching redemption which secures the resurrection of even the unjust.

CHAPTER VI.

THE JUDGE OF QUICK AND DEAD.

This is one of the official titles of the Christ. The apostles constantly presented Him in this character to their hearers, and gave great prominence to it. In the first official proclamation of the gospel to the Gentiles by Peter in the house of Cornelius, he declares: "And He charged us to preach unto the people, and to testify that this is He which is ordained of God to be the Judge of quick and dead" (Acts x. 42).

The term "quick" here is the translation of the Greek ζώντων. It occurs in several similar passages. It would have been better if the word were rendered uniformly "living," as we find it in Romans xiv. 9: "For to this end Christ both died, and rose, and revived, that He might be Lord both of the dead and the living." The objection to the archaic word "quick" is that many readers refer it to those who are to be quickened at Christ's coming, and so virtually identify this class with the "dead," who are then to be raised. The word refers to the living masses of mankind as distinct from the dead. And the two words together are designed to include both classes, and to set forth the universal character of the Messiah's judgment, as embracing all the families of the earth, both living and dead. This official title then comprehends the two aspects of His judgment which we have recently studied, and which are especially set forth in the two notable passages, Matt. xxv. 31-46 and John v. 29. In the first, as we have seen, the Christ announces Himself as about to enter upon His glory as the Judge of the living nations of men. The scene, as we have seen, is laid before the resurrection. The subjects of the judgment are not dead men raised, but living men, the wicked among whom are consigned to death. But, in John v., we have the judgment of the resurrected dead. "All who are in their graves" come forth to "the resurrection of judgment." These two great passages then bring before us this two-fold aspect of the Messiah's office as the ordained "Judge of both the living and the dead."

Here we have to enter our protest against the narrow view of this high office which prevails in the church, and has been crystallized in even its most ancient creeds. The common impression is that these words refer to a grand court and pageant of the future, and that the judicial function of the Christ is mainly that of Chief-assessor of this court, at which all mankind shall be assembled, and the eternal destiny of every one be irrevocably fixed. In order to correct this view, one needs to study well the Old Testament prophecies and promises of His judgment. We use the word "promises" because these passages, while they do not conceal the vindicatory and retributive features of His judicial work, give equal prominence to its reformatory and beneficent results. Hence all nations, and even the earth and its inanimate creatures, are invited to rejoice together because of His judgments. There is far more of promise than of threat in the announcement that He shall judge the world in righteousness (Psalms xcvi. xcviii. Is. xi. Jer. xxiii.). The great mistake in our eschatology is, that it has not brought over from the Old Testament these large and gracious views of the Messiah's judgment, with which to fill in the outlines of that larger conception of the Christ as Judge, presented in the New Testament. His office is there more clearly defined as comprehending the dead as well as the living. But its beneficence is not diminished by this enlargement. Because He is the Son of Man, all humanity is embraced by it. Not even the dead are shut out from its benefits. The resurrection of the Christ did not limit, it immensely enlarged the scope of His benign and saving work. "To this end Christ both died, and lived again, that He might be Lord, both of the dead and the living." The man who believes that death can in any way defeat His designs, or annul His promises, or limit the provisions of His grace, misses the very key to the right understanding of the Bible. From this point of view our explanation of "the resurrection of judgment," as designed to bring the dead within the sphere of His judicial reign, is seen to be required by this whole Biblical conception of His office. And indeed the context of John v. 29 requires this. For it is there stated that the reason why all judgment has been given by the Father into the hands of the Son is, "that all men may honor the Son even as they honor the Father" (verse 23). And that the term "all men" includes the dead is seen in the fact which Jesus proceeds to declare, that the execution of this universal judgment requires an universal resurrection. All who are in their graves must hear His voice and come forth. This judgment does indeed involve the trial of all men according to their works But it has also its corrective and benevolent features.

Resurrection is necessary in order to bring the generations of the dead who have not known of Christ within the sphere of that knowledge of Him which may prove their salvation, and of that salutary control which shall humble them under His mighty hand. No one would think of denying that these large and merciful aspects of the Messiah's judgment of the world, as constantly set forth in the Old Testament, apply to the *living* nations of mankind; and that future generations of living men on the earth are to be thus blessed by it. But it is commonly assumed that these promises contain no hope for the dead. We therefore need to learn that, in their deepest meaning, and in the New Testament unfolding of them, this is precisely the glory of the Christ that He is "Lord both of the dead and of the living;" that He is Judge of both, and that His office of Judge, while it includes that of Arbiter of all human destinies, embraces also those judicial administrations by which all men shall learn to call Him Lord, to the glory of God the Father; and that even the dead are to be brought within the scope of His judgment, in this wide sense of it, through resurrection.

The announcement by the apostles, therefore, of Jesus as Judge of the quick and the dead, is part of His *gospel.* It was included in the glad tidings that they were sent forth to preach. When they testified that Jesus was now raised to be both Lord and Christ, they thereby affirmed that all the ancient promises concerning the Messiah were about to be fulfilled in Him, and that these promises were so broad as to cover the realms of the dead as well as of the living. This gospel did indeed bring with it severe and searching tests. It offered no other standard of admission to God's presence than a clean heart. It foretold a purging of the world's floor by the flail of His judgments, and a burning up of the chaff with unquenchable fire. The Old Testament prophecies had intimated as much. And yet there was always a glow of light on this dark back-ground. He would send forth judgment unto victory. And so the New Testament announcements of the Christ as King and Judge of men form a part of the glad tidings of His salvation. And nothing was further from the minds of the apostles than to shut out all the generations of the dead from any interest in the good news. The fact that they longed for His coming in their own day, proves that, instead of viewing that event as putting an end to Christ's redeeming work, it would only then enter upon these wider fields of its conquest.

It is also apparent from these announcements that the Christ has already assumed this office. We have been taught to believe that "He shall come to judge the quick and the dead." So far as the dead are concerned, they do not properly come under His reign of judgment until they are raised at His coming. They are raised in order to be thus judged. But the living are all the time being assembled before His throne, and being sorted into sheep and goats. Nor are the dead, even now, apart from His control. The terms used of His investiture with His office of Judge, show that it is not the vague and distant thing which men usually conceive it to be. At Athens Paul declared that God had appointed a day, in the which He is about to judge ($\mu\acute{\epsilon}\lambda\lambda\epsilon\iota$ $\varkappa\rho\iota\nu\epsilon\iota\nu$) the world in righteousness, by that man whom He had ordained, the proof of which was that He had now raised Him from the dead (Acts xvii. 31). So again he charges Timothy (2. iv. 1) before God and the Lord Jesus Christ, who is about to judge the quick and the dead. The same Greek words are employed. And Peter (1 iv. 5) speaks of Him as "*ready* to judge the quick and the dead." And again, that "the time *is come* for judgment to begin at the house of God" (iv. 17). All these passages speak of the Christ as having already assumed this office, and as being on the point of executing it. Our exegesis of Matt. xxv. 31-46 proved to us what reality there is in this conception of His judgment. Indeed what the world, and the church also, need to-day, is such an opening of the eyes as was given to Elisha's servant, that men may see how the very atmosphere in which they live their daily life, is alive and tremulous with the chariots of His judgments. All the forces of nature are the angels of His might. Nor are we by any means sure that the judgment of the dead is wholly future. Such passages as 1 Peter iii. 19, 20 and iv. 6 convey intimations that, at least in certain aspects of it, it began when He ascended on high, leading captivity captive.

It will be seen that we are all along pleading for a larger conception of His office as Judge than has prevailed in the church,—one that will make room for both the aspects of it presented in Scripture, the retributive and the redemptive, and one that will take in the present age, as well as that which is to come. His judgment of the world in righteousness is a much nearer and broader work than men imagine it to be. The idea of a great assize is certainly a scriptural one, but it is only one aspect of His judgment. Corrective discipline, afflictive strokes that humble even the disobedient to His yoke, benignant rule, the liberation of those who are held captive by the chains of sin and Satan, and in the hands of death, the overthrow of these malign and potent enemies of man, the emancipation of the creature from their blight and corruption, the final destruction of incorrigible enemies, all these pertain to His office as " Judge of quick and dead," "the Lord both of the dead and of the living." If we view His office only in one of its functions, however important, we shall miss the meaning of the whole of it. Or if we limit the benefits of it to the living, we shall virtually deny that He is the Conqueror of death, or that there is any gospel for the dead in the fact that He died and rose again. And yet St. Peter assures us that He Himself preached these glad tidings to the spirits in prison, who aforetime were disobedient in the days of Noah (iii. 19), and that the gospel was, "preached even to the dead, that they might be judged according to men in the flesh, but live according to God in the Spirit" (iv. 6).

In order to guard against mistake, we repeat what we have often before affirmed, that these wider views of the scope of Christ's redeeming work do not require us to believe that all will at last be saved by it. They only teach that death does not cut short or limit that work, but that, in providing resurrection for all, it has provided to bring the kingdoms of the dead, as well as of the living, within its wide range of blessing.

CHAPTER VII.

THE JUDGMENT OF THE GREAT WHITE THRONE.

And I saw a great white throne, and him that sat upon it, from whose face the earth and the heaven fled away; and there was found no place for them. And I saw the dead, the great and the small, standing before the throne; and books were opened; and another book was opened, which is the book of life; and the dead were judged out of the things which were written in the books, according to their works. And the sea gave up the dead which were in it, and death and Hades gave up the dead which were in them; and they were judged every man according to their works. And death and Hades were cast into the lake of fire. This is the second death, even the lake of fire. And if any was not found written in the book of life, he was cast into the lake of fire. And I saw a new heaven and a new earth; for the first heaven and the first earth were passed away. . . . And I heard a great voice out of the throne saying, Behold, the tabernacle of God is with men, and He shall dwell with them, and they shall be his people, and God himself shall be with them, and be their God; and He shall wipe away every tear from their eyes; and death shall be no more; neither shall there be mourning, nor crying, nor pain any more; the first things are passed away. And He that sitteth on the throne said, Behold, I make all things new. Rev. xx. 11—xxi. 5, N. V.

The commonly accepted view of this passage is that it describes a simultaneous resurrection of all classes of mankind, good and evil, for the determination of their final destiny at one great assize. We shall find upon closer study that this is a mistake. It relates to the judgment of the unjust dead; and it corresponds therefore to the last half of verse 29 in John v, in which our

Lord speaks of the "resurrection of judgment." That verse gives us indeed a general picture of all resurrection. It is only from other passages that we certainly determine that resurrection is eclectic and progressive—that the saints come forth to "the resurrection of life" as a first-fruits company from among the dead (Phil. iii. 11, see Greek. 1 Cor. xv. 23, etc). The context of this passage speaks definitely of "the first resurrection" (vs. 6, 7), and of the saints as living and reigning with Christ through a prolonged period before the judgment here described. Indeed we learn from such passages as Matt. xix. 28, 1 Cor. vi. 2, that they execute it. "Know ye not that the saints shall judge the world?" The judgment of the great white throne cannot therefore include this class, and to this extent at least is not universal. We believe, indeed, that the very office to which these first-born sons of God are called, under their Head, is to raise the dead and carry on, under Him, those administrations by which the captives in Sheol shall, each in their own order, be recovered from its grasp. Hence this was made a feature in that miniature type of the kingdom of God which Jesus gave when He sent out the twelve saying, "And as ye go, Heal the sick, raise the dead" (Matt. x. 7, 8). It is probable that a barrier to the right understanding of this whole passage has been raised by the insertion into the text of verse 5, which was very likely at first a parenthetical comment put in the margin by some transcriber. The verse reads, "The rest of the dead lived not until the thousand years should be finished." The oldest manuscript, the Sinaitic, and the Syriac Version, do not contain this verse. And it certainly harmonizes better with all we have learned from the study of the Old Testament concerning God's purpose to redeem mankind from death through a resurrection, to suppose that the "times of the kingdom," here referred to as the reign of the saints with Christ, are throughout times of resurrection. The various orders of mankind would then be raised, not all at once, but as each class was fitted for it. But, whether the recovery of these past generations is admitted to be thus progressive or not, the passage we are studying, which speaks of their judgment before the great white throne, must present to us pictorially the results of that trial and judgment to which resurrection introduces them.

All our previous studies in this series have shown how vital and fundamental in the whole plan of Scripture is this truth, that, from the beginning, God has provided blessing for all the families of the earth through an anointed seed, and that this blessing can reach the vast majority of at least past generations only through their resurrection. No other passage in the Bible seems to militate against this view so strongly as the one now before us. We have already indicated, however, the way by which it may be brought into harmony with this primary truth. We have simply to regard it as presenting in a pictorial way the final results of that age, or those ages, of trial and judgment through which the nations are to be conducted by Christ and his risen saints, and to which they shall be introduced through a resurrection from the dead. The initial mistake of the old interpretation lies in its co-ordinating this judgment of the *dead* with that of the *living*, described in Matt.

xxv. It is therefore viewed as a judgment of the resurrected masses of mankind, good and bad, for their conduct in this present life.

But to this view there are these fatal objections:

1. The righteous are seen as already exalted to thrones. They are already safe within "the camp of the saints" and "the beloved city" (vs. 9). The saved of this dispensation cannot therefore be of the class who are here judged, nor must any book needs be opened in order to determine their title to eternal life. They already have it. This "book of life" cannot therefore be identical with the "Lamb's book of life" (chaps. xiii. 8, xxi. 27). It must be another book, pertaining to a new economy under which the unrighteous dead are raised and put under new responsibilities, such as a new gift of life would bring to them.

2. With regard to the results of this present trial in life, this class of men are already judged (John iii. 18, 36) and under the abiding wrath of God. They cannot attain to righteousness under the law, and most of them have never had any probation under the gospel. They are all therefore "guilty before God" (Rom. iii. 19). And not only judgment, but the death sentence has been passed upon them all (vs. 12).

3. This sentence has been actually visited upon them. "The wages of sin is death." These men had died. Sin had killed them in body and soul. They were already captives in the prison of "death and hell."

4. Their trial and sentence therefore are not set for a distant judgment day. We have already seen in our examination of Matt. xxv. 31–46, that Jesus Christ is

now the Judge of quick and dead, and that the sorting between sheep and goats and the consignment to eternal fire are now going on. Man's judgment *for the sins of this life* is before resurrection. We believe it to be essential to all right conceptions of God's dealings with mankind on account of sin, that we should regard the wicked dead, as not awaiting the awards of a remote day of judgment, but as already judged and suffering the just consequences of their sins. Was not the rich man in hell already doomed? Have not Sodom and Gomorrah already suffered the vengeance of eternal fire (Jude 7)? What else than a present judgment and a swift sentence was that by which Korah and his company went down alive into Sheol (Num. xvi. 30)? The Apocalypse does indeed once refer to a time of the dead when they should be judged (xi. 18); but the context shows that what is referred to is the time for vindicating God's saints who had died in faith, awaiting their reward.

The one fatal objection therefore to the current view of this passage is, that it makes this trial-scene to be the raising of an issue which was settled long before, the reenactment of a sentence already passed and of a penalty already inflicted. The wicked dead have been already judged and turned into hell.

II. What then is the character and purpose of this judgment of the resurrected dead? Our study of John v. 29 has already indicated the answer. The object in the resurrection of the unjust is to put them again under the trial and discipline which pertain to embodied life. This passage sets before us this fact and furnishes a vivid picture of the final results of this trial. In conformity with the teaching of all Scripture, we are obliged to view this judgment as a prolonged judicial administration. In favor of this view, we have

1. The analogy of the passage from Daniel vii. upon which the vision is based. There we have also the placing of a throne of glory. We have the same formal opening of what appears to be a great assize. "The judgment was set and the books were opened" (vs. 10). And yet what follows in the vision is evidently a continuous administration, during which all powers hostile to the dominion of the Son of Man are destroyed, and all peoples, nations and languages brought into subjection to His sceptre. So this summoning of the dead before the great white throne is to be regarded as a condensed picture of a long administration, during which the earth, the sea, and the whole empire of death and Hades give up their dead, who are thus brought under the judicial sway of the Son of Man.

2. Other passages, especially where resurrection is referred to, condense into "an hour," and present upon one plane of vision such long continued processes. "Verily, verily, I say unto you, the hour cometh and now is, when the dead shall hear the voice of the Son of God; and they that hear shall live" (John v. 25). If this refer to spiritual quickening, as is commonly supposed, the "hour" referred to lasts through the whole of this dispensation. So the hour of verse 28, during which "all that are in their graves shall hear his voice, and come forth," must be the whole period of His conquests in the realms of death for the liberation of all its captives, until the last enemy is himself destroyed. Such progressive

stages of triumph and deliverance are plainly indicated in 1 Cor. xv. 22-27. "For as in Adam all die, so also in the Christ shall all be made alive. But each in his own order: Christ the first-fruits; then they that are Christ's, at his coming. Then the end, or the fulfilment (τὸ τέλος), when He shall deliver up the kingdom to God; even the Father; when He shall have abolished all rule and authority and power. For He must reign until He hath put all His enemies under His feet. The last enemy that shall be abolished is death." All the Old Testament references to the Messiah's reign, as well as those in the New, in which the fact is plainly brought out that this reign is to be in the power of His resurrection and to embrace the generations of the dead, preclude the idea of a brief assize, and require such a long period of rule and judgment as we have supposed. We have therefore not only a warrant, we are imperatively obliged to bring this obscure passage into harmony with this fundamental fact of Scripture. And in doing so, we violate no principle of interpretation, but only follow the analogies of all the passages which set forth these great events and issues of the future. Each and all of them, whether they relate to the Messiah's reign and judgment, to the resurrection of the dead, or to the renewal of the heavens and earth, are thus comprehensive and far-reaching.

In conformity then with this principle, our exegesis of this passage would run somewhat thus:

And I saw a great white throne and Him that sat upon it. This expression indicates the perfect purity of that throne from which the Christ shall judge the world in righteousness.—*From whose face the earth and the heaven fled away; and there was found no place for them.* Many interpreters regard the phrase, "heaven and earth," in this and parallel passages, as denoting governmental systems. That all these must pass away before the coming of the perfect system is most true. But there is no warrant for refusing to regard this feature of the vision as predictive of those great cosmical changes often referred to in Scripture as included within the scope of God's redemptive plan. The whole creation is to be delivered from the bondage of corruption into the liberty of the glory of the children of God. No redemption of the human race can be complete which does not include the physical system to which it belongs, and of which it is the appointed heir (Gen. i. 26–28, Ps. viii). Hence, both Old and New Testament prophecy (Ish. lxv. 17–25, 2 Peter iii.) contain most distinct and emphatic promises of such palingenesis, and the Apocalypse ends with a glowing and lovely picture of it. This period of change is a parturition period, and hence this general resurrection of the dead is connected with and forms a part of it. And this itself confirms what has been already said of its protracted character. St. Peter assures us that we are not to measure these great steps in God's working by human standards. "One day is with the Lord as a thousand years, and a thousand years as one day."

And I saw the dead, the great and the small, standing before the throne. . . . And the sea gave up the dead which were in it; and death and Hades gave up the dead which were in them.

As the seer beholds in one picture the progressive

transformation of the "earth and the heaven," so the successive triumphs over the empire of death are viewed as one great conquest. All the dead, great and small, from earth and sea, and the depths of hell, are recovered out of the grasp of death. But, as we have seen, all analogies of prophecy, and especially as such vast and distant changes are brought within its scope, forbid us to regard the resurrection of these countless dead as simultaneous. It must proceed in ever widening circles, gathering in wider and wider harvests, according to the law, "each in his own order." Such progress indeed is indicated in the vision, which has its climax in the casting of death and Hades into the lake of fire. It thus corresponds with the progress denoted by St. Paul in 1 Cor. xv., where the advancing power of Christ's resurrection issues in the subjection of all things under His feet.

And books were opened: and another book was opened, which is* of life: and the dead were judged out of the things written in the books, according to their works.

This feature of the vision is repeated from that of Daniel. The judgment there depicted is national rather than personal. The world-power had gone through its course of evil, and now it must come to its proper issue. It must be destroyed, and the dominion of the world be transferred to the saints. The opening of the books, therefore, is the solemn assertion of God's great law of harvest. Nations, men, must reap as they sow. We know that this law must govern the resurrection harvest.

---

* The words "the book" do not occur here in the original.

And it is this to which St. John's vision relates. The "books" are the sign to us that, by God's laws of life, character is wrought into embodiment. The body gathers up and perpetuates the fruits of previous conduct. Hence, the law of resurrection is, "To every seed his own body." "For we must all be made manifest before the judgment seat of Christ; that each one may receive the things through the body, according to the things he did" (2 Cor. v. 10, Greek).

Saint and sinner are alike subject to this law. Character, in this world, is being wrought into every fibre of the body. And on the wondrously woven and folded leaves of its organism are written out the results of conduct and of life. The body is a record of the past, and a volume in which are daily written God's judgments. The resurrection opens out a new volume in man's life, but the results and recorded judgments of the past are transcribed in it. Hence, in the resurrection, the secrets of all hearts and lives will be made manifest in the form, the grade, the potencies of the recovered manhood. The Judge will not need to refer to a book as an aid to His recollection. "All things are naked and manifest before Him." Nor will men need to search any other records, in order to approve His judgments, than those which are wrought into the fabric of their lives, and determine the character of their embodiment.

But the question arises, Are these results final and irreversible? Is there no room for change, for deterioration or improvement, in this life to come? Is the new life conferred, to the unjust, an unmitigated curse? To show that it cannot be, we have only to rise from that low conception of the Messiah's work of judgment, which views it as only vindicatory and punitive, to the large Scriptural conception of it already noticed. God's great laws of life are fixed and irrevocable, as, for example, the law of heredity. According to this law, men are continually being born into the world on low planes of life and with vicious tendencies. But, even in these cases, the gift of life is a blessing and carries with it possibilities of amendment and enrichment. There is a strong *vis medicatrix* inherent in all life, an unwearying power of recovery. And therefore the life conferred at the resurrection, although burdened with the evil heritage of the former life, must be, to those who were held captive by death, a boon, and must bring with it possibilities of good. The law, "according to the fruit of the doings," must follow such a life all through its career. But, in God's great economy, the tendency of even this law is to work for the betterment of its subjects. And so the Messiah's reign of judgment must tend toward the good of even those whom He judges. It is a corrective administration. The Scriptures constantly speak of it in this character. We have seen that we must learn to view the great events depicted in this passage as the graphic strokes in a picture whose outlines are large and deep. Instead of a mere assize, we must conceive of a long judicial reign, during which the dead are awarded such kind and character of life as becomes to them a process of judgment and correction. And during it *another book of life* is opened, in which the names of those are recorded who pass successfully through this new trial of life and gain its crown.

And death and Hades were cast into the lake of fire. This is the second death, even the lake of fire. This period of Christ's reign ends with this final victory. The kingdom of the dead, having yielded up all its prisoners, is itself destroyed. The lake of fire swallows up all enemies. All things are made new. The renovation embraces, and forever unites in blessed concord, the heaven and earth. The lake of fire is called the second death, because it becomes the grave of those who had been raised out of a first death, and are found unworthy, and because it rids the cosmos forever of the reign of this fell destroyer.

And if any was not found written in the book of life, he was cast into the lake of fire.

We have already found that the term "eternal fire" denotes that devouring energy of nature by which all defective and sinful forms of embodied life are consumed. The term "lake of fire" seems to define the final form of this energetic action, by which all things that offend, and all evil doers, are finally destroyed out of this created system. Its age-long enemies, the devil and his angels, and the great depositories of their trophies, death and hell, are all alike cast into this furnace of fire and destroyed. Everything and everyone that clings to the empire of evil perishes with it. This grand result is entirely inconsistent with the idea of the perpetual existence of these enemies in endless agony in some hell of fire. Hell, in any such aspect of it, is itself doomed to destruction. And, therefore, all who are consigned to it perish with it. The idea that God will preserve in a deathless existence of misery those who fail to enter into life is irreconcilable with His character and purposes, and is utterly at war with all that is told us concerning His crowning gift of eternal life. There can be no immortal life in sin, for sin is essentially the destroyer of life. Any organism in which it is embodied contains the seeds of its own destruction. Hence, at the final summing up, " if any was not found written in the book of life, he was cast into the lake of fire."

And yet we must not make the mistake of confounding this final summing up with the sorting of mankind into sheep and goats now going on (Matt. xxv), nor suppose that there is no interval between the "resurrection of judgment" (John v. 29), and the final judgment here described. Between the setting up of the great white throne, and the lake of fire, there must be a long interval of times of resurrection, which are times of renewed trial in life, involving the opening of another book of life, suited to this new age of trial. If any fail of the crown of life under the favorable circumstances under which this new opportunity of life is conferred, they must suffer the second death. Their failure seems to be final and irreversible.

It will be thus seen that our interpretation of the judgment of the great white throne differs from that commonly received in these two particulars.

1. While the passage brings prominently before us the *results* of the great judgment process it describes, we must still view this process as prolonged through the age, or perhaps ages, to come, during which the Christ is subduing all His enemies and ridding the creation, of which He is the Heir, of all those invisible enemies

who have converted its fair fields into the camp of death. This involves the liberation of the myriads of death's captives, who "stand up" again in life before His throne.

2. This new gift of life, while it is conferred according to previous character, brings with it a new trial before its results are finally determined. If this idea is not found on the surface of the record here, it is required by all that Scripture teaches concerning the character of the Messiah's administration, and also by its teaching about death as the wages of sin, and of the redemptive character of resurrection. To make room for these important features in this passage, it is only necessary to admit the obvious principle that it does not describe sudden and simultaneous events, but sharply defines the outlines and results of great and prolonged administrations. From this point of view there is no difficulty in harmonizing it with what we have found to be the current teaching of all Scripture with regard to resurrection, that it is a "hope," and that even the raising up out of death and hell of the unjust dead belongs to the economy of redemption. This feature of the divine plan is so inwrought into the texture of Scripture promises and hopes, it is so consistent with the character of God, and with all we have learned of His plan of creation, and its progressive development of life, that we are obliged to regard it as true and incontrovertible, however we may find it hard to adjust to such an obscure passage of Scripture as the one we have been studying. If any are disposed to regard our effort to reconcile it to this passage as a failure, we beg such not to reject the principle itself. It is too well established in Scripture to be dislodged by

any single passage, and especially one so obscure as this. Still less must any man's failure to reconcile it be accepted as evidence against it. When this whole book is better understood, some way of explaining this passage will be found which will neither impair its testimony, nor dim in the least the lustre of that great principle which has been our morning star through the twilight of all Old Testament prophecy. Once admit that the fact that the Christ has been ordained of God to be the Judge of all men, living and dead, is a part of His *gospel*, that the dead are to be brought under His judicial dealing through their resurrection, that this universal resurrection is in the line of His promised redemption which, to this extent at least, is a blessing in store for all the families of the earth, and even such hard passages as this will not militate against it, nor quench the light which this great principle throws upon all the dark places in God's Word, and all the dark features of His world-long dealing with the children of men.

CHAPTER VIII.

RETRIBUTION IN APOSTOLIC PREACHING.

Our studies of the words of Jesus concerning future punishment, judgment, and resurrection, have convinced us that the destruction awaiting the sinner is an imminent peril, that hell, for him, lies this side of resurrection, that judgment has been passed upon him and sentence already pronounced, and that his future resurrection is not for these purposes, and for increase of retribution, but in the line of God's redemptive working, even where it perpetuates trial and judgment. We have also seen that that passage in Rev. xx, which depicts the judgment of the great white throne, and which, more than any other in Scripture, seems to militate against this view, may yet be harmonized with it—indeed must be so reconciled, unless we are to deny the manifold promises of blessing to all the generations of mankind through the Christ in whom all are to be made alive. All that is needed is that we interpret the vision as a prophetic picture, on one plane of canvas, of prolonged processes of resurrection, and of judgment, and of palingenesis, with special prominence given to the fact that all things belonging to the old creation, and all men, who do not yield to the transforming power of the Christ, must perish with the old order before the coming of the new heaven and earth wherein dwelleth righteousness. But as this penalty of "the lake of fire" is visited upon men who have been raised out of death to another life, it must be a punishment due for the sin of that life, and because of failure to respond to the gracious influences by which it was surrounded. The penalty for the sins of this life had already been executed, inasmuch as these men had already suffered death and had been consigned to hell, out of which they were now restored to life.

It will be perceived then that our doctrine differs from the old church-doctrine, in that it makes room for other operations in an age to come of the grace and power of God, such as are required by the fact that He has provided for all men another gift of life through the Second Man, in lieu of that which they lost in the First. This involves the denial of the view that, before all the masses of mankind who, through successive generations, have died in their sins, there is in reserve nothing but an unending hell of misery, and that not even resurrection can bring to them a single ray of hope.

Our purpose is next to inquire into the doctrine of retribution as it lies in the sermons and letters of the apostles. How did these inspired servants of Jesus interpret His words concerning the wrath to come? And how did they urge them upon the attention of their hearers?

We have recorded in the Acts the text, or the synopsis, of some fifteen addresses, made, with one exception, by St. Peter and St. Paul, who were the special bearers of the gospel message to the two classes of mankind, the Jews and the Gentiles. Most of these make some reference to a future punishment. The report of Peter's Pentecostal sermon ends thus: "And with many other words he testified and exhorted them, saying, "Save yourselves from this crooked generation" (Acts ii. 40). After the healing of the lame man he again solemnly told the people that, in crucifying Jesus, they had rejected the Christ, and killed the Prince of Life, whom God had now raised and glorified. But that still pardon and blessedness under His reign, and the fulfilment of all the covenant blessings pledged to Abraham, were held out to them upon their repentance and confession of the Name of Jesus. But every soul which should not hearken unto that prophet should be utterly destroyed from among the people (iii. 23). The national hopes involved the hope of resurrection; and so, as the priests and Sadducees were drawn around the speaker, "being sore troubled because they taught the people, and proclaimed in Jesus the resurrection from the dead," Peter testifies again to the Messiahship of Jesus, and re-affirms His resurrection, and declares, "Neither is there any other name under heaven, that is given among men, wherein we must be saved" (iv. 12). Stephen boldly charges home upon the people their long accumulated guilt. "Ye stiffnecked and uncircumcised in heart and ears, ye do always resist the Holy Ghost; as your fathers did, so do ye. Which of the prophets did not your fathers persecute? and they killed them which shewed before of the coming of the Righteous One: of whom ye have now become betrayers and murderers; ye who received the law as it was ordained by angels, and kept it not" (vii. 51–33). Although he cuts them to the heart by his sharp speech, he does not speak definitely of the punishment awaiting them. But, as they stoned him, "he kneeled down, and cried with a loud voice, Lord, lay not this sin to their charge." Later, we find Peter rebuking Simon Magus as follows, "Thy money perish with thee, because thou hast thought to obtain the gift of God with money. Thou hast neither part nor lot in this matter; for thy heart is not right before God" (ix. 20, 21). In the house of Cornelius we find him testifying to the Risen Jesus as the ordained Judge of all men, living and dead (x. 42).

In the 13th chapter, St. Paul comes to the front as the chosen witness to the Gentiles. At Paphos, he denounces Elymas the sorcerer as one "full of all guile and all villiany, a son of the devil and an enemy of all righteousness, perverting the right ways of the Lord" (vs. 10). And the hand of the Lord smote him with blindness for a season. At Antioch he warns the people of their danger in rejecting the Christ, in these words, "Behold, ye despisers, and wonder, and perish; for I work a work in your days, a work which ye shall in no wise believe, if one declare it unto you" (vs. 41). To the rude Lycaonians at Lystra, who imagined him to be a god, he seems to have uttered no such threats, but to have urged them to forsake their idols and to turn to the living God who made all things, and filled their hearts with food and gladness (xiv. 15-17). At Athens he closes his address with the warning that God, who had overlooked the times of ignorance in the past, now commanded all men to repent, "inasmuch as He hath appointed a day, in the which He is about to judge the world in righteousness, by the man whom He hath ordained; whereof He hath given assurance unto all men, in that He hath raised Him from the dead" (xvii. 31). In the 24th chapter, before Felix, he sums up the hope of the gospel he had been preaching, as a "hope toward God that there shall be a resurrection both of the just and the unjust" (vs. 15.) Before Felix, he reasoned of righteousness, and temperance, and impending ($\mu\varepsilon\lambda\lambda\acute{o}\nu\tau o\varsigma$) judgment, until his royal hearer trembled. This apostle's preaching always assumes that men by nature are in darkness, and under the power of Satan, that they need remission of sins, and salvation both from sin and from its doom (xvi. 30, xxvi. 18, 19). And the accounts of it close with his solemn testimony to a representative company of his own countrymen at Rome that the Jews were blinded to the grace and glory of this salvation of God, and that henceforth it should be sent unto the Gentiles (xxviii. 23-28).

We have thus cited, or referred to, all the passages in these specimens of apostolic preaching which refer to future punishment. The question we desire to ask from them is: Do they fairly set before men the danger of an everlasting punishment in hell?

In order to a fair reply we have to observe, first, An entire absence from these addresses of such statements and appeals as we might justly look for in view of such a danger. It is only in the way of remote inference that this doctrine could be gathered from anything contained in these first typical sermons. The strongest phrases are those of Peter, where, quoting from Moses, He warns the Jews that the rejecters of the Great Prophet would be utterly destroyed from among the people; and of Paul, at Antioch, who quotes from the prophets a warning to despisers that they shall perish. Neither of these threatenings, as first uttered by Moses or Isaiah, carried with them the idea of eternal torment in hell. And, it is altogether gratuitous to suppose that the Jews, or the proselytes, or the Gentiles, who made up the audience at Jerusalem and at Antioch, would attach any such meaning to them. Granting that a portion of the Jews of that day did believe in the eternal conscious existence in misery of some wicked men, they did not believe such a destiny to be possible for Jews. Moreover, some of them believed that the worst sinners would be annihilated. And the words of the apostles are much more consonant with that view. But, the point we make is that it is irrational to suppose that, if the apostles put that meaning upon the words of Jesus about the eternal fire which we have attached to them, they would have been so reticent concerning this inconceivable peril. If all their hearers were in danger of dropping into this eternal hell, there to be tormented, first in soul, and after resurrection, "with unspeakable torments of body and soul in hell-fire, with the devil and his angels forever," can it be possible that they would not have spoken more plainly of this awful doom. Where else should we expect the plainest utterances on this tremendous theme, if not in these first inspired proclamations? The attempt has lately been made by Prof. Austin Phelps, of Andover, to show that the silences of the apostles, as to this matter, prove that the eschatological teaching of Jesus had already been diffused and accepted, that it was a thing "fixed and familiar in the beliefs" of men. This is a most unwarranted assumption. But, granting its truth, can we suppose that a feature of such immense importance should be so uniformly left out of these appeals by which the apostles urged men to take refuge in Jesus Christ and be saved? Familiar beliefs are those upon which we most rely in urging men to duty. Or, granting that their Jewish hearers needed less to have this infinite danger held up before them, how can we account for it that the address to the rude Lycaonians at Lystra contains nothing of it, and that, while Paul spoke to the cultured sceptics of Athens of Him who was appointed to judge the world in righteousness, there is no record of his warning them that, by the sentence of this divine Judge, they would be cast into the hopeless agonies of an endless hell? Neither in his words, nor in the sneering criticisms made upon his address, is there any evidence that he alluded to this appalling issue. These Gentiles had not been familiar with the teachings of Jesus upon this point. And the most fearful conceptions of their pagan mythologies were infinitely below the horror of this awful fate. And even these were made a mock and jest of among the loungers in the Academic groves of Athens. No other view is reasonable than this, that the first preachers of Christianity did not put the meaning upon the words of Jesus to which we have long been accustomed. They did not believe that before all mankind, except the little handful of Christian disciples, there was one long night of hopeless, endless, despair. They doubtless believed that there was a great danger before sinful men, a fearful looking for of judgment, a possible loss of soul and body in hell, a failure to enter into life, and a resurrection of judgment. But even such apprehensions of wrath to come were balanced and tempered by their belief that a light of hope had arisen for all the world when Jesus arose, that, in the grand sweep of His triumph, all the promises of blessing to Israel and to mankind, spoken by the mouth of holy prophets since the world began, would be made good, that His ascension was the beginning of "times of restitution" whose widening circles should embrace "all things" (iii. 19–21), and that, therefore, the "hope toward God" covered even the "resurrection of the unjust" (xxiv. 15).

No worse fate for incorrigible sinners can be extracted from their words than their final and utter *destruction*. But even this must be such a destruction as consists with their future resurrection from the dead. What lies before them beyond that they do not reveal. Only a glimpse is here and there given of hope beyond. It is only in the epistles, written afterwards to their converts, that they disclose more of the unsearchable riches of Christ. So that, while we are not warranted in deriving a doctrine of universal salvation from these first models of gospel preaching, we are certainly forbidden by them from holding up before men the terrors of an everlasting fire of hell. We are instructed by them in more merciful views of God, and in wider views of the scope of His salvation. But while these sermons do not fit in to the long-accepted theory of future punishment, they certainly do warn men that they stand in present need of *salvation* from sin and death and hell, that this salvation is in no other name than the Name of Jesus, and that, whatever possibilities may be involved in God's gracious provision to recover the human race out of the pit of death into which sin has cast it, there is now an imminent destruction out of life and manhood, and away from the light and bliss of God's presence, awaiting every sinful man who refuses to believe on the Lord Jesus Christ and be saved.

There is one other consideration necessary to a proper understanding of these first presentations of the gospel. The apostles seem at first to have contemplated the possibility of the wide-spread conversion of mankind to Christ. St. Peter, after Pentecost, speaks to his fellow-countrymen, as if the whole nation might now submit to the risen Jesus, and so inaugurate His world-wide triumph (iii. 12–26). But the martyrdom of Stephen soon dispelled this anticipation, and the way was prepared for gathering a new spiritual seed of Abraham from among the Gentiles. Peter received Cornelius and his kinsmen and friends, as the first fruits of this harvest. But it was reserved for Paul to pronounce the definite turning away of God's electing grace from the Jews, who judged themselves unworthy of eternal life, to the Gentiles (xiii. 44–48). And to him it was gradually revealed that it was not God's purpose now to convert all these nations, but to gather from among them a chosen seed. At Antioch, only "as many as were ordained to eternal life believed" (vs. 48). The Lord encouraged him to remain a long time at Corinth, for He had much people in that city (xviii. 10). But he was forbidden of the Holy Ghost to go to other places he was intending to visit (xvi. 6-8). In such ways God was teaching him that the object of his mission was not to accomplish the conversion of all men indiscriminately wherever he might go, but to be His instrument in gathering out from these nations that chosen company who were to be God's instruments of wider blessing to all mankind in the future administrations of His kingdom. But it is only in the way of suggestion that we have in the Acts an occasional glimpse of this feature of the divine purpose. It is reserved for the epistles to plainly reveal it. But we see, in these few glimpses, another reason than that already given, why the apostles' preaching did not have about it that character we might have expected, if we must regard them as sent out on a mission to all their fellow-men of salvation from the doom of an endless hell, and to present to them a test by which their destiny should be everlastingly fixed. The fact that their preaching did not have that character is a proof that it was not designed to present this test, and that this is not the issue which is imbedded in the truth as it is in Jesus.

CHAPTER IX.

RETRIBUTION IN ST. PAUL'S EPISTLES.

We have now remarked upon the significant absence from the first sermons of the apostles of the doctrine of an eternal hell of tormenting fire. When we pass to the study of the epistles we find the same lack of evidence that the apostles put that construction upon the words of Jesus concerning future punishment which the church in later ages has fastened upon them. No one of the passages which refer to the doom of the wicked will bear the weight of this tremendous doctrine. The church would never have thought of putting this meaning upon them, had not her pre-conceived interpretation of the words of Jesus required it.

Our present contention is, that the silences of the apostolic sermons and letters upon a matter of such enormous interest can be explained in no other way than by the fact that these inspired men did not conceive of it as it has since been defined in the church confessions. It may be said that we have no right to look for definite statements of this doctrine in epistles addressed to believers. But this objection does not bear upon the fact that such statements are not found in their addresses to unbelievers. The epistles, however, do contain many allusions to the destiny of wicked men. How is it possible, if the apostles believed that the vast majority of their fellow-men were standing on the brink of such bottomless despair, they would not have given so plain a testimony in both sermons and epistles that he who runs might read?

Our examination will at first be confined to the epistles of St. Paul. A large proportion of the New Testament is taken up with these epistles. In them, more than in any other part of Scripture, the verities of Christianity are set forth in their logical relations, and as connected with God's great plan in the creation of the world and of man. Questions of human destiny are often discussed. It becomes therefore a matter of prime importance in the line of these studies, that we should inquire what these epistles have to say about retribution. We shall find:

1. That while St. Paul continually conceives of the judgment of the world as a consummation of the future, he also views it as already begun and carried on under the administration of Christ.

2. The words by which he describes the punishment awaiting wicked men always contain in some form the death-idea.

3. This punishment is always conceived of as inflicted before, and not after, resurrection.

4. He never views the resurrection, even of the unjust, in any other light than that of a " hope."

5. The salvation of the church in this dispensation is always viewed as that of a first-fruits or first-born company.

6. There are frequent glimpses in his writings of wider reaches of God's saving grace toward the unsaved masses of mankind, to be unfolded in the ages to come, after the salvation of the church in this age has been completed.

Taking up these points in order, we find that this apostle teaches:

1. Concerning judgment, that Christ Jesus is now Lord of both the dead and the living (Rom. xiv. 9), and that He shall come to judge the living and the dead (2 Tim. iv. 1). The word μέλλει, however, in the latter passage, carries with it the idea not only of a future but of an impending judgment. It must have its consummation at "His appearing and kingdom." But while He speaks of a "day of wrath and revelation of the righteous judgment of God" (Rom. ii. 5), he also says that the wrath of God is now "revealed from heaven against all ungodliness and unrighteousness of men" (i. 19). That the wrath and indignation, tribulation and anguish, which must come upon every soul of man that doeth evil (ii. 6–10), is not wholly a thing of the future, is proved by what he tells us of the Jews, as an example of the severity of God. They were already "cut off" (ch. xi). He says of them also (1 Thess. ii. 15, 16) that because they had killed the Lord Jesus and the prophets, and driven him out, forbidding him to speak to the Gentiles that they might be saved, "wrath is come upon them to the uttermost." The same thing appears in his teaching concerning Christians as subjects of the divine judgment. "We must all be made manifest before the judgment seat of Christ that everyone may receive the things in (or through) the body, according to the things he did, whether good or bad" (2 Cor. v. 5, Rom. xiv. 11). And yet all Christians are viewed as already held to a strict account before that bar. A notorious offender was delivered unto Satan by this apostle, acting in the name of the Lord Jesus, "for the destruction of the flesh that the spirit may be saved in the day of the

Lord Jesus" (1 Cor. v. 5). So also certain persons in that church had been judged and chastened of the Lord by sicknesses and death because of their unworthy behavior at the Lord's Supper (xi. 30–32). Such instances were proof that the Lord was now judging His people (Heb, x. 30), and that, in the chastisements that came upon them, they were being taught that "Our God is a consuming fire" (Heb. xii.*), and that it is a fearful thing for even the offending Christian to fall into His hands. In the view then of this great teacher, judgment for sin was as truly a fact of the present as of the future. The day of the Lord would be but the more open and intense manifestation of a wrath against sin which was even now burning, and which should devour the adversaries.

2. As to the character of punishment awaiting evildoers, it is always defined by St. Paul as a perishing or a destruction. The death-idea enters into every one of the terms employed.

Referring to the ungodly heathen, he says of them that "knowing the judgment of God, that they which do such things are *worthy of death*," they still do the same (Rom. i. 32). "For as many as have sinned without law shall also *perish* without law" (ii. 12). In the sixth chapter the service of sin is said to issue in *death* (vs. 16). "What fruit then had ye at that time in those things whereof ye are now ashamed? for the end of those things is *death*" (vs. 21). "For the wages

---

* We shall quote from the Book of Hebrews in this examination, although many of our best modern scholars assign it to some other author than St. Paul. Its theology, at least, is Pauline, and we may therefore very well include it in an effort to study the doctrine of this apostle.

of sin is *death*" (23), This term includes present spiritual death (vii. 9, 13, 24), but this spiritual state is called "death," because the end and issue of it is the "perishing" or destruction of those who are not saved from it. Hence, in the ninth chapter, he speaks of wicked men as "vessels of wrath, fitted for *destruction*" (22). In 1 Cor. i. 18, he defines rejecters of the gospel as "them that are *perishing*." The same phrase occurs again in 2 Cor. ii. 15. And that he means by this term something more than spiritual deadness is seen by his use of the same word in 1 Cor. x. 9, 10. "Neither let us tempt the Lord, as some of them tempted, and *perished* by the serpents. Neither murmur ye, as some of them murmured, and *perished** by the destroyer." In 1 Cor. xv. 18, this word can mean nothing less than the complete loss of personal being. "Then they also which have fallen asleep in Christ are *perished*." For that the apostle in this famous chapter makes all future existence for man turn upon the fact that Christ rose from the dead is plain from verse 32. "If after the manner of men I fought with beasts at Ephesus, what doth it profit me? If the dead are not raised, let us eat and drink, for to-morrow we die" These quotations are quite sufficient to dispel the false coloring with which many surround the uniform Scriptural teaching as to the penalty of sin. We have found it throughout to be the destruction of man, as an embodied being, created in the image of God and made the heir of His works. It has been confidently assumed that spiritual death, alienation from the life of God,

---

* In most of our quotations we follow the New Version, in which the same Greek word is more uniformly rendered by the same English word.

is the essence of this penalty, but that the life of man, thus severed from God, would continue forever in immortal woe. Spiritual death, no doubt, is an essential feature in man's penalty. But that it involves and must ultimateiy issue in the literal death of its victims is plain from these passages. Evidently, when St. Paul writes that if there were no redemption from this penalty through resurrection, even those who had died in Christ had *perished*, and that for us to live any longer in expectation of a life beyond is useless, "for tomorrow we die," he conceives of this death as extinction of being. His whole teaching, indeed, implies that, beneath this working of sin unto death, God has wrought in the death and resurrection of Christ to give to believers an eternal life, and to provide that death should not make an end of even the unjust. But this does not alter the fact that his ultimate conception of the wages of sin for man is literal *death*.

The same idea is involved in his frequent use of the term "destruction" in such passages as Phil. iii. 19, "Whose end is *destruction*." "Then sudden destruction (ὄλεθρον) cometh upon them" (1 Thess. v. 3). "Who shall suffer punishment, even eternal *destruction* from the face of the Lord and from the glory of His might, when He shall come to be glorified in His saints, and to be admired in all them that believe" (2 Thess. i. 9). This passage is by far the strongest in any of St. Paul's writings in its apparent support of the ordinary doctrine of endless suffering in hell. The mention of it may serve therefore to lead us to examine it in connection with our next point, which is:

3. This apostle always conceives of the punishment

of sin as inflicted upon the ungodly before resurrection. We would by no means assert that his words do not carry with them a reference to a remoter death for sin after a resurrection—the same which St. John defines as the second death. But primarily his words refer simply to that death which is due for the sins of this life, and which overtakes the sinner this side of his resurrection, and which we have seen to be more strictly defined in the words of Jesus as the loss of all that gives us present standing in life and inheritance in this system of God's works, including, beyond the death of the body, the destruction of the soul in hell. We have already seen how groundless is the assumption that the judgment scene in Matt. xxv. 31-46 relates primarily to the resurrected dead. Equally forced and unwarranted is it to assume that the ungodly despisers of the gospel, whom Paul here describes as visited at Christ's coming with an eternal destruction, are resurrected men. The men who would be saying, "Peace and safety," when "sudden destruction cometh upon them" (1 Thess. v. 2), could be no other than men living on the earth. This was the class who were to be overtaken. And hence it is altogether gratuitous to suppose that any other class is referred to in 2 Thess. i. 9 as to be eternally destroyed from his presence. Whatever this punishment may be, it is inflicted upon living men, and not upon men resurrected to be damned. It is the death that precedes resurrection. With regard to the word "eternal" ($αἰώνιον$*) it might define this destruction as (1) endless. But in

---

* This is the only instance in which St. Paul uses this word in connection with retribution.

this case we would be obliged to regard the death it brings with it as absolute and final. Or (2), giving to the word its strict etymological value, it may describe an *age-long* destruction, that is, one lasting until the resurrection. Or (3) if it be insisted that no less value than that of "endless" pertains to the word, the destruction, which is not defined as absolute, but as "from the face of the Lord," would be a banishment from His presence, and from a share in His glory, from which not even resurrection would recover them. They could be restored only to those outer circles of life and blessing which are far removed from His central glory. While we incline to the second of these explanations, the third will be preferred by those who are unwilling to admit that αἰώνιον can ever have a lower equivalent than "endless." But in either case we are obliged to regard the destruction as visited upon men alive upon the earth at Christ's coming, and as continuing through that long period which lasts up to their resurrection. And therefore the question is still open, What change will be wrought in their condition by that event? We have seen that the unrighteous of every class, in Paul's view, must be shut out from the kingdom of God (2 Cor. vi. 9, 10), that they cannot inherit that kingdom when the saints are invested with its glory. But would resurrection bring to such no recovery and no relief? Would it not bring them into some outer precinct of this kingdom? If not heirs, might not some of this class be made subjects?

Now, that some such good must be made possible is involved in all Paul's teaching about the resurrection of the dead. For

4. He never views the resurrection of the unjust in any other light than that of a "hope."

We have already seen that, in all his sermons, the hope of resurrection is an essential feature of the gospel. There is not a word or an allusion which can possibly be construed as proof that he regarded resurrection as a terror to the countless masses of mankind who had died in their sins. On the contrary he thus distinctly speaks of it as a *hope*. "And have hope toward God, which they also themselves allow, that there shall be a resurrection both of the just and of the unjust" (Acts xxiv. 15). Nothing but special pleading, in the interest of a preconceived theory, can remove the resurrection of the unjust from the category of "hope" in this passage. Accordingly, we find, when we turn to the epistles, this apostle teaching that, as death came upon the whole world by reason of the sin of the first man, so this forfeited life has been redeemed for the whole race by the obedience of the second man (Rom. v. 12–20). "So then as through one trespass the judgment came unto all men to condemnation; even so through one act of righteousness the free gift came unto all men to justification of life." No view of this whole passage which limits the blessing of restored life to a select class of mankind can possibly do justice to the parallels which run through it, or can possibly be made to consist with what it teaches about the far more abundant grace shown in the recovery. We do not indeed regard the "justification to life" provided as the ransom of all to "eternal life." For that was not the life which Adam forfeited. He was created only a candidate for this high dignity. Eternal life is of a new and higher order of life, and is the gift of God through Jesus Christ alone to as many as receive Him. But the passage plainly teaches that the life which Adam lost has been bought back for all. And Scripture knows of no other way by which it reaches all except through a resurrection from the dead. And, therefore, this must be to all a recovery and a boon. Life in manhood is an embodied life. Man is a creature holding a certain relation to the system of God's works, of which he was made the crown and heir. Death discrowns him and casts him out of his inheritance. Resurrection rehabilitates him and gives him another opportunity in life. This may bring new perils and issue for some in a "second death." But, it must bring also new hopes and opportunities. And, hence, St. Paul includes the resurrection of even the unjust in his catagory of "hope toward God."

The same view of it is required by his teaching in 1 Cor. xv. 21–28. He tells us there also that "Since by man came death, by man also the resurrection of the dead." The one is co-extensive with the other. "For as in Adam all die, so in the Christ shall all be made alive." The "all" must be as inclusive in the one case as in the other. He teaches, however, that all do not come forth at the same time, or in the same order. Christ is the firstfruits. Then they that are of the Christ, the Christ-body, at His coming.* "Then (εἶτα, after

---

* Other passages in his writings show that he regarded the resurrection as eclectic and progressive, notably Phil. iii. 11, "If by any means I may attain unto the resurrection out from among the dead." Εἰς την ἐξανάστασιν την ἐκ τῶν νεκρῶν.

that) cometh the end, when He shall deliver up the kingdom to God, even the Father; when he shall have abolished all rule and all authority and power. For He must reign, till He hath put all His enemies under His feet. The last enemy that shall be abolished is death." These words evidently refer to successive and advancing triumphs in the administration of Christ (with which His saints are to be associated), issuing in the recovery of all death's captives and the destruction of death itself. That this is a deliverance for all these captives is further shown by the inquiry raised in verse 29. "Otherwise what shall they do which are baptized in behalf of* the dead? If the dead are not wholly (ὅλως) raised, why then are they baptized for them? why do we also stand in jeopardy every hour?" These questions hint, at least, at a truth which is frequently alluded to in Scripture, that the future recovery of all mankind from death is made to depend upon the salvation of a firstfruits company.† The apostle, as belonging to this priestly company, was now, with his brethren, enduring the trials which fitted them for this place of honor and of service. They were being baptized in behalf of the dead. Their sacrifices would be useless, if they were neither to attain unto the resurrection of the dead, nor be made participants in their Lord's extending conquests over death which should issue in the recovery of all, and for which high service they were now now being baptized into Christ's death. He thus views all his sufferings as his baptism in behalf of the dead, a surrender of himself to that which would

---

*This is the meaning of the Greek ὑπέρ.   † Appendix B

issue in deliverance to them. And this brings us to our next point, which is:

5. That St. Paul always views the salvation of the church as that of a first-fruits or first-born company. This explains what would otherwise be his hard sayings about election. Nothing is plainer than that he refers our salvation to the sovereign, absolute, eternal, choice of God (Ephes. i. 4, 5, 11, Acts xiii. 48, etc). The Pelagian and Arminian quibbles by which men have endeavored to set aside this blessed truth would never have been heard of, if it had been perceived that the purpose of this gracious election does not terminate upon the little flock who are its subjects. They are chosen as the channels of a grace that shall extend beyond them to others. They are the royal priesthood of a great salvation (1 Peter ii. 9). Hence the titles by which Paul designates this body of Christ are, "Brethren of the First Born" (Rom. viii. 29, Col. i. 18), "Church of the first-born" (Heb. xii. 23), the same as St. James designates as begotten by God of His own will to be a "kind of first-fruits of His creatures." They are those who have "first hoped in Christ" before the "redemption of the purchased possession" (Eph. i. 12, 14). All these terms imply that these special objects of God's favor are not the only ones embraced in His redemption. First-born implies that there are later born. First-fruits implies a subsequent harvest. And this leads us to remark:

6. That there are frequent glimpses in Paul's writings of wider reaches of God's grace toward the unsaved masses of mankind, to be unfolded after the salvation of the church has been completed. In Rom. xi

he shows how the cutting off of the Jewish people had opened wide the door of God's grace to the Gentiles. But, "after the fullness of the Gentiles is brought in," that is, after the chosen company from among the Gentiles, necessary to make up the fulness* of Christ's body, be gathered in, then "all Israel shall be saved," and upon all those whom God had shut up unto disobedience His mercy should fall. The same thing is hinted at in chapter 15, where "the promises made to the fathers" are referred to. The germinal promise was that in a chosen seed all the families of the earth should be blessed. It is declared that Jesus Christ came to confirm these promises, and "that the Gentiles might glorify God for His mercy." That more than a moiety of these nations were to be reached by this mercy is proved by the apostle's quotations from the Song of Moses and from Ps. cxvii, in which all peoples and nations are called upon to praise God on account of it. In the Epistle to the Ephesians he declares that it is God's purpose in the dispensation of the fullness of times to gather together in one all things in Christ, both which are in heaven, and which are on earth, even in Him (i. 10). He then unfolds the mystery of the Church, as the chosen companion and Bride of Christ, in the execution of this purpose. She is His body, the fulness of Him that filleth all in all, through whom the praise of the glory of His grace is to be displayed before angels and men (iii. 8-10). He speaks of " every family in heaven and earth " (vs. 15, R. V.) as named from the common Father, and

---

*Compare the use of the word πλήρωμα in Matt. ix. 16.

prays that He would strengthen these Ephesian brethren with all power by His Spirit in the inward man to take in the wide reaches of this love of Christ, whose breadth and length and height and depth were beyond all knowledge, and the glory of which should be displayed by the church unto all the generations of the ages. In Colossians i. 20 he speaks again of God's purpose to reconcile all things unto Himself in Christ, whether they be things in earth or things in heaven, and in Phil. ii. 10 declares that unto the name of Jesus every knee shall bow, of things in heaven, earth, or under the earth, and every tongue confess that He is Lord to the glory of God the Father. Surely here are glimpses of a wider salvation than one which leaves the realms of death and hell filled with damned souls in eternal hate, rebellion and agony. It is only as we come to understand that His triumph must finally extend itself through all these regions, recovering, each in his own order, these lost captives, and restoring at least life to all, through a resurrection from the dead, and such opportunities as recovered life must bring with it, that we can rightly understand the expressions we meet with in the epistles to Timothy and Titus. We there find St. Paul instructing Timothy to see to it that the church, in her priestly capacity, offer up prayers, intercessions, and *giving of thanks* for all men. "For this is good and acceptable in the sight of God our Saviour; who willeth that all men should be saved and come to the knowledge of the truth. For there is one God, one mediator also, between God and men, himself man, Christ Jesus, who gave himself a *ransom for all;* the testimony to be borne in its own times" (1 Tim. ii. 1–6). So also he speaks of the living God, as the Saviour of all men, specially of them that believe (iv. 10). To what can this refer, if not to the fact that while believers are made the subjects of a special salvation, all men have been ransomed to another life than that which all had lost in Adam, and that there was something in this ransom for which all should give thanks? If too blind and ignorant to do this for themselves, the church, as standing for all men, should do it for them. To Titus also he writes that "the grace of God hath appeared, bringing salvation to all men" (ii. 11). But that this was not the salvation bestowed upon the church is made plain by the statement in verse 14, "Who gave Himself for us, that He might redeem us from all iniquity, and purify unto Himself a people for His own possession, zealous of good works." These varied statements are harmonized only by the supposition that the redeeming work of Christ, in securing the salvation of the church, has secured also such a salvation of all men from the ruin wrought in them by sin and death, that all have a new standing in life before God. They cannot be reconciled with the view that no portion of the human race have yet obtained any interest in this salvation but the small proportion of regenerated believers, and that before all the rest there is no hope of relief from the agony of an endless hell.

Even if, however, our readers should refuse to go with us in accepting these passages as positively sustaining this larger hope, the negative argument with which we started out remains unchanged, and cannot be assailed. The uniform silence of St. Paul's epistles upon this doctrine of an endless torment in hell proves that he did not hold the doctrine. It formed no part of the message he was inspired to deliver to men. It did not enter into the whole counsel of God which he shunned not to declare (Acts xx. 27). He was familiar, of course, with the words of Jesus from the letter of which this doctrine has been unwisely drawn. But it is impossible, if he had received these words in the sense put upon them in later times, that not a single passage in all his writings should give a clear testimony of this unspeakable peril.

Before closing this examination it is proper that we should add a few words upon the testimony of the epistle to the Hebrews. It was very likely not written by St. Paul, but all its severe statements about "a fearful looking for of judgment and of fiery indignation which shall devour the adversaries" (x. 27), and that "it is a fearful thing to fall into the hands of the living God" (31), are in entire harmony with St. Paul's views of retribution. These passages are commonly misunderstood and mis-applied because most readers overlook the primary fact that the epistle is throughout addressed to Christians, and speaks throughout of the sore chastisements that await them if unfaithful. Even the passage, "Our God is a consuming fire" (xii. 29), which, from its use of the term "our" and its whole connection is seen to relate to judgments that must come upon Christians, if disobedient, is constantly quoted as if it read, "God, out of Christ, is a consuming fire." Whereas it is God *in* Christ, a consuming fire to all the evils remaining in His own children, and who scourges every son whom He receives (xii. 6), who is here brought to view. The passage teaches precisely the doctrine of 1 Cor. v, where a gross offender is represented as handed over to Satan, as the agent of God's consuming fire, "for the destruction of the flesh that the spirit may be saved in the day of the Lord Jesus." The harshest statement of all in this epistle is, "Whose end is to be burned" (vi. 8). But this is used of unfaithful Christians, unworthy branches of the Vine (John xv. 6), and the harshest meaning they could bear is that such will be forever destroyed. But in the light of the case of the Corinthian fornicator, we may well doubt whether anything more is meant than such a burning as shall consume the whole evil structure of such a man's life, or such a fire as is referred to in 1 Cor. iii. 13-15, which must search the whole fabric of such a Christian's life work, and burn it up, if it be not "gold, silver, precious stones," and out of which he can be saved only "so as by fire." There are many passages in these epistles about which we shall go astray unless we discriminate between the absolute and final salvation secured to all believers in Christ, and the relative salvation and reward for which, in their character of "branches" or "servants" they are still on trial before the judgment seat of Christ.

CHAPTER X.

RETRIBUTION IN THE CATHOLIC EPISTLES.

Passing on to the Catholic Epistles we find the same doctrine of retribution with that contained in the epistles of St. Paul. It is only to meet the requirements of a pre-conceived theory, that any one would think of deriving from their references to future punishment the doctrine of an everlasting punishment in hell. Indeed they all relate either to threatening judgments which must overtake the ungodly in this world, or to that destruction of being which begins with bodily death, and is consummated beyond it in the loss of the soul, and the consequent ejection of the spirit into the outer darkness. But in no case is it affirmed or implied that this punishment lies beyond the resurrection. On the contrary it is something immediate and impending. The resurrection of the ungodly is not indeed distinctly taught. But there are some indirect allusions to it. And these imply that it must be even to them a deliverance.

Taking up these epistles in the order in which we find them, we come first to that of St. James. This epistle assumes throughout—as do all the others—that there is a way of life and a way of death. The last verse declares that " he which converteth a sinner from the error of his way shall save a soul from death." This indeed is the one clear, emphatic, oft-repeated testimony of Scripture upon this whole subject—that " sin, when it is full-grown, bringeth forth death " (i. 15).

Human tradition asserts that man can never die. It makes death to mean eternal life in misery. Because, forsooth, the term "death" is often applied in Scripture to that spiritual condition in which man is "alienated from the life of God," it is assumed that death never means death. But the reason why this spiritual state is so called is, that it inevitably leads to the destruction of the being that is thus severed from God. If anything is plainly taught in Scripture, it is that there can be no eternal life for man apart from Him. Hence the sinner who dies in body, must also lose his soul. His whole being is thus dissolved, and all that gave him life and heritage in manhood is gone. Such a man is *dead*—blotted out of existence as a man —but not yet wholly extinct. Personal identity must still be latent in the outcast spirit. Otherwise the same man could not be brought back through resurrection. But resurrected life, unless it become linked in with the life of God, cannot be eternal. And hence to those to whom it does not bring this highest good, a second death becomes possible. And as no resurrection is promised out of this second death, we infer that it is total and final. This view of the penalty of sin preserves to the uniform teaching of Scripture that "the wages of sin is death," its proper meaning. At the same time, it provides room for those Scriptures which assume the prolonged existence of the soul after the body dies, the subsequent extension of the death-process to the soul, the re-habilitation of the outcast spirit through resurrection in virtue of the redeeming work of Christ, before the great issue of eternal life or death, as now raised by His gospel, is finally, and for all men, forever settled.

The only other passage in this epistle which speaks of future retribution occurs in the fifth chapter; and it is perfectly consistent with this idea, that judgment for the sins of this life is visited in and after death and before resurrection. It begins with a strong philippic against rich men who had accumulated wealth by fraud and oppression of the poor, and warns them that they must reap as they had sown—that their treasures would be speedily burned up in consuming judgments, whose fires would also enwrap their own flesh. But the reference evidently is to a judgment "at the door" (vs. 9). It would be altogether arbitrary and unnatural to refer the language here used to a distant judgment day, and to torments to be inflicted upon these doomed men in body and soul after a remote resurrection from the dead. Wicked men do not have to wait until then to learn that "God is a consuming fire."

St. Peter's first epistle has the same general characteristic. It assumes that there is a death to be shunned and a life to be gained. It warns unwary Christians against the adversary who "goeth about, like a roaring lion, seeking whom he may devour" (v. 8). It reminds them that judgment is approaching—yea, that it was already beginning at the house of God (v. 17). And if the righteous could only with difficulty survive its ordeal, "where shall the ungodly and the sinner appear?" Here also the language does not comport with the thought of a far-distant assize to which those tried should be introduced after resurrection, but of a near issue of life and death in which the righteous man would preserve his soul alive, while that of the ungodly must sink into the gloom of death and hell. But, as we have repeatedly seen, all this is inflicted before the light of another life shall break in upon this darkness. It involves the utter ruin and loss of this present gift of life. It is that bankruptcy of being and bondage in Sheol which precedes resurrection.

And hence we find in this epistle a plain allusion to the fact that such deliverance is in store for "spirits in prison." It affirms that Christ, being put to death in the flesh, but quickened in the Spirit, "went and preached unto the spirits in prison, which aforetime were disobedient, when the long suffering of God waited in the days of Noah, while the ark was a preparing" (iii. 18–20). We have not time and space to enter upon a full critical discussion of the various interpretations put upon this famous passage. Orthodox commentators have seen at a glance that its surface meaning is opposed to the current teaching of the church concerning the final destiny of all men as unalterably fixed at death. And, therefore, ingenuity has been exhausted in efforts to force into the passage some other meaning than the obvious one. And yet the effort has so far failed that an increasing number of even this class of writers now accept the ancient and catholic view, which the words themselves require.

This is what the passage states:

1. That Christ, after His death and resurrection,* "went and preached."

2. Those to whom the preaching was addressed were, at the time of it, "spirits in prison" of the men who, in a former age, had despised the warning message of Noah.

We do not understand, however, that this was the same gospel offer as is made to men in this life. It is only on the arena of manhood that the gospel prize of eternal life and of joint-heirship with Christ can be won. These outcast spirits were no longer men. They must be raised from the dead before they could get back to man's estate, or be capable of reaching its high goal. But the proclamation by Christ to them of His resurrection was to them a gospel, because it gave hope of their own future resurrection.

That this was a message to the dead is further proved by the subsequent allusion to it in the next chapter (vs. 6). "For unto this end were the good tidings preached even to the dead, that they might be judged according to men in the flesh, but live according to

---

* We call attention here to a palpable mistake in the prevalent assumption that the preaching in question took place in the interval between His death and resurrection. The statement in the text is that it was in the Spirit by which He was quickened out of death that He went and preached. It must therefore have been after His resurrection. For this quickening *is* resurrection (Rom. i. 4, viii 11. Comp. Eph. ii. 5-6, Col. ii. 12, iii. 1). The Greek word for "preached" here means "heralded" (ἐκήρυξεν). This makes it probable that the direct object of the preaching was to announce the fact of His resurrection.

God in the spirit."* That "the dead" here spoken of are not the merely spiritually dead, but those who had actually died, appears in the use of the term "dead" in the previous verse: "Who shall give account to Him that is ready to judge the quick and the dead." No one would apply any other meaning to the word "dead" in this title of the Christ than the ordinary one. And therefore the same word in the next verse in immediate connection must refer to this same class. It was captives in the realms of death to whom these good news came. However, then, interpreters may quibble in the effort to evade the plain meaning of these two passages, it is evident that they lie right athwart the dogma that the eternal destiny of all men is irrevocably fixed at death. There is at least a glad tidings of a coming resurrection through a Risen Redeemer proclaimed to all the dead. That this resurrection will issue in the final salvation to eternal life of all is not here affirmed. But that it is a boon, that it brings with it a recovery of lost spirits to that heritage in life and manhood out of which they were cast, that this renewed life will bring new opportunities—

---

*This expression "judged according to men in the flesh," etc., suggests that wherever the glad tidings of Christ's resurrection are made known, whether to men in the flesh, or to spirits in prison, it is both a word of judgment and of life. It puts all that pertains to the flesh, and all of evil that cleaves to the spirit, under the ban of judgment. And it brings life only to those who acquiesce in this judgment and accept it as their just due, and who, out of deserved death, look alone to the Risen Christ for life. From this point of view it is quite possible to believe that there is a probation for resurrection, which will indeed, finally reach every man, but only in his own time and order. For none are raised who do not first hear the voice of the Son of God (John v. 25-29).

even where it brings judgment also—under the administration of the Risen Son of Man is implied in the fact that the tidings of it are "good news," and in the nature of the change itself. For what is resurrection but recovery out of that death-state which is sin's penalty? And, inasmuch as it is the direct fruit of Christ's triumph over death, how can it be otherwise than a blessing, a gift of God's grace, who provided at the first fall of man that a Conquering Seed of the woman should bruise the head of his destroyer, and raise him up out of the pit of death?

Passing on to 2d Peter we find quite a different tone to the epistle. The right of this book to its place in the sacred canon was but slowly recognized. It is now however generally accepted as authentic scripture. And certainly it bears the marks of such. Although it abounds in severe denunciations of corrupters of the church and threatenings of coming wrath, these all fit in to their proper place as premonitions of what must speedily befall the ungodly. There is no hint of a hell reserved for them beyond the resurrection. On the other hand, "their sentence now of old lingereth not, and their destruction slumbereth not" (ii. 3). He cites the instances of the evil angels, long ago cast down to hell (tartarus) and confined in pits of darkness, the drowning of the old world, the burning up of Sodom and Gomorrah, which were then adjudged to overthrow, as examples of that swift and sure destruction which shall overtake these evil-doers. For them the blackness of darkness hath been reserved* (vs. 17). In the

---

* The word "forever" is omitted in the R. V.

next chapter he declares that, as the old world perished by water, so the heavens and earth that are now, have been "stored up for fire, being reserved against a day of judgment and destruction of ungodly men." But there is no warrant for locating any of the things here threatened beyond the resurrection. These judgments attend the Lord's second coming, and are visited upon men living on the earth, just as truly as was the flood, with which they are compared. And the perdition and blackness of darkness which lie beyond these mortal strokes do not await the decision of a distant trial after a resurrection. They are immediate. Nothing in this epistle affects the validity of the principle that out of all this pit of perdition resurrection is a recovery.

But to all this it will be objected that the unrighteous are said (ii. 9) to "be reserved unto the day of judgment to be punished." The New Version translates this passage, "The Lord knoweth how to deliver the godly out of temptation, and to keep the unrighteous under punishment unto the day of judgment" If the old version be here taken as correct (and it is not grammatically impossible) then the answer to the objection is that, in every one of the instances cited for illustration, the punitive judgment overtook the offenders this side of resurrection. This was true of the evil angels, cast down to hell and committed to pits of darkness (ii. 4). So the day of judgment which brought a flood upon the world of the ungodly came upon living men and not dead men raised (vs. 5.). Such a day overtook Sodom and Gomorrah and turned them into ashes (vs. 6). These cities are said to have been then condemned (κατέκρινεν) to overthrow. Jude tells us that they are present examples of "suffering the vengeance of eternal fire" (vs. 7). The "day of judgment and perdition of ungodly men" (iii. 7), which Scripture here and everywhere speaks of as ushered in by the coming of the Lord, is never viewed as a post-resurrection scene. It overtakes men who are marrying and giving in marriage, planting and building, and who are saying one to another, "peace and safety" here on the earth (Luke xvii. 26–31, 1 Thess v. 3). All the ungodly referred to as examples in this connection had their day of judgment and were consigned to punishment before resurrection. And it is therefore out of analogy with all Scripture, and specially with the teaching of this epistle, to suppose that the apostle teaches that the wicked dead do not come to their day of judgment, nor suffer its sentence of punishment, until after that event. And here we call attention again to the fact that in every instance in the New Testament where the phrase "day of judgment" occurs, save one, the article is wanting in the Greek. The single exception is 1 John iv. 17, where believers are referred to as having "boldness in the day of judgment." Now if the Holy Spirit in the New Testament writers desired to impress upon men's minds that idea of a definite future judgment day at which all mankind, living and dead, would be assembled, we ask why has he thus departed from ordinary Greek usage and uniformly omittted the article just where we should have expected to find it? Why, in speaking of the future judgment of the ungodly, does he always say *a* day instead of *the* day of judgment? It is because the day of judgment for any man, or any generation, is not simultaneous with that of every other. He does not fasten attention, as has been everywhere assumed—and from the bonds of which traditionalism even our latest revisers were not free—upon one single, remote, universal day of judgment for which all mankind, living and dead, are reserved, but upon the fact that the judgment of all wicked men lingereth not, and their damnation slumbereth not. It will just as surely overtake them as it did the men of Noah's or of Lot's day.

If, however, the new rendering be adhered to, viz: —"The Lord knoweth how to keep the unrighteous under punishment unto (the) day of judgment," this even more directly accords with our view that the punishment precedes resurrection. If the unrighteous are now kept in guard "under punishment," then they must have been before condemned. Prisoners, sentenced to death, and who have already "suffered vengeance" (Jude 6), cannot be said to be awaiting trial. In this case the "day of judgment" spoken of cannot be for their individual judgment. The phrase must refer to that great crisis and convulsion of this present order of things, which is pre-eminently "the day of the Lord." That such a great day is approaching, all Scripture, and this epistle particularly, affirms. It also asserts that, to the then living generation of mankind, it will be pre-eminently their "great day of judgment" (iii. 7). But it is more than that. It will be a great cosmical crisis. It will especially be a time of judgment upon the evil angels. This is a class of unseen powers, whom Scripture views as having fastened this yoke of bondage upon the creature, bringing it under this blight of sin and death. These especially, as Jude tells us (vs. 6), await the judgment of the great day. There are to be great cosmical changes (2 Peter iii.) involving the whole of these present heavens and earth. They are to be emancipated from the yoke of all evil powers. The forces of nature—which is the name by which science designates the same thing—so far as they have wrought discord and death in this realm, are to be banished or subdued to the sceptre of Him who shall put down all rule and all authority and power. In this great day of judgment, therefore, there are to be liberating and merciful, as well as punitive features. And this is plainly brought to view in this chapter. The present heavens and earth are said to be "reserved unto fire." But not to a total extinction. For out of the fire arise a "new heavens and earth, wherein dwelleth righteousness." So if we must understand the passages ii. 9 and iii. 7 as teaching that unrighteous men are kept under guard unto a future day of judgment, we are not to suppose that they are then to be first tried and punished, but, as those who have been already condemned and are suffering vengeance, they are bound over to await the outcome of those convulsive throes in which the old order of creation must pass away and give birth to a new heavens and earth. That is pre-eminently the great day of *krisis*. And it is always connected with resurrection. It brings complete emancipation and redemption of body to those who are prepared for it (Rom. viii. 19-23). To others it must bring a still longer and perhaps deeper imprisonment in the realms of death. But all this pre-supposes the failure of their resurrection, and that their punishment is perpetuated by reason of it. So that from this point of view, as from every other, we see that punishment *precedes* that great change. There is nothing that requires or favors the view that the unjust are to be raised in order to be judged and punished. And there is nothing precluding that view, which is required by many other Scriptures, and which is involved in the very nature of resurrection, that it must bring, even to this class, however long postponed, liberation and another opportunity in life.

The epistle of Jude is so strikingly, both in phrase and in tone, like the one we have just been studying that, whatever remarks are made upon it had best be brought in here. The one, however, is so much companion to the other as to leave but little to be said. There is the same prediction of judgment upon the ungodly, illustrated by the same examples of fallen angels, of Sodom and Gomorrah, of the generation before the flood (vs. 14), and by others drawn from the history of Israel. We have already referred to the striking proof given in the sixth verse to the fact that wicked men are judged and punished before resurrection. A class of them are said to have suffered the vengeance of eternal fire. In a previous chapter upon this subject we saw how strong is our warrant for believing that the phrase "eternal fire" stands in Scripture for that all-devouring energy of Nature which, now under one form, now in another, consumes the bodies and souls of men, and that men are all the time being consigned to it—in death and the calamities that produce it, and in the dissolution of being that goes on after the death of the body until both body and soul are destroyed in hell. If Sodom and Gomorrah have already suffered this vengeance, then in all other cases it must be a punishment preceding resurrection, and hence differing from that "lake of fire" into which a class of the dead will be cast after the resurrection (Rev. xx.). That term presupposes still another great and final cosmical change, before which there is to be a final sifting of the resurrected dead, as there is before that a sifting of the existing generations of men. That age to come will have its own trial and day of judgment as has this.

These two epistles, last considered, are eminently the epistles of judgment. And so far as their teaching goes, we have found it all in accord with that view of man's punishment for the sins of this life which places it before his resurrection, and which makes that event an opening of the prison doors to them that are bound. There is not a single passage which requires us to locate the sinner's punishment, or which speaks of an eternal hell awaiting him, beyond that event.

There yet remain for this examination the three epistles of St. John. These contain but few allusions to future retribution. The apostle of love dwells mainly upon the love of Him whose Name is Love, and who gave His Son to be the propitiation for the sins of the whole world (ii. 2). He sums up all His gospel testimony in this declaration,—" And we have seen and do testify that the Father sent the Son to be the Saviour of the world." Unless we are to suppose that these sublime personages fail in their mission, there must be some kind of salvation in reserve for all. This we believe to be an universal redemption from death. This great recovery, in due time and order, reaches all. But, as we have often affirmed, this does not insure the eternal life of all, which only those receive who receive the Son. This great life and death issue remains the same in this world and in all worlds. The only passages which bear upon retribution are such as relate to this issue, " He that hath not the Son of God hath not the life " (v. 12). " He that loveth not his brother abideth in death." " And ye know that no murderer hath eternal life abiding in him " (iii. 15). " He speaks also of a sin unto death " (v. 16). Whether he is speaking of a Christian's sin, such as is punishable by temporal death, or of the sin of the ungodly which dooms one to a far more bitter experience of death, is not clear.

All we have then in these epistles is first, this positive testimony as to the way of life and of death which we have found to characterize all the apostolic writings; and second, the testimony of silence that this death does not mean insupportable agony, beyond the resurrection, in an endless hell. Our contention throughout is that, if this were the issue the apostles were sent out to present to men, not even the apostle of love would have left them in any uncertainty about it. Their allusions to retribution, even in letters addressed to believers, would have given plain testimony upon a matter of such fearful import. But, while these Catholic Epistles abound in references to a future judgment and to the penalty of sin, they conceive of this judgment as near at hand, and of this penalty as overtaking men on the earth, and pursuing them into that realm of death where wicked men are bound in chains of darkness until that great world-judgment when the prince of this world shall be cast out. Under the administrations then to be begun and carried on by Christ and the risen sons of God (Rom. viii. 19) resurrection shall at last liberate, each in his own order, these prisoners in the pit. And all Scripture, Old Testament and New, requires us to believe that when this deliverance shall come, it will be, not a curse, but a boon, bringing with it another gift of life under Him who is Lord both of the dead and of the living.

CHAPTER XI.

RETRIBUTION IN THE APOCALYPSE.

The study of the Apocalypse has a less decisive bearing upon the subject we have been investigating than that of the other scriptures, because of its confessed obscurity. Anyone who is acquainted with the history of its interpretation will perceive the justice of this remark. Any doctrine of retribution drawn from its pages must, of necessity, be subject to revision and confirmation by the plainer teachings of the Word. Its teaching on this subject, however, when closely examined, will be found in general agreement with what we have been already taught. It brings to view mainly the judgments which must overtake the ungodly here on the earth and in this present life. Here and there a glimpse is given of what awaits them beyond death. But there is nothing which vitiates the general principle which we have found to govern all the preceding New Testament teaching, and which determines that the tribulation and anguish which must come upon evil men overtake them in this world, visiting them with calamities and death, and shutting them up to serve out their death-sentence in the hell that lies beyond death, and which must at some distant day give up its dead. One notable passage, indeed, seems to locate this punishment beyond the resurrection (xx. 11-15). This has been already examined. But we shall have yet other remarks to make upon it.

The first words of retribution occur in the letters to the seven churches. He who searches the reins and hearts assures them that all their acts and ways are naked and open before Him, and that He will render to each one of them according to their works (ii. 23). Jezebel's children, who had been seduced by that false prophetess, He would kill with death. He speaks to them of Sardis of a possible blotting out of their names from the book of life, and to all the churches, of high rewards in store for the overcomers, to which the unfaithful shall not attain. But all these warnings fall vastly short of the threat of an everlasting hell. Indeed they all seem to fall under the head of that corrective chastisement by which the consuming fire of God's jealousy burns out the evil in His children. For in the address to that church which was the most derelict and most rebuked—that of Laodicea—these words occur: "As many as I love, I rebuke and chasten; be zealous, therefore, and repent." Even the possible blotting out of one's name from the book of life may only refer to a threatened exclusion from the first resurrection triumphs of the chosen body who live and reign with Christ, and to a bondage in death out of which the unfaithful servant will be saved so as by fire, and with the shame and suffering of loss (1 Cor. iii. 12-17). "If any man destroyeth the temple of God, him shall God destroy." But our God sometimes destroys in order to save, and kills in order to make alive. (See Deut. xxxii. 24, 36, 39, 43; 1 Cor. v. 5).

After the epistles to the churches of Asia the visions

relate to the judgments to be visited upon an ungodly world, and especially upon apostate Christendom. A rider upon a pale horse, whose name was Death, is given authority over the fourth part of the earth, to kill with sword, with famine, and with death, and with the wild beasts of the earth (vi. 8).

After the opening of the sixth seal (vs. 12-17), great political commotions are described under the symbols of natural convulsions. There was a great earthquake. The sun is darkened and the moon becomes like blood. The stars fall from heaven, and the heaven is rolled up as a scroll. The kings and princes of the earth, and every class, in terror, call upon the rocks and mountains to fall upon them and hide them "from the face of Him that sitteth on the throne, and from the wrath of the Lamb: for the great day of their wrath is come." This precise imagery frequently occurs in the Old Testament prophets in connection with great national judgments. In Isaiah xxxiv. all nations are summoned to hear. "For the indignation of the Lord is upon all nations, and His fury upon all their armies; He hath utterly destroyed them, He hath delivered them to the slaughter. Their slain also shall be cast out, and the mountains shall be melted with their blood. And all the host of heaven shall be dissolved, and the heavens shall be rolled together as a scroll; and all their host shall fall down as the leaf falleth off from the vine, and as a falling fig from the fig tree." See also Isaiah xiii. 1-13. An invasion of the land of Judea is described by the prophet Joel (ch. ii.) under the same imagery. St. Peter at

Pentecost (Acts ii. 16 20) speaks of this day of great convulsion as then introduced by the outpouring of the Holy Ghost, whose fire is a fire of judgment as well as of purgation and salvation. All these passages look forward, however, to that consummating judgment which Scripture especially designates as the great day of the Lord. And, inasmuch as it gives many indications that that will be a crisis in the natural world, as well as in human affairs, we may well suppose that cosmical, as well as social and political commotions, will add to its terrors. There are closer bonds of sympathy between nature and its highest creature, man, than we have yet discovered. But the point at which we are now aiming is to show that these terrifying and destructive judgments, whatever be their character, are visited upon living generations of men. They do not bring to view the resurrected dead.

The same thing is true of the woes announced by the seven angels with the seven trumpets (chs. viii. ix). They are visions of war, and famine, and death and plague. We have always suspected that these apocalyptic visions, as they are seen to occur in the invisible world, so they describe events and changes that transpire first in the realm of spiritual realities. Behind all this arena of human affairs there are great warring powers in an invisible realm (Eph. vi. 10-20). There are spiritual blights, and famines, and plagues that smite the souls of men and nations before these things reveal themselves in the natural sphere. Men are often smitten with death in this region before they are stricken with physical death. Locust-shaped demons coming forth from the pit, and over whom Apollyon is king, go forth on their devastating work first in the sphere of human souls. Before Mahommedan hordes, or any form of earthly enemies, can make havoc of the professing church, or desolate the nations of mankind, something corresponding to this dread vision must have occured in that spiritual realm where the real conflict for the dominion of the world is going on, and of which the sorrows and conflicts enacting on the earth are but the shadows. We believe that all the apocalyptic symbols need a new interpretation from this point of view.

These remarks, however, are apart from our present purpose, which is to call attention to the fact that these scenes of divine retribution relate to living generations on the earth, and shed no light upon the question of what lies for man beyond death. In the eleventh chapter there is, indeed, the statement that the time had come "of the dead to be judged, and to give their reward to thy servants, and to the saints, and to them that fear thy name, the small and the great." But the connection shows that the reference is to a *vindication of God's servants and saints*, who had died in the faith of their reward without the sight. In the fourteenth chapter we meet with a special woe denounced upon the worshippers of the beast, a class which we infer from a statement in the previous chapter had included the larger part of mankind. "There was given to him authority over every tribe and people and tongue and nation. And all that dwell on the earth shall worship him, everyone whose name hath not been written in the book of life of the Lamb, slain from the foundation of the world." (vs. 7, 8). It may be that the special woe in reserve for this class applies only to those of them who reject the warning of the angel (xiv. 6, 7) and persist in their beast-worship. But a third angel makes loud proclamation of this special woe, as follows.

"If any man worshippeth the beast and his image, and receiveth a mark upon his forehead, or upon his hand, he also shall drink of the wine of the wrath of God, which is prepared unmixed in the cup of his anger; and he shall be tormented with fire and brimstone in the presence of the holy angels and of the Lamb; and the smoke of their torment goeth up for ever and ever; and they have no rest day and night, they that worship the beast and his image, and whoso receiveth the mark of his name."

It is to be observed that this torment comes in a series of judgments which, as we have seen, are visited upon the living generations of men. The last plagues of the seven angels with the seven vials, which follow in the succeeding chapters, are of this same character. This single premonition of torment has been regarded as a lifting of the veil to reveal what awaits these sinners beyond the resurrection. But these worshippers of the beast cannot be supposed to have been killed before this woe falls upon them. Indeed it is stated in ch. xix. 21, that they are killed by it. It introduces an idea foreign to the whole series of judgments to suppose that this alone relates to that torment in body which tradition affirms to be awaiting lost men in that distant future. It very likely, indeed, refers to that torment of soul which is prolonged beyond the death of the body, which is a part of the death process before a wicked man's destruction is complete. But this we have uniformly found to be the punishment which precedes resurrection. Viewing this judgment therefore as a tormenting plague upon those ungodly men who, in the last days, are the votaries of Antichrist, we are precluded from finding any reference in the passage to an eternal torment beyond their resurrection. The judgment falls upon them long before that event.

It is the *smoke* of their torment which ascendeth up unto the ages of the ages. An evidence and memorial is thus given to all coming ages of the destructive judgment which has made an end of the beast and his worshippers, as the usurpers of the honor and worship that belong to God only. This accords with the evident meaning of the symbol where it first occurs in Scripture. In Isaiah xxxiv, it is predicted of the land of Edom in the day of the Lord's vengeance, "The streams thereof shall be turned into pitch, and the dust thereof into brimstone, and the land thereof shall become burning pitch. It shall not be quenched night nor day; the smoke thereof shall go up forever: from generation to generation it shall lie waste; none shall pass through it forever and ever" (9–11). Some explanation must be given to these expressions consistent with the subsequent promise that all the earth shall be renewed (Isa. lxv). They are thus limited to a visitation that shall continue to the end of the age. They may include also the idea that in the renovated heavens and earth the land of Edom shall find no place, but that the memory of it shall be blotted out forever. But they do not and cannot mean that the burning destruction of that land shall go on endlessly. In like manner we are not required to attach such a meaning to the prophetic phraseology in the Revelation. The fact that the *smoke* of the torment goes up unto the ages of the ages does not prove that the tormenting process never ends, any more than the fact that the smoke of Edom's destruction goes up forever proves that the destructive process never ends. To this it may be objected that in chap. xix. 20, we are told that the beast and the false prophet, who are both overcome by the conquering Word of God—the rider upon the white horse,—are together cast alive into the lake that burneth with fire and brimstone.* In ch. xx. 10 we read further, "And the devil that deceived them (the nations) was cast into the lake of fire and brimstone, where are also the beast and the false prophet; and they shall be tormented day and night forever and ever." It is argued that here at least the endless torment of these three, two of whom are human persons, is distinctly affirmed. But the answer to this is that we are by no means sure that the terms "beast" and "false prophet" represent individual men. In the

---

* It is to be remarked that here we have another description of the fate that shall overtake the adherents of the beast. They "were killed with the sword of him that sat upon the horse, even the sword which came forth out of his mouth : and all the birds were filled with their flesh."

Apocalypse of the Old Testament, from which that of the New partly derives its imagery, the term "beast" represents a worldly political system (Dan. vii. 11). Its being cast into the burning flame represents the utter destruction of that system whose characteristics were such that the symbol of a beast is applied to it, in contrast with that kingdom over which there is "one like unto a son of man." What these passages bring to view is probably the utter destruction of these two hostile systems, set forth under the figure of the casting into a lake of fire of their symbolic representatives, with the devil who energized them. Whatever may be true of the future destiny of the devil, no argument for the endless torment of lost men can be drawn from these passages, unless it can be proved that the two great enemies here brought to view are individual men. The analogies of Scripture, as we have seen, lead us rather to regard them as systems. In ch. xx. 14, we are told that death and hades are to be cast into this same lake of fire. And surely these are not human persons. If it be asked how systems can be "tormented," we can only reply that as they are here *personified*, so they may be represented as suffering the torment of living persons in the remediless destruction that overtakes them, and in the everlasting shame that covers them.

In ch. xxi. 8, we are told of the casting into this same lake of fire of classes of sinners who are undoubtedly human. "But for the fearful, and unbelieving, and abominable, and murderers, and fornicators, and sorcerers, and idolaters, and all liars, their part shall be in the lake that burneth with fire and brimstone; which is the second death." This passage, however, does not prove the endless torment of these sinners. It rather points to their destruction in that deeper pit of death which this Book several times refers to as the final grave of all those enemies, including death, who are to be destroyed out of that perfect order in which God shall be all in all. It is an impressive declaration that for wicked men there can be no possible place in the new and heavenly order (xxii. 15). Here it may be well for us to inquire into the meaning of that agent of divine purgation and retribution so often brought to view in these closing chapters—

THE LAKE OF FIRE.

We have all along found, in these studies, that all Scripture, Old and New, makes frequent reference to a future renovation of this present cosmos. The instrument of this renovation is the eternal fire, by which term is brought to view that devouring energy with which Nature is ever consuming worn out and worthless forms of life so that, out of their grave, may arise forms more worthy and enduring. Sinful man, in obedience to this law, must go down into this pit of eternal fire, unless the eternal life of God be imparted to him through Jesus Christ. The Son of Man, as the divine Judge and sorter of men, is even now consigning wicked men to the destructive operation of this eternal fire, while the righteous go into life eternal. That crisis which is known in Scripture as His appearing consummates this work of judgment and brings to an end what is styled this present age or world. It brings with it also a first stage in His work of cosmical change and renewal. Satan, who is the author of physical as well as moral evil, will then be bound (Rev. xx). And life will then triumph completely over death in the person of those elect saints who share with Him the glories of this administration. It must bring with it also new displays of His power and grace to the nations of mankind, who are no longer deceived and blinded by this great enemy. But this is not the final stage of His triumph. Nor does it complete that transfiguration of the old order into the new of which we have the picture in chapters xxi and xxii. A preceding feature of this *final* renovation is the lake of fire. Into it are cast death and hell and all God's enemies. The term brings to view a still deeper working of that consuming energy with which the Creator has charged this system of His works, and by which its own purgation and emancipation shall finally be effected. All its hostile powers shall be yoked into submission to His exalted Son. Its fair fields shall no longer be blighted with a curse, nor ravaged by the rude hand of death (xxi. 4, xxii. 3). All things shall be radiant with the light and buoyant with the life of God. The lake of fire is not presented to us apart from, but as preparatory to this result. It is indeed that final abyss, prepared for the devil and his angels, down into whose devouring depths must go all these evil powers who have blighted God's fair heritage, and all evil beings, including men, who are so bound up with this system as to refuse

God's way of deliverance through accepted death with Christ out of the old order, and resurrection into the new. But we shall miss altogether the meaning of the lake of fire, if we regard it merely as a place provided for the eternal torment of these lost ones. Like all God's wondrous works and ways its aim and action are beneficent. It is the bath of fire out of which the heavens and earth finally emerge into eternal sweetness and light, a home of splendor and delight for the ransomed millions of mankind. While therefore all the preceeding judgments of this book relate to the living generations of mankind who are dealt with in judgment by the exalted Christ preparatory to His coming, and so precede the resurrection, we are not surprised to find one great judgment-scene depicted as coming in after that event, and as preceding the final crisis which winds up His millenial reign. The first stage of His triumphant reign brought with it the outbirth into His life and glory of only a selected class of men. And the creature did not attain to its final deliverance. It was lightened only with the *dawn* of its full glory. But in its final throes, and with its complete emancipation, it must cast out all its dead. "And the sea gave up the dead which were in it; and death and Hades gave up the dead which were in them" (xx. 13). We have already, in examining this judgment scene, concluded that it condenses into one picture a long-continued judgment process, in which all that Scripture teaches concerning the redemptive character of resurrection must have due place. The whole scene connects itself with the great cosmical deliverance which the next chapter immediately describes.

That there are certain features difficult to understand in these closing passages which allude to future retribution, we may well admit. That there is a hopeless doom for incorrigible sinners in the lake of fire, beyond the resurrection, must be allowed. But that resurrection introduces them immediately to this doom, without any previous benefit or opportunity coming to them with the gift of recovered life, must be denied. For, as we have seen, this lies in the very idea of resurrection. It is implied in all the glimpses of it that gleam out on the pages of the Old Testament, and in the promises of the New. The point we have to consider is whether, in view of all the testimony of Scripture to the effect that some character of blessing has been secured by Christ's redemption to all the families of the earth, both dead and living, and in view of the fact that it uniformly describes the punishment of sin as a subjection to death, and to an immediate hell which long precedes resurrection, we are warranted in allowing a few obscure allusions in this unexplained book to govern or set aside the teaching of all these earlier and plainer scriptures. That they have had this undue influence is manifest. These passages seemed on their surface to teach the doctrine of endless torment. And therefore Christians have generally read this doctrine into our Lord's teaching about hell and its quenchless fires. (Mark ix. 53-50, etc.) But, as we have seen, His sayings plainly refer to a possible destruction of man's *present* embodied being in an impending gehenna. Even the judgment scene in Matt. xxv does not primarily look beyond the resurrection. A baleful glare from these passages in the Apocalypse has been cast over all this earlier New Testament teaching. Even the sermons and letters of the apostles, which do not contain a single plain reference to the doctrine of an eternal torment in hell, have been made lurid with this borrowed light. And splendid promises of restitution, spoken by the mouth of ancient prophets, have been belittled or annulled. The point for which we are all along contending is that certain great and merciful principles of divine administration underlie the whole plan of God in Creation and redemption; that these crop out through the whole of revelation and must govern its interpretation. Especially must the obscure teaching of this book of hidden mysteries yield to them. One of these deepest principles is His purpose to lift up the human race out of its pit of death through the death and resurrection of a Redeemer; requiring that, in the execution of this purpose, neither death nor hell shall defeat Him, but be made tributary thereto. The resurrection of all, therefore, must be the redemption of all to another standing in life. This itself is a boon. It does not make necessary the salvation of all to eternal life. There is a possible second death beyond the resurrection into which some sink. But neither this threatened doom, nor any threat of the darkest passages we have been examining, must be allowed to set aside this great principle, that death cannot defeat God in His great purpose to bring blessing to all the families of the earth through a conquering seed, and that His answer to the work of the devil who brought sin into the world, so that death passed upon all men, is the gift of a Second Man to be his destroyer, through whose righteousness the free gift has come to all men of justification to another life. Sinners may incur, indeed, a fearful loss of body and soul in hell before this recovery. Moreover, it can reach them only after the just judgment of God has been fully satisfied in their case. And it cannot bring to them assured deliverance from bondage to the creature. Hence their great need of immediate salvation. Let none of this class therefore, because God is a " God of hope," forget that He is also a consuming fire, and that the longer they go on in sin, the deeper must they sink and the longer must they remain in the abyss of His wrath,—the more complete must be their wreck of being, and the fewer the elements of hope in its recovery.

CHAPTER XII.

REVIEW.

We have endeavored thus faithfully to trace the doctrine of retribution for sin, as it is unfolded in the Scriptures, and to place it side-by-side with that other great feature of the divine administration, the purpose of redemption. And we have done this in the interest of the many sad and earnest souls who fervently believe the Bible to be the Word of God, and who yet are painfully oppressed in receiving its teachings about retribution, because they have failed to see how these are balanced and explained by the other side of the divine dealings in redemption.

And yet these two sides are presented to us at the very outset of revelation On the one side Adam is sentenced to what appears to be a hopeless doom. He was to die and to return to dust. No intimation is given in the sentence that this destruction was not to be final. And yet a gleam of hope is afterwards given in the promise of a conquering Seed who should bruise the serpent's head. Later on, Abraham is called to become the father of the promised seed. And it is repeatedly declared that in him and in his seed all the families of the earth should be blessed.

We began these inquiries with the conviction that God's promises cannot mean less than they convey, and that when He says "all " He means all. Hitherto the church seems to have found no middle ground between a crude universalism, which both reason and

Scripture condemn, and the hopeless damnation of that immense proportion of mankind who have died in their sins. It has therefore been compelled to divest the future resurrection of this class of every element of hope. It has thus failed to recognize one of the most vital and fundamental features in God's unfolding plan, viz., that resurrection, as a recovery of man out of that death-state into which sin has cast him, is *essentially* redemptive. She has therefore failed to see that this provision to restore all men to another life is His way of making good His original promise to bless all mankind. This does not imply that all shall at last attain eternal life and blessedness. But it does mean that this is not His final administration of grace toward lost men. It means that death cannot defeat His purpose to bless all generations, but that He will bring from the land of the enemy, and within the sphere of His economy of grace and power, those whom it has not here reached, and whom His just judgments have for their sins consigned to death and hell.

These two principles, that His retributions for sin are fixed and inevitable, but that death, sin's wages, cannot snatch His creatures out of His hands nor defeat His purposes, we have traced through the Scriptures. We have found that He is the God of the dead, as well as of the living, and that all His great promises of blessing pre-suppose, and require for their fulfilment, the resurrection of the dead.

Beginning with that profound passage, the Song of Moses (Deut. xxxii), we found that it was built up around these two principles, and that they furnish the key to the "secret things" stored up among its treasures. God's providential dealings with the world of mankind, and especially with His chosen people, are there brought to view. The claims of His righteousness, which require that they, and that all nations, be adjudged to calamities and to death for their sins, are impressively set forth. The fire of His anger must burn against them to the lowest hell (vs. 22). And yet He asserts His power over all the enemies who had brought them into this sad plight, and even over death. He who kills can make alive. And He who gave such fearful power to "the enemy and the avenger" must revenge Himself even against him, and bring in a salvation in which all nations should rejoice with His people. And that the "all nations" signified are not merely the nations of some future millenial period, but the nations also who had suffered these visitations of His anger, and gone down to captivity in death, is implied in the whole tenor of the passage. This is the very hidden truth it contains, the precious secret sealed up among its treasures (vs. 34) that, although God must allow the adversary to people his realms with prisoners, and death to lead down to hell its multitude of captives, yet even these enemies should be compelled to give back their trophies, and be consumed in the wrathful fires themselves had kindled.

These twin facts of judgment and redemption are illustrated in all Old Testament history. They are amplified in all subsequent psalm and prophecy. All intelligent readers of the Bible confess this. But all do not see that these principles overleap the bounds of death and govern God's administrations in the ages to come. And few see that this must necessarily be so. For otherwise His great promises must be miserably diminished and His purposes thwarted. And few see that His purpose in saving a chosen seed in this age has relation to His wider purpose to bless "all the nations of the earth" in an age to come. But with this key in hand, and with the firm conviction that death cannot defeat God nor annul the least of His promises, we have been enabled to find in the Old Testament abundant hints and suggestions and direct declarations of His purpose to bring future blessing to all mankind through their resurrection from the dead.

We have seen, on the one hand, that the Bible throughout reveals a definite penalty for sin. Wicked men and nations must go down to sheol. There they are held as captives—prisoners in the pit where no water is. Many Old Testament passages view this prison as a place of silence and of gloom in which the dead lie either in an unconscious state, or at best in "the miserable consciousness of not being." It is only in the New Testament that Hades is viewed as a place of torment. But this torment seems to be but the accompaniment of that destructive process which goes on there to the destruction of even the soul in hell, until nothing of man is left but a naked spirit in the outer darkness. But many Old Testament allusions to this bondage in death imply that God's pity would not forsake them even here, although driven out to the "outmost parts of heaven" (Deut. xxx. 4). "For the Lord shall judge His people, and repent

Himself for His servants, when He seeth that their power is gone, and there is none shut up, or left" (Deut. xxxii. 36). "Even the captives of the mighty shall be taken away and the prey of the terrible shall be delivered; for I will contend with him that contendeth with thee, and I will save thy children" (Isa. xlix. 25). An extended examination of the Psalms and Prophets has shown us that the captives so often referred to as the future subjects of delivering mercy are the captives in the realms of death. All minor captivities prefigure this one. Hence these captives are often spoken of as *the children of death* (Ps. lxxix. 11, cii. 20). They are viewed as captives *in the land of the enemy*, whom the Lord should ransom from the hand of one stronger than they (Jer. xxxi. 11, 16). And that unregenerate men are made the subjects of this recovery is plain from the fact that this is the very class in view in all these passages, which speak first of the sins which consigned them to this captivity, and of their subsequent release. In Hosea xiii. it is manifestly the apostate Israel, whom the Lord had rejected from being His people, the Ephraim, joined to his idols, of whom He afterwards declares, "I will ransom them from the power of the grave (sheol). I will redeem them from death; O death where are thy plagues? O Sheol where is thy destruction? repentance shall be hid from mine eyes." We have found that restoration from this bondage is promised, in due time and order, to even sinful nations that debauched and oppressed Israel, and who had been destroyed under the heaviest hand of God's judgments,—

to Assyria and Egypt, to Moab and Ammon and Elam, to Samaria and to Sodom (Ezek. xvi). Only a salvation of so wide a scope as this could meet the requirements of such far-reaching and comprehensive prophecies as that, for example, of Isaiah xxv, in which all nations are invited to a feast of fat things prepared for them by the Lord God, who shall destroy from off the face of the earth all that now hides His glory from the nations, and swallow up death in victory.

A wide generalization of Old Testament passages has thus established for us these two principles: 1. The fire of God's anger must burn against all evil-doers to overthrow and consume them in death and hell. 2. This "land of the enemy" where they lie as outcasts in bondage and gloom is not a territory beyond the reach of His conquering arm. He has provided to ransom in due time and order all these prisoners in the pit; and so, over and beyond this region of deserved judgment for sin, to make good His promise of blessing to all the families of the earth.

Coming to the New Testament, we began its study with the principle that it cannot at any point contradict the Old Christ came not to supersede, but to fulfill the law and the prophets. His words therefore were spoken in reference to this Old Testament revelation. They were designed to illumine and unfold it. All His sayings therefore about hell and the wrath to come must be in accordance with the principles we have there discovered. And nothing more is needed to bring them into such harmony, than to put all His words about future judgment, and hell, and unquenchable fire, precisely where they belong,—as relating to what befalls wicked men before resurrection. Such an interpretation of them is so natural and obvious that it is a marvel that the church should have been so long blind to it. A single passage in the most obscure book of the Bible (Rev. xx. 11-15), which speaks of a judgment of the dead after their awakening from death, has been suffered to dominate and pervert the meaning of all the earlier New Testament passages which speak of a speedy judgment for sin, and of a suffering in hell awaiting sinners just beyond the borders of this earthly life. Just where the Old Testament located sheol, there must we locate the New Testament hell. They are but the same place of punishment.* The division of this realm of death into a Hades, and a Gehenna widely separated in character and in time, is but a part of the obscuring process above referred to. It was in *Hades* that the rich man lifted up his eyes being in torment. Gehenna is only a deeper pit in that realm of destruction which the Old Testament covers by the broader name of Sheol. Were it not for some of these false notions imported into our New Testament reading, no one would have ever thought that when John the Baptist describes the Messiah's work of judgment as a burning up of the chaff with "unquenchable fire" that anything more was meant by that term than its frequent Old Testament usage implies. And when Jesus repeatedly warns men against the danger of hell-fire, and that it

---

*See upon this point Prof. Shedd's *Doctrine of Endless Punishment*, pg. 22, et seq.

is far better that they should now mortify the sins in their members than lose the whole body and soul in hell, no one would have supposed that he was referring to a future resurrection body, brought up from the grave to be damned, but to the loss of their *present* heritage in life and manhood. What he has all along in view in such passages is an *impending* destruction awaiting sinful men, and from which He sought to rescue all who would receive Him by the gift of an eternal life which would make them even now triumphant over death.

And so His words of judgment, which relate to the trial of living generations of mankind, have been treated as if they had primary and sole reference to the masses of the resurrected dead. And this too, in the face of His repeated declarations that they would overtake the world in the same way that the men of Noah's and of Lot's day were surprised, and that they would begin before that generation passed away. No one would deny, of course, that Jesus Christ is exalted to be the Judge of the dead as well as of the living. But it still remains the fact that the nations who know Him not, and who obey not His gospel, and who are consigned by Him to eternal fire (Matt. xxv. 31-46), are the living nations of mankind who pass in review before His throne. The words describe a pre-resurrection scene, and do not attempt to define what may be in the purposes of God for these doomed masses beyond their resurrection. Indeed it must be borne in mind in interpreting all these words of Jesus that He did not intend to throw the great light of His approaching triumph upon these dark shadows of judgment before it took place. He chose to wait, until after the Son of Man was risen from the dead, before illumining the minds of even His disciples to the meaning of this great event—its relation to all God's great promises in the past, and to His widening purposes of grace toward the world in the future. This explains why it is that the harshest words in the Bible about future punishment are those of the loving Lord and Saviour. The time for the full disclosure of His redeeming plan was not yet. What hope for the world was couched in His· resurrection could not yet be made known, except in the way of hints which even His chosen followers did not apprehend. And this explains why, as these studies have made plain to us, our traditional notions of a future hell of fire and threats of everlasting torment, find no place in either the sermons or the epistles of the apostles. In conformity with what we learned of the teachings of the Master, we found that the wrath to come in their view was a fearful punishment awaiting the ungodly in death and before resurrection. The harshest passage in either St. Paul's addresses or letters is that in 2 Thess. i. 9, where he speaks of an eternal destruction from the presence of the Lord and from the glory of His power. But every careful reader of the context, and of these two epistles, will see that this passage applies to a class of sinners living on the earth and who are saying "peace and safety" at the time of the Lord's coming. The resurrected dead are not brought to view. And so in the Catholic Epistles "the great day of judgment and perdition of ungodly men" is one which overtakes men on the earth. There is absolutely nothing therefore in the words of Christ, or in the words He put by the Holy Ghost into the mouth of His apostles, or upon their pens, which sets aside the force of the principles required by the Old Testament teaching, that man's judgment and suffering for sin lie in death, and in that land of darkness and bondage into which souls pass beyond it; and nothing to interfere with that great principle outlined there, but brought into clearer light in the New Testament, that this punishment is bounded for all men by a hope of resurrection which shall reach them, each in his own time and order, as the result of the ransom paid for all. Not even the doctrine of retribution as brought to view in the Apocalypse can set aside these principles. Indeed that vision is all in harmony with it. The passages which seem to be exceptional cannot really be so. Their interpretation must yield to the requirements of these great principles which underlie all Scripture, and which are fundamental in the plan of redemption it was written to reveal. This promised recovery of all from the death-state, which is sin's wages, is not the salvation of all to eternal life, but to the blessings and the opportunities of a restored human life. The Bible brings to view two orders of life, of which Adam and Christ are the respective heads. In Christ there is eternal life. Man, in union with Him, becomes partaker of the life of God and the heir of all things.

This life is freed from all bondage to the creature. It is unfettered, glorious and endless. Only the saints are raised in the fashion of this divine manhood. Other men must come forth to a life not yet freed from this bondage, and under the law of change and corruption. Such was the life of Adam at his creation. He was peccable and perishable,—only a *candidate* for the eternal life. As Scripture speaks of only these two orders of manhood, and as wicked men cannot bear the image of the heavenly, they must be raised into the sphere of a natural and earthy manhood. This leaves them still on trial and under judgment. This is "the resurrection of judgment" (John v. 29). And this we believe to be the trial of the dead brought to view in the judgment of the great white throne. The once dead in that scene are not cast into the lake of fire for the sins of this life. They have already been sent to hell for these. That lake can only be for those who fail in their second trial of life, and who are therefore condemned to the second death.

The same principles of the divine dealing in both judgment and redemption are thus seen to pervade all Scripture. All its threatenings of destructive punishment for sin are verified. And room is made for the fulfilment of all its promises without evasion or abatement. The Sheol of the Old Testament and the Gehenna of the New alike await the sinner this side of resurrection. His judgment does not wait until some far-distant assize, nor does His damnation slumber. Hell now yawns beneath him. All Jesus' words about it are rightly understood only as we thus locate them.

Resurrection for unjust men does not mean indeed what it does for the just. We may well suppose that the grade and potency of the restored life will be according to character. "To every seed his own body." But there is nothing in the severest denunciations of Jesus, nor in His most fearful threatenings of wrath, to exclude the idea that beyond this region of judgment there is hope in resurrection. All that is needed to adjust these two sides of truth to one another is to know that what is exposed to this fearful peril is man's *present* endowment and heritage in life—that he may suffer the entire loss of this, and that its destruction is final. And yet the grace of God may again take up his case, as it did that of Adam, by restoring to him another life on another basis, with another opportunity to win the crown of life which seemed lost to him forever. In no other way can the constant assertion of Scripture be made good that blessing of some sort has been procured for *all* the families of the earth through the redemption that is in Christ Jesus. If this promise does not reach over to the dead, then the greater part of these families have no share in it, and His Messianic work as Lord of both the dead and the living remains unfulfilled.

All this accords too with what we have learned from Scripture and from science of the nature of man. He is an embodied image of God. He was made to have dominion over all His works. He now stands on the summit of created life. The forces that rule in this created system, and which we call forces of nature, but which Scripture views as living powers or angels, are made tributary to him. Death, the wages of sin, disembodies man and so discrowns and casts him out of his heritage. But man has not only an earthly body, bringing him into relation to the created system. He is a living soul. The breath or spirit of God enters also into the constitution of his being, and forms within him "the spirit of a man." He is therefore body, soul, and spirit. Each one of these elements is necessary to constitute him a man. The soul seems to be an intermediate structure between the material body and the immaterial spirit. And, like the body, it is perishable. Jesus teaches that both body and soul may be destroyed in that pit of the devouring energy of natural forces to which He gives the name of hellfire. But He also teaches that the soul may survive and suffer there—how long we know not—before the spirit is cast out into the outer darkness. Whether the spirit, after being divested of these elements of manhood, retains the consciousness of its former human personality we do not know. All we know is that it ceases to be a man. A disembodied ghost is not a man. And, therefore, the destruction of such a being out of the life and estate of manhood is complete. The *man* is dead. And this death-state is emphatically the wages of sin. But just here comes in the importance of the doctrine and hope of resurrection. It is the re-investiture of the dead and outcast one with life in manhood. And just here lies the mistake of the old eschatology. It virtually denies any proper *death* of the man before resurrection. And it unspeakably degrades resurrection into an instrument of aggravated retribution and torment. It robs that which is always viewed in Scripture as a "hope" of every element of hope, and makes it an unmitigated curse. And here also it comes into conflict with what even Science teaches concerning the progress of life. It teaches that this progress culminates in man. Science is blind indeed to the fact that the goal of this progress is not the earthy but the risen man. But if it could once perceive that man is to take on another form of manhood beyond the grave, it would scorn the idea that this can be for purposes of degradation, and that Nature's grand progress toward perfected life is to be thus turned backward. No, the idea of resurrection for the unjust must be either abandoned, or we must admit that it is even for them another beginning and on a higher scale. For it lies in the very nature of life that it must build itself up into more perfect forms. And if any of its organisms refuse to yield to this law of advance toward perfection, it must refuse to make for itself a home in such. They must be rejected out of the sphere of life forever.* So that while it must be admitted that some may perish out of the line of progress, in a second death, it yet remains true that the harmonies

---

*A most thoughtful book on this subject is Prof. Drummond's *Natural Law in the Spiritual World*. It is to be regretted that this book, while it sets forth with much ability and wealth of illustration this feature of the divine economy, overlooks so much the redemptive side of God's working, even in the realm of nature. The author should have drawn from this source analogies to prove resurrection, and so have thrown the light of this hope upon the divine plan of the world. The poverty cf this feature in its philosophy of human destiny is the great defect of that otherwise useful book.

of both Scripture and of Science require us to believe that resurrection is essentially redemptive and benignant.

This view of resurrection has a far better basis however than Science can furnish. It is inwoven into the whole warp and woof of Scripture. It underlies the divine plan of the world and of man as its heir, as therein revealed. It is necessary to its completion. It is essential to any right knowledge of God. Without it we cannot rightly know His Name, which is Love, nor His Son whom He sent to be the Saviour of the world. Our conception of the very God we worship must be distorted, and our spiritual life, which consists in the knowledge of Him, must be defective. His gospel will be shorn of half its truth and grace. What the world needs, in order to know the Father, and what the Church needs, in this day of its bewilderment concerning man's destiny, and the mystery of hell, is the recovery of the doctrine of a universal resurrection, from the region of despair and unending curse, to the ground upon which St. Paul placed it in his address before Felix, when he declared his "hope toward God that there shall be a resurrection, both of the just and of the unjust" (Acts xxiv. 15). Never shall we understand the Scriptures without this key,— that the provision in Christ to make all alive who died in Adam is God's way of making good His primal redemption promise to bless through a chosen seed all the families of the earth.

It will be apparent also to any who have followed us closely through this investigation, that it leaves the Bible doctrine of present and future punishment for sin unimpaired. In stripping it of the monstrosities with which our dim views of God's plan have clothed it, we have only made it more real. We have brought it nearer to men's consciences and to their apprehension. We have emphasized their present peril. We have called their attention away from a far distant lake of fire to a present hell, on the borders of which they daily tread, and whose fires of destruction are already kindled in their bodies and souls. We have warned them of the hell before resurrection as the penalty for sin in this life, rather than of the lake of fire which awaits the issues of a life to come. We have told them that increasing sin must intensify and prolong for them this hell, that resurrection can reach them only in their own time and order, that it cannot exempt men who continue in sin from future peril, nor exempt them from a second death, and that their lives can be saved from destruction, and purified and made eternal, only as they receive Christ, and so receive power to become the sons of God. The mass of men in Christian lands have generally rejected the old creed doctrine of endless torment. Many of them have rejected the whole system of faith, of which they have been taught to believe this forms a part. Others are being deluded with the fiction that the death state is not penalty, but extended probation. There is imperative need, therefore, that the true doctrine of immediate punishment, as we have found it presented in Scripture, should be brought out and set before them; that, on the one hand, they may be deterred from sin by its just and salutary view of the wrath to come and of a Judge standing at the door; and, on the other, may gain a true view of the face of their Father, God, now masked from them by the horrid distortions which men have drawn over it, and a true view also of the work of the Divine Saviour in their behalf, who gave Himself a ransom for all, to be testified in due time.

CHAPTER XIII.

IS THIS DOCTRINE PRACTICAL?

We began these discussions with the statement that, in the general drifting away from the old belief in eternal torment, the church was in great need of a good working doctrine of future punishment. By this we mean one that is true to Scripture, that commends itself to every man's conscience in the sight of God, and one that she can fearlessly and honestly proclaim. Such an one, we believe, is that to which these studies have conducted us. It makes a strong and rational appeal to the fears and to the consciences of men. At the same time it easily adjusts itself to all that we have learned of the nature of man, and of the character and purposes of God.

1. This doctrine appeals to the fears of men. It enables us to hold before them, in strict fidelity to the words of Jesus, the great danger to which they are exposed in the loss and utter bankruptcy of that estate in life with which they are now endowed. It makes death to be a deeper and more prolonged destruction than the dissolution of the body, reaching to a possible destruction of the soul in hell. It warns them that this peril is impending and not remote, that the tokens of it are now apparent in the debasement and ruin wrought in this world in the bodies and souls of men. It warns them that this ruin will be complete in death, and that no man can survive this crisis, and save his soul alive, who does not submit to the Lord Jesus Christ as His only Saviour from sin and death. Hell in this view is not a figure of

speech, but a veritable abyss of destruction, into which wicked men must be cast, not only by the sentence of the divine Judge, but by the law of nature and of life. And this doom does not await the issue of a remote trial at a distant judgment day. It is immediate. He, therefore, who would save his life, or save himself and not be cast away—as St. Luke phrases it (ix. 25), must fly for refuge to the hope set before him in the gospel. Here then is just the doctrine of hell our preachers need, who would be faithful to the Master's words.

2. It appeals to the consciences of men, in that it reveals this wages of sin to be the result of wrong-doing, and that it is only reached through a disregard of the warnings of natural law, the monitions of conscience, and by stemming the tide of those gracious and redemptive influences with which God is ever seeking to draw the sinner to himself.

3. It is also a reasonable and scientific view of man's future. It is not rational to suppose that any organized form of life can escape destruction which is not in perfect connection with the source of its life, and which contains within itself the principle of lawlessness. Such a principle is sin (1 John iii. 4). Science teaches that all imperfect forms of life are cast into the furnace of nature's consuming forces which burn with an eternal fire. And science also holds forth a hope of resurrection in showing how even these unworthy and cast-off forms are wrought over again in this alembic of fire.

4. This doctrine appeals to the hopes and highest aspirations of men, in that it shows how they may escape this impending loss of life and of self. It gives the

promise of the conservation of all the true elements of being through the crisis of death, and of a life emancipated, purified, ennobled, and transfigured into the likeness of the glorified manhood of the Lord on the other side of death.

5. It shows how in this way of life there is no respect of persons with God. If any are now called to enter into life it is only in that way of self-sacrifice which surrenders the old man of sin to destruction in His consuming fire. For it is not God *out of* Christ, as the passage is constantly misquoted and misapplied, but God *in* Christ, *Our* God, who is a consuming fire. Every one must be salted with fire (Mark ix. 43-49). It is not *from* judgment for sin, but *through* judgment that he saves. The whole doctrine of atonement and of the forgiveness of sins needs to be re-examined in the light of this great principle. The cross is not God's arrangement by which any sinner may go scot-free from deserved penalty. It is not a device by which a special class can slip through. It is not a bargain by which a certain number of souls have been bought off from eternal torments. It is God's way of condemning sin in the flesh, and of bringing the old man in us to the altar of sacrifice to be consumed by the fire. We are saved, not by escaping the fire of His anger against our sins, but by submitting to it. The Christian accepts the judgment against himself, rendered at the cross, and his death to sin becomes the way of life. The unbeliever refuses to submit himself to the righteousness of God, and must be overwhelmed in the fire that goeth before Him to burn up all His enemies. But the principle of His administration toward both

classes is the same. Towards all that is evil in both He is a consuming fire. And without holiness no man shall see the Lord.

6. While this doctrine proclaims the terrors of the Lord, it enables us at the same time to hold fast to all the testimonies of His grace. It harmonizes the two parallel lines of Scripture teaching concerning judgment and redemption, and shows that God's terrible acts of righteousness are not inconsistent with his essential nature, Love. It shows that what He is in this world He will be in all worlds. His attitude toward sinful man is not changed by death. His judgments are never vindictive. Neither the law, nor the grace, of His administration is ever set aside. A resurrection awaits the sinner out of the pit of destruction into which his sins have cast him, as the result of the ransom paid for all. Redeeming mercy does not forsake him. And yet judgment for his sins must first be satisfied. It must be intensified and prolonged, according to his desert of few or many stripes. These terms "few" and "many," however, imply a limit. The Lord does not say the greater sinner shall be forever beaten with heavier stripes, but with more in number, and the lesser sinner with less. But the stripes, in either case, are not immeasurable. There is an end to both. From the nature of the case, as well as from the teaching of Scripture, we know that all are not freed together. And the law of all life must still prevail to make even resurrected life a burdened and a crippled one, if it be not freed from sin. There is a resurrection of judgment. To every seed his own body. This doctrine, therefore, does not encourage

the sinner to take low or loose views of the requirements of God's law, or of the abatement of its claims. It does not open any other door than the strait and narrow one which leadeth unto life. Resurrection opens no other door. It re-opens to him indeed the door of hope, but then, as well as now, any other way than the right way will end in another death and a lake of fire. Here then is a doctrine of ceaseless punishment for the sinner so long as he remains a sinner, and of eternal death at the end, if he will not humble himself under the mighty hand of God;—but a doctrine also of recovering grace that is not foiled by death, that changes not from age to age, that meets and baffles man's enemies who have dragged him down to death, by new displays of grace and power, and new conquests over death and him that hath the power of it, that is, the devil. Both these sides of truth, and both these aspects of the character and purposes of God are necessary to save us from wrong notions of His ways, and from a distorted conception of Him, in the knowledge of whom standeth our eternal life. What the world is aweary for, and what the Church is languishing for, is a right knowledge of God. No temporary success, or hold on men through their fears, can begin to compensate for the immense damage that must come to them through false or monstrous ideas of God. These underlie everything in religious and moral life. Men become like the God they worship. No greater service, therefore, can be rendered them than one which helps to remove the vail that obscures His face, and shows them that He whom they thought of as a tyrant or a pitiless judge, is the Father, whose pity for

His offspring, and whose gracious purposes, are not circumscribed by this little span of human life, but that He is the same just and loving God, yesterday, to-day, and forever.

Such is the doctrine the Church needs to give her success, because it is the true doctrine and the full gospel. The world can never be frightened by fears to Christ, nor won by a mutilated gospel. Catholic Christianity has not been able to hold more than half the lands once won. Protestant Christianity, still more severe in its dogmas about the future, discarding any relief, such as purgatory gave in the older system, has waned in all the lands of the Reformation. It is scarcely holding its own in this most favored land; for numbers are sometimes a deceptive standard. It makes much of its missionary zeal and conquests. But it is estimated that the addition to the ranks of Pagans and Mahometans by natural increase are fifty times as great as the converts from among them to Christianity. The Church has been seeking to evangelize these millions with a gospel that largely conceals the grace of God, that draws a dark veil over His face, and denies that it is glad tidings of great joy to all people. Her success either at home or abroad furnishes no argument against the trial of some new and more merciful view. The world has not been won, and cannot be, in any way that conceals from men the true knowledge of God. The Holy Spirit will not honor testimony that robs the mission of the Lord Christ of half its grace and glory. Nor can an appeal to men's fears avail which so exaggerates its terrors that the very men who utter it recoil from it, while their hearers are only dazed and stunned into stolidity or unbelief. We want a rational doctrine of hell, as well as a full gospel proclamation of Him who holds its keys, and whose resurrection shed down its light of hope among the "spirits in prison," the myriads of earth's dead who have been carried away captive into its dark domain. And we need to arouse men, not only by the hope of individual salvation,—a hope not free from selfishnesss—but by the high aim of fellowship with Christ in present sacrifice, that so, baptized for the dead, they may be fitted to take part with Him in those ever-widening conquests by which He shall recover from the land of the enemy the captive multitudes of our race for whom His soul travailed unto death. The anxious cry of the heathen, "What of our ancestors?" when they first hear the gospel, would find here its satisfying answer.

APPENDIX A.

THE TIME OF RESURRECTION.

Upon this point a variety of opinions prevail among Christians.

1. The traditional opinion is that the countless multitudes who have lived upon the earth are all to be raised together, good and bad, at the last day.

2. The extreme opposite doctrine is that of Swedenborg, which has also its adherents in various evangelical churches. It is that, upon the death of the material body, man emerges into a spiritual world in a spiritual body. Death and resurrection are two parts of but one process.

3. Many advocates of conditional immortality hold that all men, even the saints, remain unconscious in death until the resurrection, which they believe will occur at a great crisis of the future—the coming of the Lord. They believe, however, in the first resurrection of the saints, and that, after a long interval, the wicked will be raised and punished by being consigned to extinction in the lake of fire, which is the second death.

4. Others, who reject the idea of the unconscious sleep of the soul—especially in the case of the saved—before resurrection, still hold to the idea that it is eclectic and progressive. "Every man in his own order."

As between the old traditional opinion that resurrection is simultaneous, and this view that it is progressive, there can be no doubt that the latter is taught in Scripture. The passage which seems most to favor the view that all classes are raised together is St. John v. 28, 29.

But the "hour" of vs. 25 is so manifestly a period of long continuance that we are not only justified, but obliged to regard the hour of universal resurrection (vs. 29) as a prolonged administration of the Son of Man, during which He shall recover all the captives in the realms of death. And various other passages teach plainly that there is "a first resurrection" (Rev. xx. 5, 6); that there is a chosen company first gathered from the harvest fields of death (Phil. iii. 11), "out from among the dead." "They that are Christ's at his coming."

The first view, which we have classed as Swedenborgian, makes the Scripture promise of *anastasis*, or resurrection, to be simply the promise of a future life. And that man enters upon this life immediately upon death is affirmed from such Scriptures as our Lord's conversation with the Sadducees (Luke xx. 26–38), in which He establishes the fact of resurrection by declaring that God's words to Moses about Abraham, Isaac, and Jacob imply that these patriarchs were still living, and, therefore, raised out of death. The appearance of Moses and Elijah, with Jesus, on the Mount is also appealed to. Also His words to the dying thief, "To-day shalt thou be with me in Paradise." Paul's words in 2 Cor. v, also seem to imply that immediately upon his putting off of this earthly tabernacle, he would find a "heavenly house" awaiting him in which he would be at home with the Lord. Other of his writings, however, assume that during the interval preceding the Lord's manifestation from heaven the saints would be asleep (1 Cor. xv. 51; 1 Thess. iv. 13–15), out of which they would be aroused by the trumpet-sound of some signal triumph over the empire of death.

The truth, we believe, lies between these two views. The Swedenborgian view is defective,

1. In the fact that it does not give proper weight to the fact of death as the wages of sin, and of that death-state which lies beyond the grave,—the sheol and hell of Scripture. It makes death to be simply the loss of well-being, and strips of its proper meaning the sentence, "The soul that sinneth it shall die."

2. It does not appreciate the fact that man is more than "a spiritual being." He holds relation to this created system. He is destined to unfettered dominion over it. For this purpose his body is to be redeemed and the whole creation to be delivered into the liberty of his glory (Rom. viii. 19–21). While, therefore, it is freely conceded that saved men enter upon a future life at once upon their departure out of this world, and that the words of Jesus that such "never die" require this, we must also hold that they do not attain the complete glory of the resurrection state, nor enter upon its full activities, until this emancipation of the creature. The full redemption of man requires his re-investure with a body suited to a redeemed creation. Such a cosmical change seems plainly set forth in Scripture. Its closing pages are gilded with the glory of it.

Both sides of the truth concerning man's future life may be reconciled by bearing in mind what we have learned of his nature as body, soul, and spirit. We have seen that the "soul" is virtually an intermediate embodiment of the spirit, that it survives the death of the carnal body, that the righteous man saves his soul alive through this crisis, and is therefore never completely disembodied or "unclothed," while the soul of the wicked may be destroyed in hell. All that Scripture hints at, therefore, concerning the continued and blessed life of the righteous after death, is conserved by this view of the salvation of his soul. This answers all the requirements of an intermediate ethereal body. While all that it suggests concerning a future investiture of the saints with a glorified humanity, crowned on the summit of creation as its head and lord, is provided for by this view of a completed resurrection, when all things shall be made new. And all that it teaches concerning the death of the wicked, their ejection out of the sphere of man's life and heritage, and their inferior and long-delayed recovery through resurrection, is held fast to. While its doctrine of resurrection as eclectic and progressive, corresponds with that doctrine of Science which requires that cosmical changes, and transformations in created life, be viewed as proceeding by stages, and each in their own order. It can reach no one until he is prepared for it, and it can lift no one above that plane of being for which he is prepared. Scripture, however, shows that a blessed principle has been incorporated into humanity, by which those who reach the highest plane are made capable of reaching down a helping hand to those who are struggling on the arenas below. Saved themselves, they find their highest happiness in becoming saviours of others.

As to the time, then, of the resurrection of the good, we would say that they enter upon the future life at once, and in this sense are raised out of death, their souls surviving this crisis. But they do not take on that form of glorified manhood, which is the heir of all things, until all things are ready for their manifestation as the sons of God. As to the wicked, while their souls in suffering survive the death of the body, yet the light of life in them must vanish away. And resurrection cannot reach them until after their death-sentence has been exhausted. Their release seems to be connected with, and dependent upon, certain future triumphs over the empire of death and hell, and certain changes in the present natural order, which open the way for gracious intervention in their behalf by that royal priesthood of the future of which Christ is the head. We may not venture to say what anticipations or preparations for these deliverances may now be going on in the unseen world.

APPENDIX B.

THE LAW OF THE FIRST-BORN.

Much light upon the doctrines of retribution and redemption may yet come to us by the careful study from Scripture of the law of the first-born. Theology has given prominence to the individual relations which men hold to God and to one another, to the neglect of the organic relations they sustain to Him as members of one race and as united in families. In the economy of God and of nature there is a race life, a race redemption, and a race accountability. We hear nowadays much about the law of heredity. This law shows how the ancestral life lives in the descendant, how it moulds form and feature, and weaves itself into nerve-fibre and brain-tissue, and into the finer fabric of the soul. The blood that flows in the veins of each living man has been distilled in the veins of many generations behind him. Each man has to fight over again the battles with temptation in which his fathers fought. He inherits the vices of his lineage, its weaknesses and passions. Perhaps, as the penalties he incurs are those of his race, the victories he wins may also be won for them. It was an instinct of the Jewish family to look for a saviour in its own line.

The law of heredity thus connects itself with the law of penalty, the law of vicarious sacrifice, and the law of redemption. All this comes out in the Scripture teaching concerning the law of the first-born. It views the first-born as the eminent depositary and representative of race and family life, weighted with its penalties, incurring its responsibilities, and charged with the privilege and duty of its redemption.

1. The penalty of sin is corruption of life and consequent death. Cain was not the first to die of Adam's seed, but he was the most deeply infected with the taint which had come into the race-life. Eve fondly hoped that he would prove to be the promised deliverer. She said, "I have gotten a man from the Lord." But he proved to be a murderer. He was eminently, indeed, the man of nature. "Howbeit, that which is first is natural." He was the first to cultivate and subdue the earth, the first city-builder, the ancestor of the first great leaders in the world's civilization, of those who first taught men the mechanic arts and the fine arts. But he was also the first man of pride, and greed, and envy. And the way of Cain proved to be, to that antediluvian world, the way of death. Subsequent examples of first-born sons who were a disappointment, and whose eminence was along this line of natural evil which ends in death, are numerous. Especially is this fact apparent in the line of the chosen people. Ishmael was Abraham's first-born "after the flesh." But he was set aside in favor of Isaac "born after the Spirit." Esau was hated and Jacob loved. Reuben defiled his father's bed, and Judah was set above him. "Er, Judah's first born, was wicked in the sight of the Lord; and the Lord slew him." (Gen. xxxviii. 7). Ephraim was placed before Manasseh. Nadab, Aaron's first-born, offered strange fire and died before the Lord. Korah, the leader of the rebellion against Moses and Aaron, was a first-born son. Not to multiply instances, the fact is apparent from Scripture that

the first-born were viewed as specially inheritors of the curse that had come upon the race, and therefore foremost in incurring the penalty of sin which is death. The first-born of every household in the land of Egypt were stricken down by the angel of death in a single night. And even the first-born of Israel were regarded as "devoted to death," and as needing to be redeemed from it. (Ex. xiii. 15; Numbers viii. 16, 17). The worshippers of Moloch, who offered their first-born, "the fruit of the body for the sin of the soul" did so through a perverted recognition of this law of the race-life, that the "sons of their strength," were under a special obligation to pay down the wages of its sin, which is death. They knew nothing, however, of God's purposes of redemption. These He taught to Israel. The forfeited lives of their first-born were redeemed by the offered lives of the lambs slain at the passover. Thus were the first-born viewed as first-bearers of the penalty.

2. But they had also special privileges and responsibilities. They were the natural elders and princes of the people. They were the first in the line of inheritance. They received a double portion (Deut. xx. 7). And they were also priests. God says of Israel, whom He sanctified unto Himself as a "kingdom of priests," (Ex. xix. 6), "Israel is my son, my first-born" (iv. 22). The first-born of that nation, however, might be redeemed from the obligations of the priestly office. The tribe of Levi was set apart in lieu of all the first-born. And the number of them in excess of the males of that tribe were redeemed by a money payment of five shekels apiece (Numbers iii. 44-51).

3. A duty of vicarious sacrifice for the family was put upon the first-born. Their devotion to death seemed measurably to answer the claim of death upon the rest of the household, and to bring them temporary and typical exemption. The death of Egypt's first-born sufficed to the sparing of the rest. And their death was deliverance to Israel (Ex. xii. 27). The rod with which the Lord punished David for his sin smote first Amnon, his first-born. And Absalom, the first-born of another wife, after bringing untold shame and sorrow on his father, met an untimely death. Bathsheba's first-born son must die, but a younger son, Solomon, came to the throne. The first-born were thus appointed to bear the brunt of the family curse to the partial relief of the rest. But it was as priests, rather than victims, that their standing for the family was most apparent. We have seen, however, that they might be redeemed from the obligation to devote themselves to priestly functions. And this leads us to observe,

4. That these prerogatives and functions of the natural first-born could not be worthily discharged by them, and so God has selected and qualified a spiritual seed, to take the place of the first-born in a higher order of life than the natural, and who become, therefore, a royal priesthood forever. This was foreshown all along the line of human history. Cain and his offering were rejected. Abel became the true priest, offering unto God a more acceptable sacrifice. Ishmael, born after the flesh, was cast out and Isaac, "born after the Spirit," became the heir and channel of blessing. David inherits before Eliab, and Solomon comes into the place of Amnon. The

same truth was taught in the consecration of a special tribe to serve as priests in place of the first-born of all Israel. This priestly class must come into the special place of self-devotion. Their natural rights must be surrendered in service and sacrifice. They had no inheritance among their brethren. The Old Testament economy, however, could not develop in its completeness this spiritual seed. It only prepared the way for the coming of Him who was the true First-Born of the sons of men, both in the order of creation and redemption (Col. i. 15-20). The only begotten Son of God, He is also preeminently the Son of man, summing up in Himself all man's prerogatives, assuming all his responsibilities, bearing all his curse, devoted to service, to sacrifice and to death, and now standing before God in the power of an endless life, our High Priest forever after the order of Melchizedec. But He is also the Head of a body, a spiritual seed chosen from mankind, who are a church of the first-born, a royal priesthood, the first fruits of God's creatures. They, under Him, as members of His body, constitute that anointed seed of the human race who are called into the place of the first-born, with its dignities, its responsibilities, and its duties. It is by the offering of themselves in sacrifice to God that they bring salvation to their brethren (2 Cor. iv. 10-12). Jesus, the Head, so offered Himself for us, and, as the Head of humanity, for the sins of the whole world. But we are called to be sharers in His sacrifice, to yield up our old natural manhood to death, to fill up that which is behind in His afflictions for His body's sake, the church (Col i. 24; Phil. iii. 10), to lay down our lives for the brethren, to have great heaviness and sorrow of heart for our brethren and kinsmen according to the flesh who yet know not Him, (Rom. ix. 2, 3), and to be sharers in that love for the world that gave Him to be the propitiation for its sins (1 Jno. iv. 8-10). This is that spiritual seed, Abraham's true children by faith, in whom all the families of the earth are to be blessed. But they can become a blessing only as the Christ-nature is formed in them, leading them to sacrifice and service, to take upon their own hearts the sins, the woes and burdens of their brethren, to stand for them in the place of death, and so to transmit to others the power of that redemption which Christ has brought to them, and of which He is the only source to the world. They thus fulfil the first-born's duty of penalty, of sacrifice, and of redemption. Jesus, as the First-Born of humanity, did this for the race. But the race is to be saved by generations, by families and kindreds. These terms, as constantly used in Scripture, show how we are bound together by organic ties. The pious Jew was not taught to expect his personal salvation apart from that of his own people. Race-life, lines of lineage, corporate communities bound together by ties of kindred and sharing in a common ancestral life, seem to be embraced in the sweep of this redemption. The taint of evil goes down to the third and fourth generation. The second commandment teaches this. After that the remedial power in the principle of life would seem to be able to neutralize or eliminate the evil. The good effects of piety and virtue go down, however, to thousands of generations. Such is the law of heredity. And such the priestly efficacy for good to coming generations in those who rise above the level and the downward tendencies of the life of the race, and of their ancestral life. They lift up those who are to come after, and especially those of their own blood. The channels of their family life become purified. In this domain, physical and moral transformations proceed together.

It is easy enough to perceive and confess this in respect to those who come after us. But how about those who have gone before, the brethren of our lineage who have fallen in the battle of life, who are now lying maimed and captive in the land of the enemy. What reference to them is there in the Scripture promises "All generations shall call Him blessed?" Will God's faithfulness be made known to the generations past, as well as to come? Psalm lxxxix may teach us something upon this point. After proclaiming God's faithfulness in the opening verses the writer seems to raise this very question in the closing verses. He asks, is it possible that death has defeated all these promises, and made void these sure mercies of David to the generations who have gone down to death?

"For what vanity hast Thou created all the children of men! What man is he that shall live and not see death, that shall deliver his soul from the power of Sheol? Lord, where are thy former mercies which Thou swarest unto David in thy faithfulness? Remember, Lord, the reproach of thy servants : How I do bear in my bosom the reproach of all the many peoples ; wherewith thine enemies have reproached, O, Lord, wherewith they have reproached the footsteps of thine anointed."

This is but one of many Scriptures which imply that death has broken God's covenant and made void His promises, unless He shall prove Himself victorious over death, and in spite of it, find a way to bless the generations who have gone down to Sheol. But this is the very thing He sent His Christ to do. As the First-Born of Jehovah, as well as of the race (vs. 27), He was raised from the dead to perform for us the near kinsman's part, to raise up the name of the dead upon their inheritance, to gather under a new headship the generations of men, to set the scattered and solitary ones in families, to bridge the chasm between the dead and the living, and to prove Himself the Lord of both. He is eminently the Priest upon His throne for all mankind. But under Him, His brethren, who are also a kingdom of priests, and who are the first to share His triumph over death, must hold a special relation in this work to the generations and families from which they sprang. The first in the line of their ancestral life to rise into the glory and strength of the eternal life, they must especially be helpers of their brethren and kinsmen according to the flesh. These organic ties which hold men together as one in race, and lineage, and family are made too much of in Scripture for us to deny that they will have no place in the unfolding of God's redemptive plan. That plan provides for the salvation of a chosen seed out of all kindreds and tongues, a first fruits unto God and the Lamb, who fulfil in blessed completeness the office of first-born to their brethren. Saved themselves, they become saviours of others. Paul, as one born before the time, became a first-born priest toward a saved remnant of his brethren. This remnant, according to the election of grace, became the first fruits of all Israel (Rom. xi). For if the first fruit be holy, the lump is also holy. First-born from the dead imply later born. The first-hopers in Christ are the first-ordained vessels of His grace in the dispensation for the gathering together in one all things in heaven and on earth (Eph. i. 10–12).

We shall not be far out of the way, therefore, if we conclude that the "kings and priests" of God's kingdom are to be occupied in saving ministries, which shall prove them to be indeed brothers born for adversity to their captive brethren, who, for their sins, have gone down as prisoners in the pit, who have lost their heritage of life and blessing, and who, on earth, were ignorant and out of the way because no man cared for their souls, or told them the way of life.

And what motives from this point of view open up to us for faith in, and devotion to, the Lord Jesus Christ, beyond the selfish one of individual salvation. We are called into fellowship with Christ in His sufferings, being made conformable unto His death, not only that we may attain unto the resurrection from among the dead, but that, like Him, we may help others to attain it. If we fight this battle of life through to victory for ourselves, we shall help others of our kind in the struggle. We become princes and priests to our own kindred in this larger field of God's working to bless all the kindreds of the earth. And what new power would such a gospel carry with it to the heathen. It would mean to the Chinaman, for example, taught to reverence his ancestors, that God was calling him into fellowship with His Son, that, as sharing in his sacrifice and service he would be qualified to bring this divine healing and salvation within the reach ot his ancestors who had died without the sight So might he be baptized for the dead. Faith on the Lord

Jesus Christ would thus acquire that larger meaning given to it in the first sermons of the apostles, where faith for ourselves as individuals is merged into a broad faith in Him as a Messiah for the race, anointed to restore all things and to be the Judge, in the large Old Testament conception of that office, of both the living and the dead. And the eternal life to which we are invited, and which stretches out before us in boundless prospect, would be seen to be no life of selfish ease and indolent enjoyment, but a life filled up with royal and priestly ministrations which shall show forth unto the ages to come the manifold wisdom of God, and bring Him glory by the church unto all generations, world without end.

A full view of this whole subject requires us, however, to note that there was such a thing as " a cutting off from among his people," repeatedly spoken of in the old Testament (Ex. xii. 15, 19; Lev. xvii. 4, 9; xx. 3, etc.). No encouragement is given, by this principle of family priesthood, to men to go on in sin in the hope of such future intervention in their behalf. For sin must surely be punished under the righteous government of God, and men may place themselves outside of, and beyond the reach of those remedial agencies which God has provided, and through which His forgiving grace follows men even to seventy times and seven. All we are assured of is that death cannot forever interrupt all these lines of God's gracious working. But, beyond that gracious intervention which has secured for all a recovery from death, there lies the possible peril of a final cutting off by the second death, beyond which God has not chosen to lift the veil.

INDEX.

A Divided Church an imperfect witness 2
Ages 130
Aionion 113, 126, 129. 189
Agents of God's judgments, 72, 99, 107, 156.
Alger, quotations from ...78, 81, 82
Andover Review 44
Angels, connected with the powers of Nature, 38, 39, 99, 107, 156.
Apocrypal Opinions 78
Assyria 58

Babylon 55
Babylon—type of world-religion 68
Baptized for the Dead 198, 267
Baptism of Fire 89
Beast and False Prophet 222
Blessing for the Dead ... 66, 193, 265
Body, Soul and Spirit, 101, 128, 141, 242, 257.
Book of Life 161, 166, 168, 216

Captivity Captive 64
Christ, appearing of, 107, 121, 126, 224.
Christ, the Deliverer 124
Christ, the glorified Man, 110, 113, 120, 144.
Christ, judge of the living and dead 113, 151, 154, 172, 268
Christ, the only Saviour 245, 247
Christ, the Prince of Life 114
Christ, the perfect Man 107
Christian Consciousness 134, 135
Christian Liberty 1
Church, a chosen seed, 160, 182, 194, 233.
Church, a first born company, 159, 226, 263, 266.

Church, a first fruits 159, 194
Church, a priestly company, 159, 193, 258, 262.

Day of Judgment 139, 207, 209
Day of the Lord 209, 218
Dead the, defined as Captives, 27, 33, 45, 47, 49, 53, 55, 59, 233.
Death, Egypt a type of 45
Death, idea of 27
Death, the enemy of God and man 18
Death, the penalty of sin, 32, 98, 100, 101, 121, 141, 186, 187, 201, 241, 260.
Death, to be destroyed 20
Devil and his angels ...108, 130, 210
Devil has the power of death ...109
Demons, }
Devils, } 37, 140, 143
Destruction, *qua homo*, 101, 180, 187, 201, 242.
Disciples, law of life for 96
Diseases, due to satanic power ..109
Dives and Lazarus 98, 138, 236
Doctrine of the Magi 77, 83
Doctrine of the Pharisees 82, 141
Dragon, the 52
Disembodiment, penal, 143, 192, 242

Egypt, type of Sheol, 45, 47, 53, 56, 58.
Election 194
Endless Punishment, not taught in the Old Testament 5, 77
Eternal Fire 77, 122, 126, 212
Eternal Fire, a fact of Science, 104, 224.
Eternal Fire, a servant of God, 114
"Eternal Hope" 9, 130
Eternal Life 106, 170, 191, 268

Index.

Eternal Life, its mastery..........114
Eternal Torment, unscriptural,178, 183, 196, 198, 200, 213, 228.
Evolution 106, 243

Farrar, Archdeacon..............9, 81
Fire...................................14, 17
Fire, the old man must be consigned to........................ 91
First Resurrection..................159
Forgiveness of Sins.................249

Gehenna........80, 81, 82, 90, 94, 112
Gentiles, God's dealings with, 25, 195.
Gentiles, promised deliverance through resurrection, 66, 67, 75.
God, our Redeemer...............18, 62
God, character of, 8, 133, 134, 171, 244, 250.
God, a consuming fire, 35, 42, 71, 90.
God revealed in nature 104
God, right knowledge of..........251

Hades......................26, 45, 97, 233
Heaven and Earth............165, 210
Hell...................121, 173, 206, 236
Hell, first mention of 13
Hell, not a figure of speech.....248
Hodge, Dr. A. A., quotation from 127
Human race, bound by organic ties....................................264

Idolatry..............................37, 38
Intermediate state, for the wicked, penal.......................245
Israel, lost tribes of 63
Israel, unregenerate, to be redeemed through resurrection 62

Jewish Liturgy...................... 22
Jewish opinion............77, 141, 178
Josephus, quotations from..83, 141
Judgment, a present fact, 120, 125, 170.

Judgment before resurrection, 92, 102, 118, 128, 140, 162, 173, 189, 203, 206, 208, 236.
Judgment, broad view of, 146, 152, 157, 164.
Judgment, disciplinary.........30, 36
Judgment, not a mere assize, 152, 168.
Judgment, powers of Nature the agents of............74, 99, 107

Kingsley, Charles................... 78
Kolasis, meaning of................131

Lake of Fire............169, 212, 224
Law of heredity.........168, 259, 264
Law of the first born...............259
Life, development of.........105, 243
Life, remedial power of......168, 204

Man, an embodied image of God 98
Man, destiny of................142, 241
Man, his punishment..........98, 242
Man, not inherently immortal, 201, 240.
Man, tripartite nature of 101
"Mercy and Judgment,"......9, 81
Millenarianism...................... 63
Missions, basis of............252, 267
Mystery of Evil..................15, 39

"Natural Law in the Spiritual world," 243
Nature, constitution of............105
Nature, forces of, execute the divine judgments.......107, 156,
Nature, Satan's power in, to be overthrown 40, 41, 210
Nature, to be renewed.........71, 109
Nature, viewed as sharing in man's sin......13, 36, 39, 42, 210

Old Testament, Eternal torment not a doctrine of, 7, 22, 75, 133, 134.
Old Testament, low views of its Inspiration 43
Old Testament, resurrection taught in 43, 54, 122

Index. 277

Old Testament, summary of, 87, 235, 239.
Outcasts..................53, 65

Phelps, Prof. Austin...........178
Plumptree, Dean............ 83
Prince of this World...... 14, 19, 40
Punishment of Sin............ 98
Punishment inevitable........25, 110
Punishment, Old Testament idea of..................28
Pusey, Dr. 9, 80, 81
Probation closed............161
Probation for resurrection.......205
Probation, future............241

Rabbinical doctrine......78, 81, 141
Rephaim............27, 45, 50
Restitution......41, 78, 109, 165, 224
Resurrection eclectic..160, 192, 257
Resurrection its meaning not at once unfolded............238
Resurrection, not simultaneous, 160, 166, 254.
Resurrection of judgment, 69, 138, 167, 250.
Resurrection of life............142
Resurrection Redemptive, 18, 43, 47, 50, 57, 83, 122, 144, 192, 196, 211, 244
Resurrection taught in the Old Testament 40, 47, 53
Resurrection, Time of..........254
Retribution in Apostolic Preaching 173, 238
Retribution in St. Paul's Epistles..................183
Retribution in the Catholic Epistles..................199
Retribution in the Revelation...215
Retribution, inevitable, 231, 240, 245
Review..................230

Salvation of Infants............148
Salvation through Judgment, 89, 96.

Salting with Fire............95
Satan 15, 19
Satan bound 225
Science, teachings of...105, 243, 248
Second death........92, 147, 160, 201
Septuagint............20, 44
Sermon on the Mount............94
Sheol......26, 27, 45, 49, 97, 139, 233
Sodom and Samaria........66, 162
Song of Moses............10-23
Soul, distinct from Spirit, 101, 128, 256.
Soul, destructible............101, 247
Soul, pertains to embodiment, 138, 139.
Spirits in Prison............203
Spiritual discernment needed......2
St. Paul on Retribution......179, 183
Summary of New Testament doctrine 235
Swedenborgian view.........255, 256

Talmud 81
Targums.................. 82
The Gospel.........154, 172, 252
The Lord will judge His people, 17, 35.

Unquenchable Fire............71
Use of term in Old Testament, 72, 74.
Use of term in New Testament, 90, 95, 236.
Universalism not taught, 131, 157, 170, 227, 230.

Way of Cain............260
Way of Life 249
Westminster Confession........5, 178
Wrong Method of Inquiry..........8

Zoroastrian Doctrine............80

Index of Scripture Texts.

GENESIS.

I., 26–28 165
II., 17..230
XII., 3.......................................69, 172
XXII., 18..229
XXXVIII, 7......................................260

EXODUS.

IV., 22...261
XII., 15–19.......................................268
XII., 27..262
XIII., 15...261
XIX., 6..261

LEVITICUS.

XVII., 7..37
XX., 3...268
XXVI., 25...32
XXVI, 41–43..................17, 30, 147

NUMBERS.

III., 44–51......................................261
VIII., 16..261
XVI., 30...162

DEUTERONOMY.

IV., 19 38
IV., 24...72
IX., 3 99
XVII., 2...38
XX., 7..261
XXIII., 27..40
XXVIII...26
XXX., 4...33
XXXII., 22–24..........................99, 123
XXXII., 10–23.........................216, 231
XXXII., 36.....................35, 147, 234
XXXII., 43...................37, 67, 195

JOB.

I., 12–19..109

III., 18.......................................27, 45
XIV., 10–12.......................................26
XVII., 16....................................27, 45

PSALMS.

VIII., 2 ....40, 165
IX., 17...27, 137
XXII., 27–31..................................148
XXXVI., 6...36
XLII., 9...40
XLIV., 16..40
XLIX., 15..45
LXVIII., 18–22................................47
LXVIII., 49.....................................109
LXIX., 1–4.....................................111
LXXVII., 8.....................................136
LXXIX., 10, 11......................46, 234
LXXXVI., 9......................................69
LXXXVIII., 10–12...........................45
LXXXIX., 265................................265
XCII., 9 29
XCVI. 152
XCVII., 3............................35, 42, 72
CII., 18–20 ....46, 234
CIII., 7–9...............................20–32
CIII., 20, 21. 38
CVI., 43–45.....................................30
CVII., 2..40
CXVI., 3–9, 15, 16..........................49
CXVII...195
CXLI., 7..23
CXLII., 4–7.....................................48
CXLIII., 3–16..................................48

PROVERBS.

XXIX., 1..32

ISAIAH.

I., 24–27..42
II., 18..37
IV., 4...57, 77
XI 152
XIII., 1–13.....................................217
XIX., 24, 25....................................66

XXII., 14	27, 82
XXIV	25
XXIV., 21–23	37, 59
XXV., 8	44, 124
XXV.–XXVIII	50
XXVI., 8	42
XXVI., 8–21	51
XXVI., 14	26
XXVI., 17, 18	44, 51
XXVII., 1	40, 52
XXVII., 12	53, 65
XXX., 18	42
XXXIII., 14	6
XXXIV., 1–4	217
XXXIV., 8–11	73, 221
XL., 1, 2	31
XL., 26	37
XLII., 22	27, 53
XLIII., 1	53
XLIX., 5	40
XLIX., 5–10, 24, 25	55, 234
LI., 6–14	56
LI., 39	26
LVII., 16	33
LXIII., 9	41
LXV., 17	41, 165
LXVI., 14–24	72
LXVI., 24	6, 95, 133

JEREMIAH.

VII., 20	73
X., 11	37
X., 24	57
XVI., 4–16	57, 59
XVII., 27	6
XVIII., 4	73
XXI., 12	6, 73
XXX., 10–17	58
XXXI., 10–16	58, 234
XXXII., 7, 11, 26	45, 59
XXXIII., 5	59
XXXIII., 44	59
XLVIII., 47	66, 75
XLIX., 6, 39	45, 66

LAMENTATIONS.

III., 34	27

EZEKIEL.

XVI., 53–63	66, 235
XX., 47	74, 99

XXXIII., 22–32	28
XXXVI	60
XXXVII., 11–14	28, 61
XXXVIII	74

DANIEL.

VII	119, 163
VII., 11	148, 223
XII., 2	6, 133

HOSEA.

XIII., 9	44
XIII., 14	44, 62, 124, 234
XIV., 4	62

JOEL.

II	217

MICAH.

VII., 7–10	30, 33, 36

HABBAKUK.

III., 5	72

ZEPHANIAH.

II., 11	37
III., 8	74
III., 14–20	64

ZECHARIAH.

IX., 11	33, 64
X., 8, 9	65

MALACHI.

IV., 1	74, 89

MATTHEW.

II., 17, 18	59
III., 10–12	88
V., 29, 30	94
X., 7, 8	159
X., 28	94, 101
XI., 23	98
XIII., 41, 42	107
XVI., 27, 28	119

280   *Index of Scripture Texts.*

XVIII., 8, 9	94
XXIII., 15, 33	95
XXIV., 29–35	120
XXIV., 34	237
XXV., 31–46	112, 115, 151, 156, 189, 237

MARK.

III., 29	147
IX, 43–50	95, 249
XIII., 3	117

LUKE.

I., 46–55	123
I., 68–79	123
I., 70, 71	41
II., 29–32	123
VI., 27–37	137
IX., 25	248
X., 19	109
XI., 14–18	109
XII., 47	249
XIII., 16	109
XVI., 19–31	98
XVII., 26–31	208
XX., 26–38	255
XXI., 28	120

JOHN.

III., 18	138, 147, 161
III., 36	147, 161
V., 23	153
V., 25	163
V., 28, 29	113, 138, 151, 153, 162, 163, 205, 254
VIII., 52	114
X., 28	114
XII., 31	14
XV., 6	199
XVII., 2	113

ACTS.

II., 16–20	217
III., 19–21	175, 180
III., 21–26	124
IV., 12	175
VII., 51–53	175
IX., 20, 21	176
X., 38	109
X., 42	151
XIII., 10	176
XIII., 41	176
XIII., 48	19
XVI., 30	177
XVII., 31	156, 177
XXIV., 15	129, 180, 191, 244
XXVI., 6	43
XXVIII., 23–28	177

ROMANS.

I., 19	185
I., 32	186
II., 5	185
II., 6–10	185
II., 12	186
III., 12–19	161
V., 12–20	122, 191
VI., 23	186
VII., 9, 13, 24	187
VIII., 19–21	67, 69, 109, 130, 211, 256
VIII., 29	194
IX., 22	187
XI	195, 266
XIV., 11	185
XIV., 9	151, 153, 185
XV., 8, 9	124, 195
XV., 10	20
XVI., 26	129
IX., 2, 3	264

I. CORINTHIANS.

I., 18	187
III., 13–17	199, 216
V., 5	186, 199, 216
VIII., 2	2
X., 9, 10	187
XI., 30–32	186
XV., 18	187
XV., 22	122, 164, 192
XV., 23	159
XV., 32	187
XV., 40	143
XV., 51	255
XV., 55	4

II. CORINTHIANS.

II., 15	187
IV, 10–12	263
V., 1	142, 255
V., 10	144, 167, 185
VI., 9, 10	190

GALATIANS.

VI., 7, 8	91, 145

EPHESIANS.

I., 4, 5, 11	194
I., 10	195, 267
I., 12–14	194
I., 20–23	113
II., 2	109
III., 8–10	195
III., 15	195
VI., 10, 20	217
VI., 12	39, 109

PHILLIPIANS.

II., 10	196
III., 10	263
III., 11	159, 192
III., 19	187
III., 21	143

COLOSSIANS.

I., 14	14, 120
I., 15–20	263
I., 16–18	133
I., 24	263
I., 20	196

I. THESSALONIANS.

II., 15, 16	185
IV., 13–15	255
V., 2	189
V., 3	188, 208

II. THESSALONIANS.

I., 9	128, 187, 189, 238
I., 8	108

I. TIMOTHY.

II., 1–6	197
IV., 10	197

II. TIMOTHY.

IV., 1	156, 185

TITUS.

II., 11–14	197

HEBREWS.

II., 14	20, 109
V., 7	111
VI., 8	199
IX., 27	139
X., 27	198
X., 30	35, 186
X., 31	35, 198
XI., 30–32	186
XII., 23	194
XII., 29	14, 35, 186, 198, 249

JAMES.

I., 15	200
I., 18	194
III., 6	102
V., 9	202

I. PETER.

II., 9	194
III., 19–21	156, 157, 203
IV., 5	156
IV., 6	156, 157, 204
IV., 17	156
V., 8	202
V., 17	202

II. PETER.

II., 3	206
II., 4	207
II., 9	139, 207, 209
II., 17	206
III.	165, 207, 210
III., 7	208, 209

I. JOHN.

I., 1, 2	106
II., 2	213
III., 4	248
III., 15	213
IV., 8–10	264
IV., 10	135
IV., 17	208
V., 10–12	12, 218

JUDE.

Verse 6	210, 211

Verse 7......................67, 162, 208
Verse 14.................................211

REVELATION.

II., 23 216
III., 5-16................................216
V., 13.....................................109
VI., 8.....................................217
VI., 12-17..............................217
VIII.......................................217
VIII., 16..................................55
XI., 18..........................162, 219
XIII., 8..................................161
XIV., 6-11.............................219
XV., 3, 4.....................11, 20, 146
XIX., 20................................222
XIX., 21................................220
XX., 5...........................160, 255
XX., 9...................................161
XX., 10.................................222
XX., 11-14...109, 114, 148, 158, 223, 226, 236
XXI., 4 ....61, 109, 225
XxI., 8..................................223
XXII., 3........................113, 225
XXII., 15..............................223

The Fire of God's Anger.

PRICE.

Single copy, . .	$ .75
Sent by mail, ...	.80
Three copies to one address, .	2.00
Five copies to one address, . . .	3.00

The usual discount to dealers.

For $1.00 this book will be sent with "Words of Reconciliation" for three months.

ALSO BY THE SAME AUTHOR,

The Mystery of Creation and of Man.

Price, by mail, ... $ .80

Address orders to

L. C. BAKER,

No 2022 DeLancey Place,

Philadelphia, Pa.

WORDS OF RECONCILIATION.

A NEW MONTHLY MAGAZINE.

DESIGNED to bring to the attention of the Church the truth which is in order to her ultimate unity. To this end much attention is given to the questions which concern man's place and destiny in the unfolding plan of God and the place which the Church holds under it, in the belief that she cannot be drawn into unity until she obtains a truer view of the goal toward which all things are tending.

Living questions of the day, in their bearings upon these great issues, are discussed in this magazine.

The duty of the Church to hold herself and her authorized creeds open to the larger views of truth which the Spirit of God is bringing before her in these last days is also urged.

A new principle of interpretation, drawn from the Bible teaching concerning the resurrection of the dead, is proposed as the true solvent of the mysteries of future punishment.

TERMS.

$1.00 per year in advance.

Three copies to one address, ... $2.25
Clubs of five or more, ... 70 cts. per copy

Volumes I and II are bound. Volume III will be bound at the close of the current year. These are sent, postage-paid, for $1.00 per volume, two volumes for $1.75, or three volumes for $2.50.

SPECIAL OFFERS.

"WORDS OF RECONCILIATION" for one year, with Vols. I and II, $2.50
"WORDS OF RECONCILIATION" for one year, with "FIRE OF GOD'S ANGER," 1.50
"WORDS OF RECONCILIATION" for one year, with "MYSTERY OF CREATION AND OF MAN," 1.50
"WORDS OF RECONCILIATION" for one year, with both of the above, 2.25

Address all orders to

L. C. BAKER, Editor,
No. 2022 DeLancey Place, Philadelphia, Pa.

www.ingramcontent.com/pod-product-compliance
Lightning Source LLC
Chambersburg PA
CBHW032102230426
43672CB00009B/1612